Can AI Proclaim Christ?

CAN AI PROCLAIM CHRIST?

A Theological Investigation of AI's Performance
of Christian Proclamation

NICHOLAS ALAN KEUNE

WIPF & STOCK · Eugene, Oregon

CAN AI PROCLAIM CHRIST?
A Theological Investigation of AI's Performance
of Christian Proclamation

Copyright © 2025 Nicholas Alan Keune. All rights reserved. Except for brief quotations in critical publications or reviews, no part of this book may be reproduced in any manner without prior written permission from the publisher. Write: Permissions, Wipf and Stock Publishers, 199 W. 8th Ave., Suite 3, Eugene, OR 97401.

Wipf & Stock
An Imprint of Wipf and Stock Publishers
199 W. 8th Ave., Suite 3
Eugene, OR 97401

www.wipfandstock.com

PAPERBACK ISBN: 979-8-3852-5572-6
HARDCOVER ISBN: 979-8-3852-5573-3
EBOOK ISBN: 979-8-3852-5574-0

VERSION NUMBER 082725

Unless otherwise indicated, Scripture quotations are taken from The Holy Bible, New International Version®, NIV®. Copyright © 2011 by Biblica, Inc. Used with permission of Zondervan. All rights reserved worldwide. www.zondervan.com.

Scripture quotations marked (ESV) are from The ESV® Bible (The Holy Bible, English Standard Version®), © 2001 by Crossway, a publishing ministry of Good News Publishers. Used by permission. All rights reserved.

Scripture quotations marked (SBLGNT) are from the SBL Greek New Testament, copyright © 2010 by The Society of Biblical Literature and Logos Bible Software. Public license. All rights reserved. https://www.sblgnt.com/license/.

Dedicated to my eldest son, Caleb,
who will be raised in a world saturated with AI
and reminds me constantly that we must reason well
about the faith of Christ.

CONTENTS

Common Abbreviations | viii

1 Introduction: Why Discuss Artificial Intelligence? | 1
2 Outline of the Argument | 5
3 Addressing Likely Misconceptions | 16
4 Understanding Artificial Intelligence Systems | 21
5 Generating an Utterance | 45
6 Using Concepts-Meanings in Texts | 69
7 Authority in and Derived from a Text | 128
8 The Spiritual Event of Proclamation | 181
9 Drawing Conclusions | 193
10 Final Exhortations | 198

Bibliography | 209
Subject Index | 215
Author Index | 217

COMMON ABBREVIATIONS

AI	Artificial Intelligence
LLM	Large Language Model
ML	Machine Learning
NLP	Natural Language Processing

1

INTRODUCTION: WHY DISCUSS ARTIFICIAL INTELLIGENCE?

For over a decade, I was a Christian working a secular job involving applied machine learning (ML) and artificial intelligence (AI). I would often speak publicly about the practical implications of AI and get deep into the technical details about how AI could and could not yet be used to transform how humans worked with the world. I witnessed the rise of AI systems that used natural language in the same ways as human individuals and communities, which raised several nagging questions for me as a Christian and a theologian. Has anyone been brought to saving faith in Christ through an interaction with AI? Is it possible for someone to have a faith experience interacting with AI, and if so, can that go beyond the accurate statement of propositional truth? If a human performs a text that is generated by an AI system, does that change the outcome of these questions, and if so, how do we describe what is happening between the various parties? How should the community of faith build up and strengthen a new believer who has had such a positive and revelatory faith experience from AI? How should the community prepare for the opposite situation, where potential believers have a growing distrust and skepticism due to presumed human authors being revealed to be AI? Reasoning about AI in theologically and linguistically robust ways would go on to motivate this book.

When AI is talking about God, there are at least three aspects to consider. These aspects are not mutually exclusive. However, each represents a different set of priorities when looking at the relevant data.

1. AI is a tool to evaluate for use in the community of faith. It may be rejected or warmly approved, but AI is being thought of as primarily a tool for humans in the community of faith to use. Human actions and their effects will be influenced by the use or absence of AI. This is a question about applied AI.

2. AI-generated texts will impact how people interpret texts in general. The increasing prevalence of AI-generated texts means that a growing portion of readers will question if a text is written by a human or an AI. When a reader expects a human author and later realizes it was an AI author, there is potential disillusionment. Readers may choose to protect themselves against future disappointment through thorough skepticism, doubting texts and authors. This is a question about the general impact of AI on interpretation.

3. AI-generated texts that proclaim faith in Christ and urge others to adopt the same faith as Christ may be indistinguishable from human-generated proclamation. The question will be what criteria can be used to differentiate between human- and AI-generated texts. If this data cannot be found in some location (such as in the semantics of an autonomous anonymous text), then the question will be what data can help make this differentiation.

The primary focus for this book is the third of these aspects. A thorough treatment of the third question will resonate with arguments for the first and second. However, the focus of this book needs to be more precise than is possible when evaluating all three at the same time. I will focus on specifically Christian proclamation (unlike number two). I will focus on the unintentional implications of AI generating Christian proclamation (unlike number one). A word relating my argument to these other aspects will help clarify my focus on number three of the aspects above.

The first aspect is a very practical matter, but one that will need to be tailored to the specific circumstances of a situation and community of faith. To this end, I have recently started working with churches who are looking for specific training and consultation on this topic. Many others are writing on these practical and applied topics. Advocating for the use of a tool comes from using that tool oneself, so a faith leader who spends some time practically working with AI will come to have an opinion on its applied practical use. However, this leaves open the more holistic question about how use of this tool, even if effective in the short term, will impact communities.

The second aspect is very important for appreciating the impact of AI on future generations of believers independent of its specific use within their community of faith to help with proclamation. The second aspect looks at the impacts of AI, even without AI being used at all within a specific church. The impact of AI on the trust of texts can potentially even happen vicariously, through awareness that other people are convinced that AI is using language like a natural language user. In articles elsewhere I focused on the limited argument that there will be reader disillusionment driven by AI. The intention was to show how AI-generated meaningful texts, which are misconstrued as human generated, will produce disappointment. Arguing for a potential misconception is easier than arguing for the reality of AI generating texts that, by some criteria, are indistinguishable from human-generated texts.

In short, the first aspect is important but particular and specific to a contextual situation. The second aspect is generally important and carries importance outside of the purely Christian focus of this book. The arguments made in a general context are less focused on attributes that are important to make the strong claim that AI-generated texts are, for good reason, indistinguishable from human-generated Christian proclamation.

The overwhelming answer from this research will be that AI can and will make Christian proclamations to varying degrees of completeness. Linguistically, AI can satisfy the expectations with natural language use and infer propositional content that is recognized as Christian proclamation. Hermeneutically, theories that are bound to the author, text, and reader will be unable to conclusively identify AI authors. A reader or critic of a text cannot reliably differentiate AI and human authors when interpretation is limited to the data expressed within the communicative act. The reader or critic is unable to reliably differentiate an AI from human author when limited to the text, and absolutely not as a precognitive or preconceptual step. The same interpretation will be tried before knowing if an author is human or AI, and this precipitates a growing skepticism of authors following improperly set expectations of authors who are revealed to be AI systems. The determinacy here would require something like unmediated access to authorial intention, which is an unrealistic and impossible expectation. As a result of this key requirement being impossible, we will need to conclude that in interpretation we cannot expect or demand the determinacy needed to differentiate humans from AI authors.

In terms of ethics and sacramentalism, there is a similar indeterminacy. The receiver may not know how to authenticate the proclamation. Alternatively, the receiver may know the process, but determining the nature of the author may require ideal private knowledge. In ethics, there is the tension between localized novel use of concepts that are recognized as continuing in the same trajectory, against the dissemination and agreement over the normative operative rules of the community. In sacramentalism, determinacy would relate to some idealized authentication, such as unmediated access to God's illumination and will. In both cases, there is a lack of public information needed to determinately infer the nature of the author.

Differentiation is unknown or unreliable when based on the linguistic event itself. Ethics and sacramentalism will encourage a different hermeneutic that locates the communicative act within a story-formed community. Locating the proclamation within a lived experience of suffering for Christ provides a preconceptual and nonliterary means to authenticate the truth claims of the proclamation. For hermeneutics, this means expanding what is admissible to the discussion about authorial intention. The goal is not a reconstruction of the author's intention, but the augmenting of the meaning conveyed by the medium of the text with additional public data that gives the words a traditional meaning and the truth claims a lived authentication. "Traditional meaning" in this sense is that the use of words as diachronically modeled.

Propositions gain specific significance, authority, and authentication because of the experience of the author as evidenced outside of the text and through the performative communicative act. There will obviously be times when the recipient lacks this direct knowledge (such as seeing the living story-formed community or the life of the apostle). If this was always accessible, it would make the criterion an immediate and complete solution. Short of that immediate resolution, reasoning about the story-formed dimension of the performance and the practices[1] needs to be appreciated and sought. We should encourage such a hermeneutic for all people, not only for the academic exegete. It will help as a positive means to escape the otherwise all-encompassing skepticism of being unable to differentiate the nature of authors, and ultimately trust the authentication and truth claims that are being presented as truth.

---

1. To use concepts and language used by Stanley Hauerwas (story-formed) and Alisdair MacIntyre (practices), which will be explored further.

2

OUTLINE OF THE ARGUMENT

When AI systems are used to generate text, the ostensible goal is an output that is indistinguishable from one created by a human author. Quite often the desired text is entirely novel, in which case a human-generated text is not readily available. In other cases, a synthesis of existing human texts, or a summarized synthesis, is the goal. The generated text may be inaccurate or may not at all seem like what a human would have written based on the human authors we've previously read. Yet, regardless of the level of success or the specific task, when an AI system is being used to generate text the expectation or definition of a good response is one that is indiscernible from a human text. The goal of all involved parties—from the developers building and testing the systems to the humans who are providing various prompts to the AI systems—is oriented toward an AI-generated text that meets the various expectations we have of a human-generated text. As AI systems pursue this objective, we ought to reckon with the possibility of their success and the impact of meaningful or humanlike AI-generated texts on readers and interpretive communities. This book will ask these questions in the context of Christian hermeneutics, framed around a simple question:

> Can AI theoretically and practically generate Christian proclamation?

There is growing evidence of AI systems being able to produce linguistic skills that are equivalent to those of humans. The humans involved in prompting the AI to generate humanlike texts are often satisfied with the results, and humans who are not privy to the generation process are increasingly unable to discern when an AI was or was not involved. An example from a work colleague will help illustrate the impact.

I recently spoke with a work colleague who went through a messy breakup with his longtime girlfriend. As he was going back and forth via emails and text messages with his girlfriend, he began to have AI process the messages for sentiment. He wanted to know if his girlfriend was gaslighting or manipulating him, and, of course, he wanted to validate his own tone. Eventually he began to use AI assistance in writing his messages, hopeful that it would help his tone and objectivity. When things finally reached the end and he broke off the relationship, he had a final email message where he could no longer guarantee the authorship. His own messages had become increasingly AI inspired or authored. Was this final breakup email written by his former girlfriend? What portion of the amalgam was hers? If none of the final email was written by a human, had he broken up with an AI? He realized that the words had the same impact regardless of the authorship, and that, by the end, even if she had read out some prepared remarks for my colleague he would have doubted that it was fully authored by her. In the words of the linguist, even the verbal performance of a text could not guarantee the lack of an AI authorship behind the scenes.

Now that AI can write texts that can be anonymously presented as human generated, we must ask what this does to our hermeneutics. Centuries of hermeneutics have presumed that the only scenario that produces a meaningful text is one that begins with a human author. With this assumption, the linguistic and hermeneutic models sought to equate the written and the verbal communicative acts, locating the intentionality and physical presence of the speaker in the anonymous and autonomous words of the text. Now that the reverse engineering of authorship cannot be guaranteed to correctly lead to a human author, what needs to change about our hermeneutics?

If an AI can produce novel text—brand-new strings of words about ideas—and can speak about any range of topics discussed, can an AI apply theological concepts to a situation? The question is quite different from looking up a text by Luther or Aquinas or reading Scripture via an electronic medium. This is a question about an AI system producing a brand-new application of theological concepts to a new situation and context. How should this encourage the community of faith to respond? This project surveys various linguistic and hermeneutic theories, along with empirical AI research, to affirmatively answer that AI systems should be considered capable of generating Christian proclamation, based on the evidence internal to the text of the proclamation. Based on that insight, this research proposes some critiques to existing models that are now more dangerous than helpful, and provides some alternative proposals that can help the modern reader avoid the bewilderment of my colleague. It is better to have a hermeneutic that proactively is ready for AI-generated texts than one that is adopted after the disillusionment of thinking a text was human authored and finding out it was an AI (or the reverse realization that one's human acquaintance writes like an AI).

For an AI to generate meaningful applications of Christian theology, it would need to meet the general criteria expected of Christian proclamation. This begins with general linguistic skills but quickly expands to hermeneutics and ethics. The goal of reviewing these theories is to identify criteria that could differentiate AI from human authors. I found that most were ill-suited to the task. The fight against skepticism and autonomous texts had led hermeneutics to strongly defend the presence of the author in a text; an innocuous innovation that seemed harmless before the same arguments and evidence used for respecting an author became arguments for respecting an AI author. Many of the models commonly used for hermeneutics place assumptions on the inferred author, and this maneuver makes it difficult to subsequently differentiate the nature of the author (particularly for these assumed attributes). When these attributes include intentionality, or moral virtues, it is clearly problematic.

HISTORY OF CHRISTIAN PROCLAMATION

The practice of proclaiming the gospel of Jesus as the crucified and risen Christ started face-to-face. Physical presence was quickly followed by proclamation via texts across time and space. The first generation of Christians turned to written texts due to the need to proclaim Christ without an embodied authorial presence. Selections from the first generation of letters between Christians was so well approved that these texts become large portions of the New Testament. The remainder of the New Testament canon was, from its origin, intended as a written record proclaiming the works and faith of the Christ across time and space, and, not rarely, without specific authorial attribution.

It is not an exaggeration to describe the historical development of the Christian community of faith as a religious movement organized around a set of texts. Christianity did not have generations or centuries of tradition before a written Scripture, and communities were deeply involved in intraregional correspondence and debates over theological concepts.

Proclamation in absence was already in place during the first generation of Christians. Writing down proclamation in itself was not novel, for it is procedurally akin to the practice of the prophets of Israel and the apocryphal apocalyptic writings. Almost the entirety of the history of the Christian community is filled with the practice of proclaiming the gospel despite separation by location and time between author and reader. To this was soon added the distance of language and culture, as the Greek Scriptures reached un-Hellenized peoples. Virtually the entire community of faith has therefore participated in proclamation in absence (via consuming the New Testament). Proclamation of the gospel, and adjacent-proximate concepts like dogma and doctrine, have an extensive history that is relevant to the idea of proclamation via proxy or proclamation via absence, and elucidate the worth of better understanding how this practice interacts with recent technology developments. For Protestant theology, Scripture (itself a written proclamation) has the highest standard of authority, and this necessitates a serious understanding of the propositional truth conveyed in the written form. Proper treatment and discernment of the propositional content in a written communicative act is accordingly a critical theological capacity.

THE PROBLEM

Framing the problem needs to start by understanding the parties involved in a proclamation, and therefore what could be involved in the criteria describing proclamation. Generally, models describe three parties in the communicative act: the author, the text, and the reader.[1] Each is described in their contingent context and in strict or loose relationship to the others. These relationships allow assertions about one party (for instance, the text) to derive from attributes more basically held by one of the others (for instance, the intention of the author). Theories that give freedom or obligation to the reader depend on certain attributes about the text or author respectively. If a reader is obligated to respect the author of every text, then respect will be paid to an anonymous author who may very well be an AI system.

To avoid rampant relativism about the meaning of canonical text, many Christian theories choose to argue against an autonomous text and reader. Arguing for a determinate meaning depends on and is justified by the nature of an author and relationship to their text.[2] If the theory espouses

---

1. A relationship between these parties is present even when a theory minimizes one party, such as the knowability of the author. Even if "[the written work's] 'anonymity' is part of its very structure," this structure and the experience of the communicative act expresses and relates to an author, albeit one where the reader lacks direct knowledge. Eagleton, *Literary Theory*, 119.

2. This expectation is shared by theories holding a determinate view of meaning in a text. In general, a high view of the determinacy of the propositional content in a text is

a unified hermeneutic, meaning this respect is not exclusive to Scripture, then these expectations are applied to all texts. Accordingly, these inferred characteristics of authors become projected onto AI authors. When these theories include minimal recourse to external criteria outside the parties of author, text, and reader, then they will have grave difficulty discerning between AI and human authors and predicating only what is appropriate to each.

One of the historic reasons for this situation is the intention to have a unified hermeneutic that applies equally for Scripture as normal human-generated texts.[3] In recent years this desire for universality appropriated and built on the radical translation of linguists, who sought and found universally applicable relationships of natural language users to language. The results of Bruce Marshall build off of the formal logic of Tarski; the hermeneutics of Vanhoozer adopt and extend the interpretation frameworks of Hirsch and Searle. These two are not outliers, for most Christian thinkers sought a universal hermeneutic across Scripture and other texts, and the academically inclined built atop the works of linguistics, sociologists, and functional grammarians. It is quite helpful to learn from other fields, and the problematic assumptions in these models were not introduced by linguistics. Marshall rightfully observes, "Theology should seek to bring under its own discipline the most plausible account currently available to it, not the account that makes its own job go more smoothly."[4] When our models are no longer productive in the world, such as being ambivalent to human versus AI authors, we need a more plausible account.

My research will engage and synthesize various (primarily modern) thinkers who approach the communicative act of texts from various vantage points. Vanhoozer extends and applies the thinking of Hirsch, Juhl, and Plantinga (who have their own related proposals) to create a deterministic view of meaning in a text. Marshall defends an epistemic model that is inherently based on the Trinity. Hays seeks to induce the rules of a New Testament ethics from the canonical texts based on a hermeneutic cycle beginning with understanding the whole of each of the authors, before

---

derivative of the nature of the author. A singular proper reading tends to derive from a singular authorial intent, given the author is a more singular and stable locus of meaning than the text (diachronic linguistic changes) and the interpretative community/reader (diachronic and synchronic variations in culture).

3. Zimmerman articulates the desire for "universal application" of rules about hermeneutics: "Both the theologian and the philosopher, at least in hermeneutics, desire a universal application of their theory." This lofty goal creates complications for Christian thinkers, as it is difficult to include the Canonical witness as a text alongside texts that are produced by human or nonhuman agents. Zimmerman, *Recovering*, 46.

4. Marshall, *Truth*, 233.

inducing synthetic concepts and metaphors that reflect the whole. Hector proposes to work with concepts without availing himself of a correspondence system of concepts, building on the cultural-linguistic patterned deployment of norms and theologians Schleiermacher, Barth, and Soskice. Lindbeck advocates ecumenical healing by proposing a rule theory that applies cultural-linguistic concepts to how the covenant community understands and continues rules via a grammar that flexes without breaking due to divergences in opinion. This is only a sampling of the various important thinkers who will be dialogued with to let their understanding of utterances, concepts-meanings, and authority in texts speak into the question of an AI system being capable of generating proclamation.

Each of these programs approaches the important generalized problem space of how we deal with theological concepts in communicative acts, and these theories, to varying degrees, achieved their immediate contextual objectives. However, their success came when their scope of being judged was necessarily limited to a time before AI systems existed in the manner they do today. They were proposed in a world where language was not as aptly modeled mathematically nor systematically and pervasively generated by nonhuman agents. We should not be dismissive when observing assumptions about intention, determinacy, and meaning that, in the original context, often seemed to be making precise and well accounted assertions about the truth of reality. However, we should not ignore the presence of new data.

This research shows that we must revise our hermeneutics proactively. When current hermeneutic models are applied in the presence of meaningful AI-generated texts, the resulting conclusions predicate human attributes of AI authors. For some, this would be an acceptable conclusion (that an AI can intend, have sentience, or even sapience). If these conclusions are objectionable, as I expect to be the case for many, then it ought to motivate change. It ought to motivate a reconsideration of the triad of author-text-reader, which also means adopting frameworks and models that can go outside of linguistics and the boundaries of semantics. My version of such a proposal will be revisited at the end of this book. I will argue that a paraconsistent truth system will avoid the limitations of semantics-linguistics, and a corresponding evaluation of lived experience can become a fourth factor in the hermeneutic triad. But before turning to the solution, we must exhaust our understanding of the problem.

THESIS

AI systems are producing texts that are recognized by individuals and interpretive communities as indistinguishable from human proclamation. These meaningful texts satisfy criteria readers expect from Christian proclamation. As a result, readers increasingly are unable to assume a human author is behind a text, even if this text is a Christian proclamation of faith.

The criteria a normal reader expects of proclamation will come from discourse analysis, hermeneutics, linguistics, theology, and philosophy. The descriptions and criteria of proclamation will be grouped around proclamation as utterance, its communication of concepts-meanings, its commerce in authority, and its experience as a sacramental event.

> Proclamation is an utterance conveying concepts-meanings that, if taken true, would be consistent in a belief system that is also consistent with the faith of Jesus Christ. When taken true, proclamation invites the spiritual experience of sharing truth with the physically absent and spiritually present Christ.

Christian proclamation is first an utterance. Each utterance is comprised of concepts and meanings that create understanding in the audience. The understanding and implicit truth present a claim to being an authoritative understanding or ordering of truth. The projected world of concepts, meanings, and authoritative truth will be processed as a contextual event in which the recipient has a demand to turn to God and receive from God his self-disclosing revelation.

The result of a positive taking true of proclamation is the spiritual experience of sharing in the truth that is provided by the Christ. The propositional and noetic content of proclamation is no less and no more special than the bread or the wine of the communion table. What composes a proclamation is critically important for its role in an event that is beyond the physicality or created nature of the participating elements (both the words and the communicating agent). It is incorrect to collapse the event into the elements: it would be the error of confusing the elements with the movement of God in the event involving the elements.

The spiritual attributes of proclamation are critically important, yet distinct from the propositional considerations. Therefore, the working definition has intentionally separated the spiritual comments into a reflection and meditation on the event involving the elements of proclamation. *When taken true, proclamation invites the spiritual experience of sharing truth with the physically absent and spiritually present Christ.* The event only is an experience for the one who is open to the experience of Christ. Furthermore, the event of communion with Christ is predicated on the decision by the human receiver to take true the claims of Christ and commit to the belief system of Christ that was lived, leading to death upon the cross after a life of the divine will incarnated in mortal flesh.

The belief system one commits to is that of the Son of God going to the cross. The believer is uniting their faith to a faith that acts by choosing death on the cross. It is faith committed behaviorally to sacrifice lived under the shadow of the cross and the glory of the King of kings. One cannot accept or participate in Christ's truth commitments without living the life of following him and participating in his physical sufferings for the spiritual gain of unity with God. Accepting his faith as true means accepting his sacrifice as life. As we address the noetic content, we should stay attentive to the spiritual effect of taking true and participating in the faith of Christ. We are not focused on merely the propositional, but how these words demand a lived response. As my colleague noted in his own experience, the effect of the words may have a life of its own beyond the authorial process.

METHODOLOGY

1. Review four *aspects* of Christian proclamation:
    a. As utterance
    b. As the use of theological concepts-meanings
    c. As making an authority claim about the faith of Jesus
    d. As a spiritual event

2. For each aspect, consider the important *attributes* of that aspect of proclamation. For example, the utterance aspect has an attribute of context and intentionality.

3. Each attribute will either contribute new *criteria* or reinforce existing *criteria*. The running list of criteria will describe what a text would need to be able to do and look like to be reliably recognized as Christian proclamation.

4. The research and theoretical analysis will demonstrate that there are no reliable pragmatic means (e.g., using public data within the communicative act) to determine if the original author of a proclamation was human or AI. Even if the data presented by the text suggests the text is Christian proclamation, the reader will be unsure if the author is human.

5. The negative implications of authorial indeterminacy will be discussed. There is potential for significant disillusionment when misattributing an AI-generated text to a human. Hermeneutic theories that uncritically predicate things and responsibilities of the author will exacerbate this problem.

6. The positive potential of using data outside of the communicative act, such as the story-formed community of faith and paraconsistent logic, will be proposed to mitigate disillusionment without rejecting outright the value of texts.

Starting with a proclamation as an utterance will ground the subsequent discussion in linguistic theory and concepts. The technical ideas of an utterance will provide a foundation for deeper engagement with the concepts and meanings carried by these utterances. Given the foundational nature, it is less surprising that it is virtually impossible to remove the ambiguity of authorship at this level.[5] Through each major topic (proclamation as utterance, carrying concepts-meanings, expressing an authority, and being a spiritual event) the focus will be on criteria that should be expected of Christian proclamation. After clarifying the use of these criteria in various theories, we will ask how well-suited AI systems are to meet these expectations. Research and data presented herein will showcase the reality of AI systems that can produce content indistinguishable in many criteria from human Christian proclamation.

GOALS

The primary goal of this research is to begin dialogue. AI systems have the potential to produce propositional content that satisfies the noetic aspects of Christian proclamation and become a source of confusion or skepticism for the spiritual and sacramental elements of proclamation. The existence of meaningful AI-generated texts will impact our general relationship as readers to authors. Both the directly Christian-like text, and the general-purpose prevalence of meaningful AI-generated texts demand an adapted hermeneutic model.

---

5. This lack of discernment is exacerbated by the reality of ambiguous digital communication. It is hard to guarantee the origin of a digital message, and in digital context, it is more prevalent and possible for human agents to perform or claim as their own content generated by an AI system. However, note my colleague's example. By the end of the breakup he would have questioned even a live performance.

The linguistic skills of composite AI systems have been shown to surpass our expectations and begin to look like natural language use.[6] We once believed there were limits that AI systems could not pass, such as the distributional semantic theory. The expectation was that, at best, an AI would pick words based on the statistical distribution of the word in the total available linguistic corpus. Such language use would look like sentience but not sapience. It would be a diagnostic response to a stimulus but would not reflect commitments or inferences based on language use. Surpassing this limit is the movement from patterned use to novel use of language. Novel use of language means that AI-generated texts may be recognized as contributing to the direction of the meta-conversation, participating in the literary tradition, and even shaping how human interpretive communities are minded. When we recognize an AI system as writing something meaningful, or we know things because of interacting with an AI system, we are inviting the AI system to participate in the literary and epistemic history of our communities. We are shaping our reality by our engagement with language, and thus language is increasingly of indeterminate origin.

Resultingly, it is only responsible to reinvestigate problematic theories that fail to differentiate, or worse, grant human attributes of AI authors based on the exercise of linguistic skills (producing a meaningful text). The first goal is to highlight the limitations of these hermeneutic models and proactively encourage better models that can avoid some of the greatest risks posed by AI-generated meaningful texts.

The second involved goal is to illuminate potential improvements to theories that commerce in the involved concepts of utterances, concepts-meanings, and authority. Investigating the ability for various hermeneutic systems to differentiate against AI inadvertently revealed significant shortcomings. These were not the initial focus, but after realizing these lapses, it became apparent that there is urgent need to revisit many hermeneutic theories.

The third goal is to motivate dialogue. How can the community of faith fill up what is lacking in the noetic or propositional proclamation of an AI system? How can the community *do* and *be* proof beyond well-reasoned propositions about faith? When AI directs a seeker to the human community of faith, will they find a living faith that by its life proves that God gives it life beyond death? Will they find those who have received faith revealed by the Spirit and participate in the sufferings and eternal hope of

---

6. Arai and Tsugawa, "Large Language Models." This early research summarizes from a cognitive linguistics perspective many of the same observations that this research seeks to put in dialogue with specifically Christian proclamation as a subspecies of specialized communication.

the Son? Loving new believers in the age of AI texts succeeds or fails on our understanding of what is lacking in the propositional affirmations. Training a person with more propositions of the faith of Christ (e.g., the catechetical propositions) is tone deaf to what these individuals need as authorization and discipleship. Study, discipleship, and preaching ought to learn and surpass the expectations or experience of AI proclamation.

We can no longer assert with a clear conscience that "only persons say something to someone about something."[7] Let us nuance what AI proclamation[8] lacks. Such nuance also helps the community safely and consciously use AI-generated texts. When done with suitable nuance and augmentation, the resulting hybrid performance can produce a rich and complete proclamation and evangelistic effort. Cross-cultural contextualization is more feasible with a system that can not only translate but contextualize. We can use tools like AI to understand our own barriers to communication and our limitations. Teaching can be positively impacted, for teaching is both a propositional and a lived commitment: there exists propositional content that is viable for augmentation or automation with AI. The focus of this research will not be to propose novel use of AI for these purposes, but this ought to be legitimized and motivated by this book.

The fourth and final goal is to call our human proclamation to a higher standard than AI systems can produce. If the community of faith ever finds that human proclamation is no better than AI proclamation, we ought to call our human proclamation to a higher standard. A failure to differentiate lived faith from the propositional text of faith is reminiscent of 2 Cor 3. Will we repeat the same fear as Moses and fail to shine the glory of God? Or will we participate in the reality of God being with us in the Christ?

---

7. Vanhoozer, *Meaning*, 217.

8. The general consensus of this research will be that criteria outside of the text are most promising in differentiating between human- and AI-generated proclamation. The need for evidence outside of the text itself raises an important challenge that will not be able to be fully examined; the case I call "spooky proclamation at a distance." If a human performs the content created by an AI system, is there anything still lacking in the proclamation? For example, if the human participant is truly living in Christ, and speaks the generated words with the experiential approval and conviction of their truth, then is this performance any less authentic, effective, or evangelistic than otherwise? Or if the person so influenced by a human performance of AI content comes to faith, could this individual then also bring others to a faith that is consistent with that of the Christ?

3

ADDRESSING LIKELY MISCONCEPTIONS

THIS BOOK WAS WRITTEN *by one human (Nicholas Keune), without AI assistance in the writing process.* Most people ask the question, not as a commentary on my writing, but due to the QED impact on the argument that an AI-authored book about AI authorship would suggest. My goal is the hermeneutic and theological discussion, which would not be furthered purely by the case that AI can advocate for its linguistic abilities.

This research could be seen as highly critical of specific hermeneutic models, particularly those of Dr. Vanhoozer. A critique of existing hermeneutic models was not my original intention, and I would not be satisfied with only this as the outcome of the research. The conversation is much broader than Vanhoozer. As for my specific treatment of his hermeneutics, I have also written a scholarly article intending to remediate his hermeneutics by using his own ethics. My proposal in that article suggests there is a great value that can be redeemed in his thinking, and that his own works suggest a path toward this that is coherent with my general proposal. I want to make it clear that none of my comments are meant to attack or diminish the value of these models; they were selected because of my respect for the authors and their treatment of the respective topics. However, since the data suggests certain responsible reactions to their models, I will responsibly advocate for these changes.

This research will not argue for the "general intelligence" or humanity of AI systems. The arguments that suggest we cannot differentiate human from AI authors are meant to create a tension, akin to proving a null hypothesis that motivates a reconsideration of the experiment and assumptions. AI authors and human authors are distinct, but the current models do a poor job of describing or assisting in this differentiation. I will exploit how existing frameworks predicate human attributes (e.g., intention) to the author of a text based on the evidence within the text. The conclusions are meant to prove the danger of the models, not justify and legitimize the conclusions that AI systems possess these attributes, status, or relationships of authority.

This research is not only for Christian hermeneutics. Unacceptable yet logically consistent conclusions demonstrate the need for new theories based on foundational assumptions of linguistics and hermeneutics. We need to accommodate how we appropriate these foundational assumptions about how humans interact with texts, so that we can prepare for the impact of AI-generated texts in the presence of these assumptions. I am confident that the usefulness of general-purpose hermeneutics will improve by incorporating these findings from the community of faith. These proposals challenge the pedantic models of hermeneutics in the academy and ideally encourage our human proclamation to a higher standard. I hope to propose ways to safely and thoughtfully weigh the impacts of using content of a lower standard (human or AI-system generated). The applications are diverse, reaching in both directions: toward the academic consideration of proclamation, hermeneutics, and foundational basic constructs (truth, meaning, being, and becoming), and in the other direction toward how the community of faith ought to proclaim the formative word and teach the community to seek the word of God from his revelation.

The argument applies to all readers of texts, not only the unbelievers who are the least qualified to evaluate the theological concepts of an AI-generated text. A possible class error is to fixate on what is discernible to the unbelievers, compromising the criterion of well-reasoned use of theological concepts. The best judge is someone who is in Christ and participates in his presence for the community of faith. Slight errancy or heretical views may be more readily observed by the expert, but it would be a disingenuous objection to proffer a hypothetical ideal or omniscient human to distinguish authorship when the consideration at hand is for a nonbeliever. The primary focus for this research is the evangelistic case or, more precisely, the AI system that is responding to an inquiry that reasonably seeks to understand the faith of Christ and participation in his life. There are important questions raised about the dynamics of norms within the community of existing believers, leading to discussion of the reciprocal authority of theological concept usage and experiential authentication of such concepts. The potential authority claims of an AI-generated text will pose critical questions about the attributes of authority, with compelling impact on ecclesiology, theology, and missiology. In terms of authority, are our norms derived from an authority in Scripture, in tradition, or from an external (profane) source such as reason?

Not all the theories mentioned herein are equal in quality or scope. A reader might confuse my dialogue with theories for approval of said theories. To have a wide aperture of consideration, each facet of proclamation and the related descriptions will contain rival concepts and frameworks. My goal is not to adjudicate the best model for each aspect, attribute, or criterion. The goal is an expansive synthesis of many (but certainly not all) of the high priority attributes in each aspect. This is particularly true for aspects that are quite expansive, such as theological use of metaphor or analogy.

We're not judging who is united to Christ and will receive life in him. This book will consider the effectiveness of proclamation toward someone receiving and participating in the faith of the Christ. We can look for all the propositional truths of Christ's incarnation, death, and resurrection and, furthermore, for corresponding performances in the lives of the individuals in question. However, the assessment of belonging to Christ is for Godself. We lack the data to, in Bonhoeffer's terms, confirm we've moved from the penultimate to the ultimate.[1] This investigation cannot exhaust the eschatological mystery of being like Christ himself[2] and seeing him face to face,[3] but will address the reality of seeking after these ends and our preparation that God flourishes into fruitful crop.[4]

JOHN SEARLE'S CHINESE ROOM

There is a specific thought experiment from John Searle that merits a quick discussion prior to engaging in this project. His Chinese room experiment is a popular way to differentiate between a system functionally using language, and the system having "understanding" of language. His thought experiment is summarized as follows:

> Imagine a native English speaker who knows no Chinese locked in a room full of boxes of Chinese symbols (a data base) together with a book of instructions for manipulating the symbols (the program). Imagine that people outside the room send in

---

1. Bonhoeffer describes proclamation as the penultimate that is in service of the ultimate, and reminds that "the purport of the Christian message is . . . that one shall be like Christ Himself." Bonhoeffer, *Ethics*, 124.
2. See Col 2.
3. See 1 John 4.
4. See Matt 13:1–23; Mark 4:1–20; and Luke 8:4–15.

other Chinese symbols which, unknown to the person in the room, are questions in Chinese (the input). And imagine that by following the instructions in the program the man in the room is able to pass out Chinese symbols which are correct answers to the questions (the output). The program enables the person in the room to pass the Turing Test for understanding Chinese but he does not understand a word of Chinese.[5]

The thought experiment can be very compelling, and many raise their hands and insist that the system cannot at all understand language, even if it can functionally use this language in every scenario and case that one could test a human or native language user. Even if one accepts his argument uncritically and completely, his argument is tangential at best and possibly entirely perpendicular to the case of this research. My goal, as stated above, is not to prove that an AI can understand language, but that the use of language by an AI system can and will be recognized by others as functionally proper use of language, and therefore there will be impacts on how readers interact with various texts. There is a significant difference between an AI understanding language and an AI generating meaningful texts. Understanding is an ontological claim about the author, while meaningful texts describe the product of an author in a context.

Searle uses his thought experiment to argue against a functional definition of language, whereby language use justifies making certain ontological claims about the author. His argument rejects the fallacy of arguing from the consequent, specifically arguing against the claim that meaningful use of language logically necessitates an author who can understand. The formal structure of his argument presents that the functional description of language use deals with a different matter than claims describing the nature of the author. Recall, this is my own position above regarding the topics being perpendicular.

Searle's thought experiment does not deal with an argument focused on the functional nature of language. Provisionally accepting that an AI does not understand the language it uses does not diminish the potential impacts of AI-generated texts on the readers who recognize the AI as generating meaningful texts. The functional use of language (and recognition of language use) explains how these literary events will impact an interpretative community. My argument is that AI can generate texts that a reader recognizes as meaningful. If the reader is liable to reach the conclusion that an AI text was produced by a human, then there will be important implications from AI using language to create meaningful texts. Hopefully Searle

---

5. Searle, quoted in Cole, "Chinese Room Argument," para. 6.

has helped clarify the path forward for this argument and has rounded out the discussion of what it is not.

4

UNDERSTANDING ARTIFICIAL INTELLIGENCE SYSTEMS

1. AI was built on ML techniques for pattern matching.
2. AI systems have implemented techniques to mimic the language processing and generation of humans (natural language users).
3. The behaviors of these systems reflect the characteristics of natural language users, and are properly described with linguistics terminology due to exercising the same functional characteristics.
4. AI systems can intentionally be designed to optimize their natural language use, and will increasingly be impossible to differentiate from human authors.

Out of necessity, this chapter will use a mixture of technical terminology from computer science, applied mathematics, and linguistics to present a foundational understanding of AI. When new terms are used, they will be explained using examples and a brief explanation of why this term is relevant to the discussion of AI-generated texts. Where technical terminology makes the discussion jargony, the hope is to maintain accessibility through less technical examples. What follows will provide a workable history and model to discuss what these systems already are doing or, based on research, could be designed to perform.

AI and ML are domains of applied computer science that have been researched and advanced for the last several decades. There is no universally adopted way to disambiguate these two terms (*AI* and *ML*), but in current discussions the term *AI* is often used as a catch-all. *Machine learning* is the study of techniques for computers to perform tasks that were not explicitly programmed. These techniques in general allow a computer to observe patterns in data and then act based on new observations. One common application for ML is in natural language processing (NLP). Natural language processing has been used in recent years to produce systems that produce behavior that is labeled *artificial intelligence*. The label *AI* is primarily ex post facto (based on observation after the fact). If the system produces results that are recognized by humans as resembling natural language use or reasoning, then it is called AI.

AI is a rapidly advancing field. Concepts and approaches continue to evolve. Some of the research (e.g., reasoning models) did not exist when this project was started, and new capabilities will soon follow. It would be impossible to state the long-term state of the art, but that isn't important to express the direction of change outlined above. One alternative would be a negative definition (one that tries to define AI systems by what they cannot do), but given the state of the art is changing, a negative definition seems even less stable. The conclusion of this chapter is that AI is intentionally designed to express the same characteristics as human language use, and as it gets better at this task, AI will increasingly be impossible to differentiate from human authors. The argument will be outlined in this chapter, before exploring the nuanced details that go into those characteristics.

There is no turning back. Even if all AI systems were to immediately cease to exist, the epistemological and theological conundrums posed by the current situation would need to be addressed. It is much more likely that future systems will increase the ability to produce communicative acts. As these systems produce higher quality communication, based on the criteria used by linguists and human readers alike, it will be harder (read: less justified, pragmatic, credible) to differentiate AI communicative acts from those of humans.

BUILDING ON MACHINE LEARNING

Machine learning is a field of applied computer science using algorithms to identify patterns. Pattern matching is particularly interesting as an applied science where the execution of these algorithms is intentionally designed to arrive at an execution capability that was not intentionally designed. A complex set of rules defined by a human is less interesting than a programmatic means of arriving at a novel result not explicitly intended by the human creator.

The initial and intentional design of the algorithms specify a way for the computer system to process the problem of identifying patterns based on some sort of data signal. The resulting procedural-algorithmic ability to identify those patterns is empirical. In machine learning the former is often called a *classifier* (the general class defined by the human designer) and the latter a *model*. While some classifiers of ML employ deterministic processes for producing or *training* the specific model to identify patterns from the data signals, the more interesting examples are stochastic. This means that given the same data inputs, the resulting model will vary. In Aristotelian terms, the model is the *accident*, and the classifier is the *essence*. With more advanced classifiers these accidents may diverge significantly and be exceedingly mathematically unique, meaning the model is derivative of the experience of training of the model.

Classifiers have been applied for many decades in specific point industries and use cases. In 2014, this author worked on several projects where applied ML was used in the domain of predictive maintenance. In 2011 this author was doing the same for financial forecasting. These projects were not novel. Applied ML had proven its capabilities for *classifying* data and for *generating* new cases based on prior context.

Classification is the process of training a model to correctly identify some predicate of a given data point (also called a *case*, an *event*, or an *observation*). One of the textbook examples is using a classifier to identify the type of a plant based on metrics related to the plant leaves. For this type of classification, "correct" answers are needed to confirm how effective the model is performing, and these correct values are called *labels*. After training the model on some portion of the total available data corpus, the resulting model will be given data without labels and be evaluated based on the accuracy in providing the correct label as annotated in the data that was not used during training.

The implementation details for generating new content are more eclectic, given the context that can be considered is significantly more complicated. To illustrate, in order to produce the label of one data point, a model would use at maximum all the other attributes of that data point. In contrast, to generate a temporal extension (a new data point that is at a point in time beyond the last observation of the input data), the model would ideally avail itself of all the attributes of every prior data point. The scope of context made generation a more complicated task and would be exacerbated by research and newer architectures that further expanded the data under consideration.

Approaches to the question of how much context should be used when generating a new data point often use the human brain or the human eye as a source of inspiration. In both cases, the biological example provides inspiration for programmatically implementing math that will define the influence of new training data on the system during training. For all types of models this can in general be called the *learning function*. Emulating the brain, various types of *neural networks* were developed. Emulating the eye, various types of *convolutional networks* and *kernel functions* were developed. In a broad over-simplification, the former attempted to build procedures that would capture more context based on a more resource-intensive architecture and carry this forward in an attention matrix, while the latter focused on efficient ways to decide what data was acceptable to lose and summarize into data kernels.

Neural networks gained popular attention when systems using these models began to beat humans in advanced strategic games (e.g., Go and Chess). In a neural network, the designers can decide the number of layers and the number of neurons in each layer. Each isolated neuron is responsible as one input in a potentially extremely sophisticated action. The determination of a next-best action is therefore distributed across the responsibility of each of these individual actors. Architectures within the neural network family diverge in how they assess the success of training and provide feedback during training.

One very important long-term architectural concept that was proven by the rise of neural networks was the idea of a system where multiple ML processes work together toward a goal. Specifically, the work in Go and Chess was based on Generative Adversarial Networks (GANs), where multiple neural networks play against each other, with the objective winner leading the direction of the ongoing training of the eventual system. GANs showed the advantage of multiple actors working together or against each other to produce better results, which would later become a widespread system design.

Another important area of research that would be incorporated in newer models pertains to the learning function. In a neural network, an important question is how downstream decisions/results of external neurons should change the weighting of upstream neurons based on the success of using those pathways (for example, a feed-forward mechanism). If all the data were shared back, then the whole series of layers would essentially collapse into a single layer. Advanced concepts were researched and empirically tested for allowing each layer and neuron to have a *memory,* and this memory would help guide either training or the execution of the trained model. During execution of the trained model, the path taken is the *activation* of those layers. Layer activation is analogous to the activation of multiple neurons in a human brain when responding to some stimulus.

The recurring question is how to manage the right context. Context was particularly difficult when working with NLP. When generating new data (for example, to finish a sentence) there is not only the context of what has come before, but there are all the potential words in the language as next data points. High quality *inference*—namely, evaluation of the potential options—requires that our natural linguistic expectations are met for heuristics like coherence and function. Naïve approaches took a purely distributional semantic approach: what is the most statistically occurring next word, or what word semantically is statically the closest. An overly simple statistic model failed to optimize for natural or ordinary usage of language. Convolution networks used approaches from the human eye to reduce down context (analogous to organizing a series of words into sentences and clauses), and these functions borrowed *kernel* functions as a term from cognitive and generative linguistics.[1]

The watershed moment came when new research on how to model words (*embeddings*) was combined with a new architecture (*transformers*) for managing the context (*attention*) needed for generating natural language. In November 2022 there was the public release of one such resulting system, and it made much of the world stop calling these systems machine learning and recognize their actions as AI. The first of these systems provided an interactive interface (bidirectional chat) that would prompt a response from a large language model (LLM).

These offerings quickly evolved into AI systems: composite architectures with multiple components, performing intermediary tasks to improve the quality and nature of the generated content. The first generation of AI systems became a sensation for the ability to quickly generate extremely sophisticated natural- or ordinary-seeming language. Subsequent evolutions have added layers of *reasoning* and *judgment* (using the self-descriptions of practitioners in the field: these terms are not meant to suggest the analogs to the human characteristics they are modeled upon implementing). Multiple components working together is an *agentic* approach to dividing or iteratively working through complex problems and has given rise to these systems legitimately rivaling the reasoning intelligence of humans.

---

1. Simon Dik and Noam Chomsky used these terms decades before AI and ML implementations.

MIMICKING THE LANGUAGE PROCESSING AND GENERATION OF HUMANS

The ability to produce natural language and respond to natural language in a manner evocative of a human is inherently and importantly related to the concept of *embeddings*. The critical research here was laid by a paper published in 2013 titled "Efficient Estimation of Word Representations in Vector Space," but more commonly referred to as the Word2vec paper. The implementation details for the architectures needed had not yet been developed, but this research proved a quite "surprising" find: the mathematical means of computing the differences between semantic terms

> can be answered by performing simple algebraic operations with the vector representation of words. To find a word that is similar to *small* in the same sense as *biggest* is similar to *big*, we can simply compute vector X = *vector*("*biggest*") − vector("*big*") + vector("*small*"). Then, we search in the vector space for the word closest to X. . . . When the word vectors are well trained, it is possible to find the correct answer (word *smallest*).[2]

The paper describes a functional use of language that had been predicted by the generative grammar school of linguistics, who argued that language is the implementation of innate and universal rules. The paper provided empirical proof a mathematical representation of semantic terms could allow plain vector mathematics to produce coherent language use.[3] To use an example, with proper vector representations of the words *king*, *queen*, *man*, and *woman*, a program could calculate the vector difference between king and queen, and adding the result to man would get woman. Natural users of language understand these metonymies by which pairs of words are related in transformation or distance. The Word2vec paper produced data in support of this being achievable in a consistent and procedurally meaningful way using techniques that were available to computer science. The barriers to producing coherent natural language were dramatically lowered.

Generating natural language also meant dealing with the consistent problem in this brief history: how to deal with the scope of data to use during generation and during training. A major solution for this problem came in 2017 with the advent of *transformer* architectures announced by

---

2. Mikolov et al., "Efficient Estimation," 5.

3. Modern computer science has focused on optimization of matrix calculations for decades, as this is also critical to most image manipulation processes. Representing linguistic knowledge in vector spaces, and then expressing linguistic skills as mathematical operations in these spaces meant that all of the decades of research in this field could be immediately put to effective use by these AI systems.

the paper "Attention Is All You Need." One of the motivating ideas of this research was to "[dispense] with recurrence and convolutions entirely"[4] by providing a new means ("attention") of dealing with sliding windows of context within natural language. The proposed approaches provided ways for parallelization of the attention, meaning both training and execution would be dramatically scaled. Using the prior learnings from eye and brain functional-biological design, these parallel context windows could be mathematically summarized. The algorithms implement a behavior parallel to how native speakers track the movement of "thematic frames" and anaphoric chains of reference.[5] This architecture provided both a means for mathematically modeling the coherence of a text in terms of higher order concepts (discourse, narrative, tone), and for dramatically improving the feasibility of these systems through the performance impacts of parallel execution.

The resulting systems began to accumulate empirical results. These data were not only in the laboratory of research teams like Deep Mind, but after November 2022 became available in the personal experiences of consumers across the world. Seemingly complex *prompts* (strings of words) could be procedurally processed into small contexts which in aggregate would produce a meaningful and increasingly accurate higher order communicative activity.

Reflecting the Characteristics of Natural Language Users

One of the important considerations in contemporary research in AI systems is how the semantic model produces empirical results that surpass the expectations of a distributional semantic system. This area poses a very relevant question: are the results of AI systems reducible to the expected statistical patterns of our language usage or is there something fundamentally different that happens when an AI system generates texts? Does the combination of context, attention, dense vectorization, reinforcement, prompting, and other procedural factors produce a system that, at the system level, is doing something more or distinct from a distributional semantic system? Research suggests the surprising answer is yes, and this realization has motivated the current research program applying these findings to Christian proclamation.

If LLMs were only statistical models of language (distributional semantics), this would manifest in the ways that languages are mapped to

4. Vaswani et al., "Attention Is All You Need," 1.
5. See Runge and Dik.

each other. For example, this limitation would manifest in how *skills* learned in one language would express in other languages.[6] Research in December 2024 investigated neuron activations to investigate this process. First, they were able to identify the regions within the latent vector space that are associated with different languages, and then remarkably found that a similar language task (e.g., writing poetry) would have similar activation patterns across different languages. This shared activation pattern suggests what the authors termed "a 'Lingua Franca,' a common semantic latent space that allows for consistent processing across languages."[7] The primary focus of the research was to improve the generalization of "language-agnostic activation pattern[s],"[8] yet the bare empirical results suggest that the process of LLM generation is distinct from a purely statistical pattern matching system.

Skills being transferred across languages is evidence against the assumption that the model is simply well trained in continuing use of language based on repeating prior human examples. In fact, few humans randomly code switch in the midst of a line of reasoning. It is nontrivial for humans to express advanced linguistic skills learned in a different language (for example, giving directions in a non-native language, or writing poetry in a non-native language). Data such as cross-language skill transfer, and the empirical observation of these cross-language latent spaces should dispel any academically honest doubt that an LLM is doing more than very effectively repeating and parroting series of words observed in the wild.

Large language model performance of linguistic tasks can also be compared to human performance to elucidate questions about their distributional semantic nature.[9] One example of this is the precision and proper use of vague terms related to quantifiers such as *few* or *many*. A distributional semantic model expects that an LLM will better match human (natural language user) behavior for vague quantifiers, given the difficulty in building a sufficient statistical pattern of association for exact quantifiers. The contextual nature of the truth conditions that would need to obtain for exact quantifiers argues against a distributional semantic model being more effective at those linguistic tasks than at the use of vague quantifiers. However, the data from this research disproves the expected results derived from a distribution semantic description of an LLM.

---

6. For illustration, consider a model trained to generate poetry in English that is then prompted with the expectation to generate poetry in Korean.
7. Zeng et al., "Converging to a Lingua Franca," 1.
8. Zeng et al., "Converging to a Lingua Franca," 1.
9. Enyan et al., "Are LLMs Models of Distributional Semantics."

The conclusion of the authors is that "either we must revisit our assumptions about what distributional semantics can capture, or we must determine at what point a model trained only on the distribution of text ceases to embody the distributional hypothesis."[10] The net result is an expansion of the range of capabilities that an LLM is seen to exhibit, either under the auspices of distributional semantics (motivating questions about cognitive linguistics, our linguistically minded nature, and the relationship of language to reality), or by recognition that an LLM can, through various techniques, surpass the limitations of distributional semantics. Either possibility grants greater credence to the suggestion that an AI system can produce texts that satisfy the linguistic skill requirements of proclamation, at least from a cognitive-linguistic and semantic perspective.

In December 2024 a group of researchers proposed an approach to modeling the behavior of LLMs based on the philosophy of language.[11] Their hypothesis runs parallel to the contentions of my own thesis. Despite different goals their argumentation, based on various research and concepts of design, is extremely aligned with the conclusions of my own research. I will not exhaust these points at this time but will consider some key points before elaborating the technical capabilities of these systems.

The related proposal of that research fits the label of *anti-referential*. This school of thinking, contrary to the limitations of the distributional semantic hypothesis, allows for "concepts of substitutable expressions and anaphoric expressions."[12] Properly predicating these capabilities of AI-generated texts is critical to argumentation regarding thinkers like Hector as he extensively relies on anaphoric concept usage as the criterion for proper concept use.[13] In the subsequent analysis, the researchers argue that "it is appropriate to consider the inference in LLMs as material rather than formal inference,"[14] and that the Fregean idea of contextualization of a word in a sentence is maintained by a model using a transformer architecture.[15]

---

10. Enyan et al., "Are LLMs Models of Distributional Semantics," 2.
11. Arai and Tsugawa, "Large Language Models."
12. Arai and Tsugawa, "Large Language Models," 6.
13. Hector, *Metaphysics*.
14. Arai and Tsugawa, "Large Language Models," 8.
15. In layman's terms, due to the attention mechanism being based on a decomposition and weighting of a moving window of context within a larger textual segment, the meaning contribution of each semantic element is based on the shifting context of the larger language unit, up to the entire discourse (if permitted, given the size and computational limitations). Long sentences or discourse units can dramatically shift their meaning based on an emphatic clause or a change in anchor through overspecification in the last words. For example, "I will clean my room and wash the dishes and take care

In terms of anaphoric use, the research showed an example neuron view, whereby an *induction head* was used to properly resolve a demonstrative.

A significant note from the researcher warns that "LLMs are only open to truths of the world via the humans involved in providing training data and RLHF [reinforced learning from human feedback], and these truths can be easily distorted by humans."[16] Other research cited will suggest that case study and ethical conclusions can be directed toward various goals, but this comment succinctly and importantly suggests that a system can be designed with a specific goal of Christian proclamation as a so-called distortion. My thesis certainly does not hang on the fallacious idea that every LLM will proclaim the Christian message, nor that this will occur in every communication. Instead, my thesis will obtain if the possibility of this occurrence is demonstrated, and the criteria for considering this proclamation are sufficiently met. The warning from this paper is a good indicator that this is indeed a result which obtains.

AI SYSTEMS DESIGN IMPROVES NATURAL LANGUAGE USE

Fully enumerating the most advanced AI systems would become almost immediately obsolete and would run at best tangential to the primary focus of this research. What will be fruitful is consideration of the technical and mathematical underpinnings of current systems that are highly analogous to human cognitive-linguistic procedures. The results are linguistic skills that testify to advanced communicative acts. These further details are a means toward the primary focus of analyzing the potential for distinguishing the generated proclamation content of AI systems versus human agents.

Tokenization is the procedure by which the text that is inputted (the prompt) and the output results (a response, or in linguistic terms, an utterance) are materialized. A stream of text needs to be broken into chunks for processing by computers, much as sounds and morphemes need structuring to be processed by humans. In terms of computers, approaches range from breaking apart words into consistently sized chunks (tokens) for processing, to breaking based on larger units of semantically and syntactically meaningful content. Toward the former end of the spectrum, the text is broken in a machine-optimized manner. Toward the latter, the tokens represent meaning in a manner more analogous to the human thought processes of

---

of the errands" has a very different sense when the final clause "when pigs fly" is added. Arai and Tsugawa, "Large Language Models," 8.

16. Arai and Tsugawa, "Large Language Models," 12.

discourse and rhetoric analysis. The smaller units allow each individual contribution to be a smaller impact on other behaviors, the primary one being attention.

Vectorization builds upon how the stream of text is broken into tokens. Vectorization is how the specific chunks (tokens) are represented (mapped) onto a multidimensional vector space. This mathematical representation can then be used to model relationships to other vectors, producing a semantic space. Various vectorization approaches exist, optimized for capturing different aspects of these semantic similarities. An optimal vectorization facilitates the vector math done by the AI systems to produce high-quality results (generally those that are perceived as more humanlike).

A cursory consideration of various vectorization approaches shows how technical approaches to vectorization follow and could be considered implementations of theories about language. The same theories linguists propose to model and approach language are used to design the algorithms used in these systems. Therefore, the resulting interactions with meaning and significance should be expected to carry a similar burden and practice.

The simplest version of vectorization is "one hot," where tokens are encoded by a unique position on a vector that grows with the size of the vocabulary during training. A more sophisticated approach is to break text into n-grams and then create vectors for these, which are then used for training the probabilistic relationships used in embeddings. N-grams are combinations of words, so a three-word-long n-gram would be similar to the game played by humans of composing a three word story.[17] Vectorization-built larger semantic units means that more explicit relationships can be modeled at that level, similar to the idea in linguistics of not looking at the morpheme but the word situated in a clause or nearby context (and ultimately within the sentence or discourse). Term Frequency-Inverse Document Frequency (TF-IDF) is an approach that builds a statistical heuristic for the vector based on the larger corpus used for training and the localized context of a document. The lessons of word studies and hermeneutics for dealing with the notorious occurrence of hapax legomenon are reflected in how TF-IDF looks to relevance within a document versus a corpus in attempting to derive a meaning. The long-standing assumption was that these approaches would approach an ideal statistical distribution of language in order to preserve semantic or lexical meaning. However, more recently the pragmatic effect mirrors behavior that exceeds just semantic distributions,

---

17. This was a concept the author personally implemented back in 2016 with an earlier generation of ML and NLP techniques.

with novelty, metaphor, and projections of the semantic space that exceed the optimization for semantic distribution.

Embeddings build upon vectorization in a manner explicitly focused on representing the semantic aspects of the token. Embeddings go beyond vectorization to build dense vectors that represent the semantic meaning of a word.

The parallels to linguistics will emerge from looking at the implementations of vectorization models in general. GloVe is an example that was launched in 2014 shortly after research into vectorization began being published. GloVe builds a vectorization model based on the statistical distribution of words, with the goal being a relative vector distance that approximates the semantic similarity.[18] The context of each word is modeled based on co-occurrence probability built around two vectors. During training the model learns a multinomial logistic regression of the probability of the two vectors, which can then be used to compute the cosine similarity or absolute Euclidean distance between vectors as an expression of the magnitude of semantic similarity (or to optimize for the most locally similar vector to a goal). In layman's terms, two lines representing different parts of the semantic meaning are combined together to precisely identify one object.

The implementation of GloVe is predicated on the understanding that the important meaning or sense of a word can be mathematically expressed and procedurally estimated (to an acceptable accuracy) by using two vectors representing the same word. The strategy of using two vectors is an implementation of the same concepts and formulations provided by linguists and philosophy-of-language specialists. Hector discusses the idea at length (from Davidson) of "triangulation,"[19] concluding that a language user can uniquely pick out "only one object" based on the intersection of two lines of perspective. Hector's usage is intentionally capturing the idea of "continuing out from" some base coordinates, where he proposes doing so with two lines of continuation to triangulate a unique picking out. In his framework, such triangulation allows concepts to express the continuation of an existing trajectory and provides for the Davidsonian idea of using two unique continuations to produce a singular picking out of an item. This helps Hector avoid the metaphysical use of correspondence and concepts, which is conceptually core to his proposal.

The theoretical and conceptually motivated ideas of Davidson and Hector are empirically and pragmatically demonstrated by the means of vectorization in AI systems (and independently in other natural language

---

18. Pennington et al., "GloVe."
19. Hector, *Metaphysics*, 158–59.

processing applications). This collision of concept and implementation within AI systems gives further validation to the confidence of an AI system being capable of procedurally implementing and executing concepts to obtain a sensemaking communicative act converging in quality to the most thoughtful human native language users.

Embeddings are an important subset within vectorization, where the semantic meaning of the described unit is the primary focus. Embeddings allow the results of AI systems to mathematically represent and optimize for many of the ideas of cohesion. Lexicogrammatical semantics and grammatical data about a word in context are only the beginning of what effective embedding strategies produce. Currently there is a continuous effort to expand the efficiency and precision of these implementations, and advanced models continue to seek to mathematically model more and more of the context that is also important to those directly or adjacently studying language. Coherence of semantics and grammar have expanded to model the flow of thinking in a sentence (for example, embedding via sentence-BERT, or Bidirectional Encoder Representations from Transformers) or other larger units of discourse.

The quality of embeddings is evaluated along the ability to model the higher-order coherence of a plot, situation, tone, and register, and to manage complex natural-language practices like ellipsis, anaphoric references, and other nuanced lexical rules. An interesting related phenomenon is the ability for these systems to deal with improper spelling and grammar in the human provided prompt. Modern AI systems will make sense of a formally incoherent string of letters that to a patient native-language user (or an AI system) can be processed as meaningful data. The human transposition of letters to rehabilitate a misspelling was not immediately expected as a skill of LLMs.

Approaches for implementing these improvements are varied. Sometimes this is by working with larger units of thought (recall sentence-BERT). Others have improved the training process itself (which is ripe for improvement, as this is an unsupervised training process in which the model arrives at its trained result based on the initial design and architecture). Focusing on the training process helps, for instance, with the peculiarities of language not being efficient or explicitly rational. Homonyms and polysemy are difficult, while contronyms are exceedingly difficult to mathematically model without intentional approaches. An example of the latter is the Most Suitable Sense Annotation (MSSA)[20] and intentionally improves a multi-

---

20. Ruas et al., "Multi-Sense Embeddings."

sense embedding model for representing words with multiple or colliding meanings.

Recent research has shown that the semantic spaces produced by currently advanced LLMs are surpassing the expectation of training to estimate semantic distance by producing "categorical hierarchies . . . represented as subspaces in a linear space."[21] Empirical observation of this behavior in the activations and semantic latent spaces of LLMs argues against the linear representation or semantic distribution hypotheses in favor of a more robust inference or model-theoretic semantic. Large language models are, by merit of their training, producing latent spaces that employ a sophisticated set theory to create taxonomical structures in their semantic subspaces, as driven by the optimization of the goals for these systems established in training. This allows for logical conclusions to be properly tested, as there is an asymmetry that otherwise does not exist in a purely linear semantic distance-based model. In practical terms, this means an LLM can properly distinguish between use of a semantic term in a protasis versus the apodosis, mathematically representing these very different contexts in terms of subsequent logically justified inferential claims. Large language models so enabled will not try to claim all men to be Socrates but will find all to be mortal.

Intentional AI System Design

Model and system design have expected points of strong similarity to the processes of working with concepts as an individual or collective language user, and processes for justification and normative taking true by interpretive communities. The comparison is not perfect (it does not need to be dogmatically followed and is offered for ease of conceptualization) but my research primarily presents parallels between the attributes of model design and individual language users, while the attributes of system design implement intersubjective aspects of communicative action (either located within the individual participation in the community of communication, or with a loci external to the self and within the community and interpersonal institutions itself).

Recent developments in AI systems have focused on an agentic system design, where individual *agents* are responsible for specific parts of a holistically sophisticated task. This concept applies to the modality of generation (for example, an agent good at linguistics, another one good at creating images, and another at doing mathematics accurately), agents to decompose

---

21. Arai and Tsugawa, "Large Language Models," 10.

and orchestrate the activities of other agents, and agents to apply various criteria before the response is provided. To simplify the conceptual discussion, I will overload the term *model design* to include the various aspects that fall into the design of the agents themselves, and then *system design* will discuss the coordination of these to produce a greater systemic behavior.

When discussing model design in this framing, the primary focus is on LLMs or other sorts of language models. As expected, the design choices of these models implement learnings and understanding of human native language users in order to produce high quality results. In many cases, the convergence of what is optimized for the computer science objectives of an LLM and what is pedantically predicated by linguistic theory is uncanny. This is the outcome expected by the generative linguistic school, or those who hold to maximal models for semantics.

Attention mechanisms draw on the modeling of the human eye, where the field of vision is broken into smaller subdivisions (kernels) that are then summarized. The important or salient part of the kernel is all that is extracted at the end of this process of recursive summarization. The attention process for efficient information representation also follows the expectations of functional grammar and discourse analysis: meaning shifts depending on the level of aggregation. This practice is well known for exegetes of languages like Koine Greek, where an anchor clause at the end of a long sentence may dramatically shift the meaning.

Attention mechanisms provide a process of recursive summarization that parallels the models used in functional grammar. The process for attention summarization uses matrix mathematics to weigh and calculate the most important data that should be focused on.[22] Functional grammar describes a similar process for modeling meaning. According to the functional grammar and kernel model of Dik,[23] sentences are expressed as aggregations of regularly formed kernel sentences. Dik's own effort was shared as a computer program at the time of his research, demonstrating the ready applicability and implementation in the computer sciences.

The challenges of attention mechanisms recall the important process of finding the right level of detail to represent during training a neural network. The learning function is one of the most dramatic impacts to the quality of the resulting model, and the reason has a very clear linguistic parallel. When training of a data stimulus, the goal is a global or generalized model, not an exact repetition of the source data. For example, use of

---

22. There are multiple algorithms to deliver this result, with one popular example being SoftMax.

23. Dik, *Structure of the Clause*.

a paradigm is not the same as rote repetition. To properly train a model, we need to learn the proverbial paradigms. We don't want to just repeat the tokens/words/n-grams that are observed in the training corpus. This focus on abstraction as part of the process is critical to generating content that is not explicitly the training material and yet is coherent with the training material. In mathematical terms, it is a matter of allowing an appropriate amount of noise (added data) or lossiness (loss of data) that will produce results that can continue a literary context without repetition of prior art.

Advances in attention mechanisms reflect the linguistic movement away from morphology and toward the sentence or the discourse unit being the carrier of meaning. New models work with alternating attention (moving between global and local), with a rotational approach (RoPE) being a common implementation. Again, the mathematics pursued to produce high quality empirical results converges on the same conclusions of linguists, many of whom have moved toward discourse analysis.

Parallel to the construction of sentiment in a human mind, an effective and high quality LLM is not creating a single stream of attention. Multi-headed attention mechanisms provide the ability for parallel points of attention, meaning a turn of phrase or specific referent can dramatically shift the attention of a text. This practice is well known, particularly for exegetes of languages like Koine Greek where the emphatic placement of verbs, which themselves encode a potentially anaphoric subject, can often follow many clauses and words with their own localized importance. The human mind can struggle to remember references, and this same limitation can impact too large of a context window for an LLM to process, yet despite the inherent difficulties, both employ pragmatically similar techniques to maintain focus on the right content.

One of the other techniques shared by these language users is the idea of various *activations*, determining how influential those layers are in the activity manifested in the system. One of the more popular approaches is GeGLU,[24] an approach to using gated linear units to drive activations of the layers. When building the model itself, the designers make decisions about the shape of the layers (how wide they are with multiple units, and how deep they are with multiple layers). GeGLU is a family of layers that allows for these varied activations, which is extremely important for efficient *transfer learning*. In transfer learning, the relationships that were trained from a general-purpose corpus are then refined to be specifically and deeply specialized for a specific domain.

---

24. Shazeer, "GLU Variants Improve Transformer."

The initial training of a model will produce the *initial weights* to be used for attention of the context. The training process will often begin with very large datasets and computing clusters, yet recent advancements have allowed the costs and access to these capabilities (of a high quality) to be dramatically reduced. After the initial training, the transformer architecture is ready to be dynamically influenced and interacted with. The completed model is a *pre-trained transformer*, which, if used for generative purposes, will often be called a Generative Pre-trained Transformer (or GPT). Development-cognitive linguists may be interested in parallels here to the cognitive development of native language users, but this is outside of my primary research focus.

When a user interacts with a GPT, it is by providing *prompts*. These are written in natural language and responded to in a manner that increasingly reflects human behavior. The prompts are processed into the attention of the GPT so that the response is highly tailored to the context set by the human. This can be as imperative as telling the GPT the domains of expertise to draw upon or giving the GPT instructions on how to decompose and recompose a problem (as in chain-of-reasoning prompting), or as seemingly innocuous as using polite language and telling the GPT it has had its morning coffee. In a heuristic that parallels human communication and the need for cooperation,[25] these aspects in a prompt will dramatically change the quality and nature of the responses. A whole discipline for *prompt engineering* focuses on how to produce prompts that will have the greatest efficacy.

While a GPT has already been trained for general inference, there may be domain- or application-specific details that need refined weighting. This can be done with *fine-tuning*, a process that changes the weights of the model in a persisting manner. Examples would be taking a general-purpose GPT that has the ability to draw inference from a wide range of vocabulary and embeddings and adding specific embeddings for a domain like medicine or academia. This process of generalized training and then specialized training produces higher quality results than a model trained only on the small, limited corpus of data for that specialized domain. This observation in the behavior of LLMs reflects a kindred observation about human use of concepts. Pannenberg echoes the idea that domain specificity finds a firm foundation in generalized capabilities and, in making his case, draws further still on Schleiermacher: "Religion and its content were not additional to the ordinary reality of ourselves and our world."[26] The generalized aware-

---

25. An important example is the "cooperative principle" highlighted by Cotterell and Turner, *Linguistics*, 258.

26. Pannenberg, *Systematic Theology*, 139.

ness of the world is quite helpful for our own human *transfer learning*, and the resulting applications have much richer capabilities than the narrowly trained models that begin and end with a specific domain.

When not going through the process of fine-tuning a model, there can still be context buildup that helps appropriate the attention of the LLM. This is called *few-shotting* in contrast to *zero-shotting*. In a zero-shot situation, the user is seeing if the LLM can produce high-quality results on the first exposure to a specific language task or context. The quality of the generated results will often dramatically improve, particularly with difficult tasks, if the LLM is prompted with multiple examples or feedback is provided on multiple examples. Similar to traditional training, this reinforcement process allows for the customized weights to shift, meaning the results of the attention mechanism can better align with obtaining the goals of the user.

Furthering AI System Design

An individual LLM or GPT can produce remarkably humanlike content. However, just as teams of humans coordinate to bring the best out of every member, systems built by coordinating the best work product of several AI components has the goal of surpassing any individual model on its own. These combined systems have the lofty goal of equal or superior performance in tasks (including linguistic ones) versus human capabilities. The weaknesses of a single GPT are often mitigated by counter-balancing agents (a *panel of experts*). Just as a single interpreter may be more inclined to mistake than the committee or consensus of an interpretive community, particularly one of experts, the systems that are composed of multiple GPTs and agents are less prone to obvious errors and more capable of refined quality outputs.

Agentic AI systems (another example of the shorthand *AI systems*) allow individual parts of a process to be subdivided and optimized. This is being done in a way reminiscent of GANs, where multiple neural network models would play each other to see which was empirically proven to be the best model, and to drive further learning for an idealized target model. A GAN approach allows AI models to reinforce their own behavior without active human intervention. In terms of AI systems using LLMs and GPTs, this concept also motivated the general idea of "LLM as judge," where an LLM is used to score the results of some other process.

Early in the use of LLMs, it was found that they were effective at judging arbitrary input based upon enumerated criteria. Attention can be very intentionally influenced with prompt engineering, and this can be directed toward an LLM exercising expert-level analysis of some input content/text. Large language models are stochastic and therefore do not have the repeatability of a deterministic system, but when it comes to a relative evaluation, they have strong performance versus the discernment of human judges and can scale to process dramatically larger volumes of input data than human expert judges.

One reason why LLMs were first used as judges was to see if the resulting compound systems could filter out and protect against LLMs *hallucinating*: making inferences that are not correct. Hallucinations, just like human misconceptions, are often presented as facts with evident confidence. Using a separate LLM to evaluate the truthfulness and accuracy of the generated response has become a powerful way to quickly assess the quality of the results and iterate on these results in the case that a judgment rules against the veracity or quality of the initial LLM response. An LLM or AI agent serving as judge will still be stochastic; however, multiple AI agents judging in concert has shown to dramatically increase the reliability and quality of the resulting generated communicative acts. One empirical study found that this means AI systems can become more truthful than humans when debating, given the AI systems had a lower propensity to lie than the comparative human participants.[27] This humorous observation raises a fair objection: AI systems should not be compared against a standard of perfection. These systems are being compared to humans, who also intentionally or by weakness fail to execute linguistic skills with perfection.

Hallucinations (incorrect statements presented as facts) are particularly dangerous given other aspects of human communication related to the natural receiver of language. The principle of charity[28] is an example of how humans are inclined to believe that most of what they hear in a communicative act is true. Similarly, Plantinga argues that the very composition of the human mind for language by God our Creator disposes humanity to make sense and seek truth in what is heard or received.[29] Our inclination toward expecting most of what we hear to be true is an implicit assumption with processes like radical translation[30] or radical interpretation. The very possibility of this radical case of language usage is predicated on assumptions built from observations and logical extensions from native language use.

27. Aryan, "LLMs as Debate Partners."
28. This will be discussed extensively in chapter 6 on concepts-meanings, beginning under the section "Epistemic Assumptions in Natural Language." Concepts-meanings is the second of the three major sections describing aspects of a proclamation (as utterance, as conveying concepts-meanings, and as expressing authority).
29. Plantinga, *Warrant*, 14.
30. Quine, *Quintessence*, 124.

Playing language games by the assumed rules and cooperating in order to have a bidirectional communication is the expectation.

The inherited effect is that nonhuman participants are granted a similar degree of good will. When we consider that it is not inherently clear if a communicative act originated in an AI system or a human author, it becomes increasingly difficult to pragmatically and proactively know if the principle of charity or cooperation is being performed with a human or an AI as the other party. If a communicative act is received without the context of knowing if it originated in human thought or an AI system, what approaches to interpretation are possible for the human interpreter? Further complicating matters, if a human performs a communicative act (reading a text out loud), the audience still may not have a non-question-begging determinate way of validating that the text which was read (or for that matter, memorized) was not one provided by an AI system.

We could accept a persistent and debilitating skepticism against all communication now that AI systems are capable of producing human-like content, or we can thoughtfully reason about the implications of our pragmatic,[31] cultural, and philosophical assumptions, in addition to our potentially generative-linguistic biological and societal design, on the inclination to take true and interpret AI-system-generated content in a manner undifferentiated from human authors. Human optimism toward communicative acts is important to introduce in the context of hallucinations. The charity principle is one example of how natural language usage disposes humans to take things as true until sufficient reason for disproving has been provided, meaning that hallucinations by AI systems are liable to not be detected immediately (unless the reader has a strong existing and conflicting knowledge of the subject matter).[32]

Another humanlike augmentation that has been added to individual AI models to produce empirical quality improvements is giving the AI system access to well-known resources or references. When a well-researched human is asked a question, they may turn to a bookshelf and retrieve a book or turn to a set of research notes prepared on the topic. Turning to a trusted and well-known resource dramatically improves the results and

---

31. "We can be clear about breakdowns in translation when they are local enough, for a background of general successful translation provides what is needed to make the failures intelligible." Davidson is one of many linguists who argue that the failure of language demonstrates the overall rule of the success of language for communication. Davidson, *Essential Davidson*, 203.

32. The primary focus of this research is on texts, but hopefully it will not be lost on the reader that the discernment of authorship is not limited to just written text. This is particularly true given the reality that humans have performed AI-generated content with the intention of it being presented and received as having a human origin.

performance of a human answering an esoteric or difficult question. The AI system parallel is *Retrieval Augmented Generation* or RAG. When working with the vector space of the embeddings, embeddings can be added that correspond not to words but to references to external resources. The vector space is already enriched and clarified with difficult concepts, but RAG adds specific external specialist resources to be made available within a response. The resources that correspond to these embeddings can either be provided directly as part of the generated response, or the internal content can be used for other processes and AI agents/processing. The net result is a higher quality result due to reliance on trusted references, which are referenced contextually due to being related to the whole of the vector space of potential inferences in the same way as any other concept or semantically modeled unit of thought.

Another attribute of AI system design to highlight is the structuring of problem-solving/multistep communicative acts as *chain of thought* or *chain of reasoning*. Humans are notoriously opaque in their honest reasoning about the procedure taken to arrive at a communicative act. Either from neglect or intention, humans often struggle to understand what "made us say or think that." AI systems produce clues that help to identify the internal processing, and using these has proven important to help researchers and participants in interactions with AI systems have confidence in the reasoning that produced a final result. An expert on a given subject may know if an AI system has hallucinated a falsity, but even a nonexpert can follow (and potentially object to) reasoning that leads to a given generated result. Without domain expertise, a larger population of human participants can still evaluate the truthiness of each individual step in a complex process. If the human participant does not understand or have confidence evaluating every step of the process, they may still have greater confidence by having the wherewithal to evaluate these proceedings.

Recalling the nature of humans in processing communicative acts, these explanations may also serve to convince a dubious human of the accuracy of incorrect content by giving a well-reasoned account for an erroneous trajectory of thought. This possibility cannot be discounted. Addressing the human participation in this communicative act leads away from the important foundational context about the attributes of an AI system, and deviates from the focus of research: applying the abilities of AI systems to their utterances concepts-meanings, and authority that can provisionally be qualified and evaluated as Christian proclamation.

System design also improves the quality of inference through reinforcement learning. There are two primary types of reinforcement learning, where the models are trained or fine-tuned using an external third-party judge to provide feedback. The highest quality feedback is generally expected from humans, who can evaluate if a response is correct or meets certain standards of epistemic quality. In this procedure, the AI system is implicitly participating under the authority of a human community of judges. There is no "volitional" participation (the AI system did not seek human reinforcement) as the AI system was designed to participate in incorporating this normative authority. The secondary approach is to scale the reinforcement process by using models or other AI systems (compound systems interacting with compound systems). This is different than a single AI system including an LLM as judge in the inference pipeline, because this feedback is being provided prior to inference time (during training). In anthropomorphic terms, it is like the difference between a good pedagogue teaching a pupil how to think (reinforcement learning), and a team responding to an answer with one member telling another that their work was wrong. The more scalable and exciting is clearly the former, where all future system-executed inference is improved.

Research in the field of AI is currently yielding dramatic results, and one of those areas of dramatic improvement is in synthetic reinforcement learning. Significant research in synthetic reinforcement learning was published during the course of my own project, shifting the perception of the quality of this method, and reflecting the rapid pace of significant contributions to the practical efficacy of these AI systems.[33] The dramatic launch of a top-tier AI system based on reinforcement learning demonstrated to the world and the AI community the quality that can be achieved with the latter type of reinforcement learning. The research showed that a sophisticated use of group relative policy optimization would allow a cohort of synthetic (nonhuman) reinforcement feedback to drive better overall efficacy from an accuracy and a presentation perspective. The result of a reward mechanism inserted in the multistep reasoning was a production model that can "improve its reasoning capabilities autonomously."[34] This is a procedural (system design) implementation that allows for the model to be guided in a pedagogically meaningful way without humans being the scaling bottleneck.

The design raises interesting cultural-normative questions about relative authority that are partially beyond the scope of this research. In the research of R1, the researchers themselves were surprised by the empirical findings that reflect the process of student learning. The model experienced an "aha moment" where the system determined that additional processing time was necessary for a specific step. It is worth a direct quote

---

33. DeepSeek-AI et al., "DeepSeek-R1."
34. DeepSeek-AI et al., "DeepSeek-R1," 7.

from those researchers: "Rather than explicitly teaching the model on how to solve a problem, we simply provide it with the right incentives, and it autonomously develops advanced problem-solving strategies."[35] This raises questions for the nature of pedagogy as a process of developing the minds of students, and potentially important philosophical, cognitive-linguistic, and behavioral questions about the primitive source of more advanced reasoning (particularly when not expressed by a human agent).

SUMMARY

AI increasingly writes like a human. This has been a cursory review of the ways that AI systems use language to produce texts that are increasingly recognized as showing the attributes and behaviors of natural language use. AI systems have implemented the predictions and theories of functional grammar that describe the process of properly working with language. It is a very functional view at this level, and the results are meaningful. Humans recognize this language use as contextual, intentional, and natural. These texts are more than mere reproduction. AI uses words based on their literary use, not rote definition. AI models the communicative context so that the whole composition is coherent. AI use of language maintains the tension between a normative use (based on training to identify prior use) and novel use (using language based on the specific context). Commitments within a discourse and across a conversation are reflected in the subsequent commitments, satisfying the inferentialist criterion for how sapiential humans *describe* instead of merely *labeling* the objects of their texts.[36] Inferential descriptions are reflected through the "inferential consequences, either immediately practical . . . or for further classifications"[37] that are semantically evidenced in AI-generated texts maintaining description commitments through the attention mechanism.

The field of AI research is broad and constantly evolving, so these capabilities will continue to mature post the publishing of this book. No survey could be capable of staying ahead of a constantly growing and evolving field

---

35. DeepSeek-AI et al., "DeepSeek-R1," 8.

36. The object of a text is its intention, and therefore it is important to *describe* more than merely *label* this object. Describing the object of a text reflects a more meaningful and committed language use. Description with persisting commitments is the higher standard applied by inferentialist thinkers like Wilfrid Sellars: "The expressions in terms of which we describe objects . . . locate these objects in a space of implications, that they describe at all, rather than merely label." Sellars, "Counterfactuals, Dispositions, and Causal Modalities," 306–7.

37. Brandom et al., "Intentionality and Language," 11.

like AI. Instead, the goal is to highlight some of the concepts that will be critical to describing the ability for AI to produce Christian proclamation.

5

GENERATING AN UTTERANCE

THE FIRST ASPECT TO focus on is proclamation as an utterance:

> *Proclamation is an utterance* conveying concepts-meanings that, if taken true, would be consistent in a belief system that is also consistent with the faith of Jesus Christ.

1. What attributes are expected because Christian proclamation is an utterance?
2. How do these attributes show up in Paul's Letter to the Romans?
3. What criteria in the models of linguists describe these attributes?
4. How does AI text perform on the criteria:
   a. Contextuality
   b. Linguistic intentionality?

A proclamation is a written utterance. Cotterell and Turner define an utterance as "when a sentence is used in the real world, whether it is spoken or written."[1] It is no longer theoretical (like a sentence) but is expressed through context. Many linguists stress that the situational context of an utterance is a critical factor, particularly for sentences that describe a belief or position versus pointing to and describing some part of objective reality.[2]

---

1. Cotterell and Turner, *Linguistics*, 22.
2. Wittgenstein, *Zettel*, §§ 532–34.

Discourse analysis,[3] where linguists consider the authoritative claim made in a situational context, is built on the analysis of sentences.

The theoretical and practical comparison along the expected attributes of a human utterance will be the first foundational step of illustrating that AI-generated content can be reasoned about in direct comparison to human proclamation and evaluated based on meeting the criterion expected of the human variant. Utterances have attributes that are critically important as predicates of proclamations, and therefore this category stands as a proper and beneficial descriptor. After explaining why utterances are an effective descriptor, my attention will turn to the attributes that are so apt, and the suitability of AI-system communications as a qualifying instance.

As a quick clarification, it is not the claim that utterances are exhaustive in describing all human proclamations. However, the goal of illustrating how an AI system can meet the criteria normally expected of a human proclamation will be fully satisfied by meeting this one class or subclass of proclamation (textual proclamation).

WHY UTTERANCES?

Throughout this research, the referenced linguistic, hermeneutic, and philosophical approaches to the use and meaningfulness of language share a common emphasis on the contextuality and concreteness of an utterance. Utterances clarify the focus on a contextual, historical, accidental event of a communicative act. This disambiguates a mistaken focus on individual words or only limited dimensions of a text, and forces AI systems to accommodate this wider range of possibility and simultaneously more specific application.

Cotterell and Turner explain (with the quoted support of Hirsch, Juhl, and Thiselton) that "text of written discourses are not to be interpreted as if they were contextless sentences to be read in the abstract and so capable of multiple meanings."[4] Additional consideration should be given to the "context and social context which generally gives determinacy to a speaker's meaning" such that it goes beyond the "contextless sentences [which] may have many possible meanings."[5] Vanhoozer emphasizes both the context

---

3. Cotterell and Turner present the claim that a focus on utterances versus sentences allows for the discussion to move from abstract sentences/linguistics into practice and implication. This is absolutely critical for a partially empirically driven consideration of AI capabilities. Cotterell and Turner, *Linguistics*, 22.

4. Cotterell and Turner, *Linguistics*, 63.

5. Cotterell and Turner, *Linguistics*, 63.

and the historical conventions around the original event that is encoded in text.⁶ Wittgenstein draws the clear connection between a specific event of communication and the event of conveyed meaning: "Only in the stream of thought and life do words have meaning."⁷ Hirsch grounds meaning in the intention of the author,⁸ not only the symbols themselves.⁹ Ricoeur presents the historically situated utterance as an event, with a conveyed meaning tightly bound to the discourse content.¹⁰ This survey shows differing terms used as a proxy for utterance (e.g., an *episode, communicative act, event, performance*) but they are all referring to this shared sense of a specific realized experience of communication in a specific context that has moved from meta-language to concrete use.

An individual's most obvious and (meaningfully) uncontroversial interaction¹¹ with an AI system is the intentional prompting of such a system and the reading of the resulting text. In this experience, humans specifically seek out access to an AI system and initiate a communicative action by expressing themselves in text processed by the system. In response, the AI system will attempt to produce a textual reply.¹² The human communicates a prompt, and that language input is then used to set attention for the AI system, adjusting its generative vector space to the solution space evaluated to be most meaningful. In more complex compound systems, the response will be processed and evaluated for meaningful relevance to the original prompt and then provided back to the requesting human. The response of the AI system is adapted to the shared context of the prompt (which does not need to be real; it is correctly understood as the intention of the human participant to set a hypothetical context). The AI system attempts to produce a response in the context of the interaction, and compound systems may attempt several times to satisfy the expectations of the prompt. This

---

6. Vanhoozer, *Meaning*, 243.
7. Quoted in Thiselton, *Two Horizons*, 38.
8. Quoted in Thiselton, *Two Horizons*, 38.
9. Hirsch, *Interpretation*, 225.
10. "If all discourse is actualized as an event, all discourse is understood as meaning." Ricoeur, *Interpretation Theory*, 12.
11. As was alluded to prior, there is always the potential for a seemingly human interaction to have originated in an AI system. Individuals have submitted research generated by AI systems. Pastors have preached sermons written by AI systems. Correspondence of both serious and trivial matters have been permeated with completely AI-generated content, or content augmented by nonhuman agents (such as type-ahead suggestions).
12. Other modalities, such as video, audio, and images are commonplace, but the purview of this research is focused on textual interactions.

diligence and preserved context exhibit the principle of cooperation[13] in which is generally expected but not always provided by human communicative agents. According to Cotterell and Turner's principle, the AI system is doing a substantially good job in cooperating with the intended exchange.

A cursory note is important for a class of models of linguistics and hermeneutics that I will not extensively cite, specifically those that fully exhaust the meaning of the communicative act in the text itself. Various theories have this similarity that otherwise might not be closely associated. The relevance of each within this diversity to the current research is trivialized due to this similar emphatic focus on the text. The shared procedure of inflating the content of the text means that the linguistic skill (to produce the text) fully satisfies the communicative act (meaning and, where relevant, authority).

Such theories create an ambivalence toward the author.[14] Whatever agent can produce the strings of written marks has achieved the same communicative act. They are not avoided for their conflicting results, but for being too ready to grant AI systems full equality of meaning and sensemaking as human compositions. There is not much to argue a fortiori if the text on its own, as a series of symbols, is presumed to bear the full weight of a text's meaning. In that case, a truly random keystroke generator would suffice if the symbols struck the right order.

In addition to elevating the total meaning to the text (for instance, the relationships of the signifiers as in structuralism), these models are inclined to bracket away the relationship of text to the world. Bracketing away the world further removes the potential to disambiguate the humanity of an author. External criteria from the world can otherwise serve as important positive external criteria for Christian proclamation. In both of these ways, such theories are too readily supportive of AI systems being capable of producing the same texts as humans. This is not to reject the value of theories like structuralist hermeneutics outright, but to observe their lack of utility in qualifying Christian proclamation more stringently than others.

Related but distinct, it is important to consider the determinacy of the utterance's context in the case of a textual communicative act. The distinguished disciplines of textual criticism, form criticism, and textual history

---

13. "Make your contribution such as is required, at the stage at which it occurs, by the accepted purpose or direction of the talk exchange in which you are engaged." Cotterell and Turner, *Linguistics*, 261.

14. Agreeing with Eagleton: "[The written work's] 'anonymity' is part of its very structure." If the text is anonymous, then there is no recourse to spooky proclamation at a distance. AI can produce content that cannot be discriminated from human proclamation, given the same linguistic skills are achieved. Eagleton, *Literary Theory*, 104.

attempt to distinguish the "true" and "historical" circumstances in which a text was produced. The ambiguity of human-produced context is further exacerbated when the question is not about the historical contingencies but about the text being produced by a human or an AI system. Without direct and unmediated access to the creation of the text, it is virtually impossible to create an unambiguous, publicly observable chain of custody by which the recipient can guarantee that a text did not originate with an AI system. This is one of the most pressing areas of concern for those interested in the ethics and honesty of a textual composition being produced by humans. The often-intractable difficulty in discerning the authorship of content validates that this is not a trivial task.

THE ROMANS EXAMPLE

Textual utterances should be considered universally important to Christian proclamation due to their compositional role in the canonical Scriptures. In particular, the Epistles were an exercise in communicating applied theology juxtaposed with reinforcing that teaching in the context of imperfect recipient churches who needed correction and guidance. The Letter to the Romans is an example that will form part of the initial contemplation for each chapter related to the criteria of a proclamation (utterance, concepts-meanings, and authority).

Paul begins by asserting his confidence in the Roman church, which he has not met directly.[15] His instruction is not a reminder of behaviors that the church had directly observed from Paul. Neither had he inculcated these based on his prior evangelistic work in Rome. He had not even visited this church yet, as attested by the internal evidence of the text. The Roman practice and manner of actively living as the community of faith is therefore being reshaped based on propositional content delivered via the modality of text.[16] Without forestalling, the possibility of this authority and impact

---

15. Rom 15:14–5: "Πέπεισμαι δέ, ἀδελφοί μου, καὶ αὐτὸς ἐγὼ περὶ ὑμῶν, ὅτι καὶ αὐτοὶ μεστοί ἐστε ἀγαθωσύνης, πεπληρωμένοι πάσης γνώσεως, δυνάμενοι καὶ ἀλλήλους νουθετεῖν. τολμηρότερον δὲ ἔγραψα ὑμῖν ἀπὸ μέρους, ὡς ἐπαναμιμνῄσκων ὑμᾶς, διὰ τὴν χάριν τὴν δοθεῖσάν μοι ὑπὸ τοῦ θεοῦ" (SBLGNT).
"I myself am convinced, my brothers and sisters, that you yourselves are full of goodness, filled with knowledge and competent to instruct one another. Yet I have written you quite boldly on some points to remind you of them again, because of the grace God gave me."

16. Regardless of the ontic performance of the text in an embodied manner. The embodied nature of a performance of a text can be similarly applied to any reading of a text, given the role of the reader in mediating the text to themself.

is made possible by a shared supposition pool (faith in Christ) with the recipients.

Observing Romans, two subsequent questions arise. There is an important hermeneutic question of "How do we today understand a communication which was public-shared, but set in a context that is now private to us?" There is also an important authority question of "How could such a text be authoritative with Paul absent and never having been present?"

Prior to these questions, in Romans there is an affirmation by example of the historical and ontic reality of proclaiming Christian faith in absence, with propositions (injunctions, exhortations, rhetoric, and narratives) directly conflicting with and overcoming traditions. This was not only the intention of Paul, but it was realized. The long-term effect of Paul's letter influenced their behavior as reflected by the records of Eusebius that the Roman church received this letter well, including the critique of their pride and divisions. Therefore, there was, at a minimum, the effort by the very first Christians to have proclamation as a textual utterance and, at maximum, there is evidence that this produced a great effect by disrupting by way of "bold reminders" the truth system that the Roman community of faith was called to and capable of in Christ.

FRAMEWORKS FOR UTTERANCES

Linguistics in the broadest sense provides a framework for understanding the mechanics of communication, with this being focused on utterances for the duration of this research. The question is embedded within many subsequent topics (e.g., philology, philosophy, theology, sociology) and these range from the very abstract to precisely and contextually applied.

Within each discourse or domain there exist many differing approaches, and this survey is not meant to either prioritize these views nor to provide a grand unification of what intends to be dissonant. Instead, I have selected a small number of thinkers who express a diversity of approaches and are important as linguistic bulwarks or foils referenced by the thinkers otherwise profiled and considered in the remainder of this research.

These thinkers include those focused on the philosophy of language (e.g., Davidson) and those who are very applied or even empirical in their thinking (e.g., Hirsch). It will be valuable therefore to review the context of their overall program before these criteria are applied to AI systems to see if they are likewise capable of meeting these expectations. Where the criteria or general frameworks provided are satisfied by AI systems, the question will be raised (but not resolved herein): Does this criterion being satisfied by a nonhuman agent motivate further refinement to the assumptions of these models, or alternatively stress the need for (existing or new) provisions (such as ontological stipulations) that must obtain for these frameworks to hold? Philosophy of language is often the foundation used by subsequent theories (e.g., hermeneutics) that will adopt and extend the assumptions and commitments of linguists.

Peter Cotterell and Max Turner: *Linguistics & Biblical Interpretation*

The ostensive goal of *Linguistics & Biblical Interpretation* is to bring together linguistics and biblical interpretation.[17] Their project discusses *meaning* (derived from the syntactical evidence), *significance* of the meaning (understood in various frames of reference from the original audience to the current reader), and then *significance* of the whole (the tension of contribution and particularity between meaning of the part and the whole).

Their approach to the third question is purposefully framed in the context of discourse units.[18] They are experts in advanced Koine studies, using nuanced frameworks such as the latest in verbal aspect-*Aktionsart* and markedness theory (local and global syntax). Their program is built upon a foundational contention that so much of the meaning in a text is directly extracted by thoughtful consideration of the text-as-it-is and the various syncategorematic configurations. The meaning found internal to the text does not exhaust the meaning but becomes the epistemic bedrock for the hermeneutic tussle between meaning of the whole and the part. Their focus is explicitly biblical interpretation as a model set in the context of the much broader general linguistics. Commonly the primary focus and attention is on the relationship of a reader to the canonical text, although their program is partially argued from noncanonical examples, demonstrating a more ambitious unified vision of hermeneutics.

A realist attitude toward the determination of the meaning of text can help navigate this hermeneutic tussle. For example, we can accept a strict correlation between a text and a determinate and specific communication act: "[Texts] are representations of definite acts of communication given in

17. Hirsch, *Interpretation*, 10.

18. My introduction to this resource was through Campbell and Carson's *Advances in the Study of Greek*, where a chapter is devoted to the burgeoning (since the 1990s) focus on discourse analysis. Many of my own personal biases in understanding utterances are in strong agreement with the effectiveness of discourse analysis, particularly in highly discursive language examples like New Testament Koine Greek. Not all languages are so aptly described with discourse techniques or by functional grammar.

particular contexts by specific people, for definite purposes and this matrix of properties is determinative for at least some levels of their meaning."[19] The uneasy ambiguity of the latter "some levels of meaning" is immediately resolved by focusing on the *discourse meaning*.[20] This fixed the notionally proper meaning in the historical reality of the meaning for the original discourse in the context of prior communication between the involved parties (which is particularly relevant for the Epistles). Texts have historical context and intention, just as other linguistic utterances.

Their approach to deriving significance in a responsible manner is largely based on understanding the "shared presupposition pool"[21] of the communicating parties and appreciating the dynamics of discourses. An excellent example is their very enlightening consideration of participation in communication through the context of John 3, raising the question of how much Nicodemus was participating in the historical event. Considering the presupposition pool introduces the ideas of shared concepts-meanings that are relevant to the participating individuals (not necessarily the full historical reconstruction). The interplay of authority in a discourse is shown by how the discussion obeys the rules of discourse, such as cooperation. Importantly, looking at the rules of real discourse avoids the idealism of an ideal (phantom) participant: someone who is always actively responding, saying what they think, and aware of all the possible facts and perspectives present in their historical context. Real discourse does not look like that. Accordingly, our reading ought not place too much emphasis on what is left undone versus our own idealized reconstruction.

Cotterell and Turner's program is not intended to reason about texts that are produced by AI systems. They describe natural language use. As a result, their theory describes the use of language that AI systems have implemented. Their shared presupposition pool is the abstract description of what is implemented for an AI system via a rich embedding space saturated with semantic concepts for the intended discourse. I often use the concept of a shared supposition pool to explain what an embedding or semantic space is. We know the former due to our use of natural language, and the latter is a mathematical implementation of the former. The expectations and behaviors of a native language user were implemented via transformer models and attention mechanisms, while the flow of a discourse was learned by processing discourses during training. Research has shown a great deal

---

19. Hirsch, *Interpretation*, 63.
20. Hirsch, *Interpretation*, 64.
21. Cotterell and Turner, *Linguistics*, 90–97, 100–1, 249, 257, 259, 262, 270, 282, 301–2, 314–15.

of success while suggesting the opportunity for further enrichment through system design (and further research).[22] Cotterell and Turner have described what natural language users do, and this provides a first blueprint of the functional behavior that an AI would need to satisfy to be recognized as a natural language user.

Key ideas raised by Cotterell and Turner are the existence of a *shared presupposition pool* between participants, and the need for minimal cooperation in a discourse. Our working definition of a shared presupposition pool follows the definition used by Cotterell and Turner: the words that have a public sense across the involved participants, often due to similar experiences or exposure to related ostensive or abstract referents and shaped by other ideological and cultural influences on the understood relative meaning of words. For example, technical language exists within specialized domains, and this technical language forms a shared presupposition pool with other practitioners. The concept of *cooperation* is familiar to most natural language users: both/all parties must cooperate to some minimal degree. When this cooperation is lacking (we're talking over each other or about different things) it will be evidenced by the discussion going silent.

Donald Davidson

Donald Davidson was a major influence in the philosophy of language and served a foundational role for other thinkers we will consider. Davidson also interacts with Quine and Tarski, who together give a comprehensive view of the field. As Cotterell and Turner advocate in their intro, there is much learning to be gained from profane study of linguistics. The description of natural language usage is not exclusive or privileged for the community of faith. To stay relevant as an evangelistic faith, consideration of general linguistics and epistemology is paramount.

Davidson takes a sternly realist and rational approach to language. His position on concepts like metaphor and the epistemic content of communication is extremely pragmatic. We communicate to mean what we said. His view accordingly veers into classical logic and a closed system of language: "Sentences of the theory [the speaker's truth system] are empirical generalizations about speakers, and so must not only be true but also lawlike," while the lawlike nature describes a truth value that can "support appropriate

---

22. Li and Wang, "TACOMORE." This research suggests that there is room for further development and the potential of building compound systems that use design to optimize for and implement various more advanced linguistic skills.

counterfactuals."[23] For Davidson, use of language commits us to an empirically realist truth system, as assessed by the speaker. The functional use of language expresses the commitments of the speaker. His ex post facto pragmatic approach accepts the heuristic that using language with an implied truth commitment means that is the commitment of the speaker. This is particularly important for the discussion of AI making commitments. If an AI text only needs to stay committed *discursively* to have a truth commitment, then this criterion can be met through the use of language to make an argument. AI doesn't need some ontological will that is committed to truth, it only needs to use language in a way that functionally is recognized as making truth commitments for the reader to recognize the AI author as operating within an understandable truth system.

Davidson's afterthoughts on this theory illuminate the logical fallacy that makes the differentiation between human and AI authors so difficult. Quite simply, we are communicative creatures so we are conditioned to think that meaningful texts are the byproduct of meaningful human intention. To use Davison's language, if we read an anonymous veridical text, we assume this relates to properly organized beliefs possessed by the author. When the reader's judgment is limited to the text, it is extremely difficult to justify thinking that the author does not believe what they are writing. Classical logic gives us two options: a radical trust that the author believes what they are saying, or a pervasive skepticism that no author can be trusted.

Ideally, the observer would escape the fool's dilemma of choosing between these options. Perhaps the reader could defer a commitment, as with an evidence-preserving nonclassical logic system. The reader could recognize the fallacy of going from the consequences (a meaningful text with an intention to discuss an object) to an assumption about the causes (an author who holds those beliefs). Either option would mitigate (delay or avoid) improper attribution of character to the supposed author based on the nature of their text. Unfortunately, this fallacious attribution is so common it is expected for ordinary natural language users (laypersons). Many hermeneutic models proposed by experts in the field (see Vanhoozer, Hirsch) urge the reader to make such assumptions about the character and ontological standing of the author based on the texts received. This is ultimately the problematic observed by this research, and it connects all the way back to how readers and listeners interact with language when described by the linguists. The challenges describe our fundamental use of language and precede other commitments (such as Christian faith).

---

23. Davidson, *Essential Davidson*, 162.

In more formal logical terms, both human authors and AI authors can produce texts that are veridical, propositionally meaningful, and in discourse reflect the intention of a specific object. Therefore, the meaningfulness of a text cannot be attributed exclusively to a human author, even though an intentional human author is one possible cause of an intentional text. For generations there was an exclusivity, leading writers like Hirsch and Vanhoozer to muse about seagulls writing texts with no intention. There absolutely is a causal relationship between an intentional human author and the intention encoded in the meaning of a text. We cannot assume that the latter (meaningful text) implies the former (human author). Furthermore, we only have public access to the latter (the text) and do not have public access to the intention (which often is inferred from the text itself), which means the case will always need to proceed from the evidence of the consequent, which cannot logically assure us of the normally expected antecedent.

Meaningful texts no longer inherently mean intentional authors. We now have AI systems producing texts that are recognized as intentional. It is common for an AI to be tasked by a human (via prompting) to produce texts with an intention, and the human participant recognizes the task as accomplished by recognizing the generated text as showing the desired intention. Henceforth, it is unsafe to naïvely assume a direct correspondence between a meaningful text and an intentional human author. Davidson is helpful for highlighting another way in which this fallacious attribution may cause the reader to expect a set of beliefs in the AI system based on a veridical reading of the text.

Davidson's theory is not a theory of truth (and he regrets describing it as a coherence theory), but he strongly insists as bedrock that "belief is intrinsically veridical."[24] For Davidson, belief has a relationship with truth by way of meaning. This is a crucial connection to explore as the connection between truth and meaning can provide an extrapolation or substitute for properly predicating belief of an AI system based on its communication. Davidson's goal is a theory that "allows us to say ... what someone who understands that speaker, or those speakers, knows,"[25] and this means we are trading in the successful conveyance of epistemic content. Prioritization of the understanding of the recipient and their cognitive experience of the text precludes external realist obligations on the human character of the author,

---

24. Davidson, *Essential Davidson*, 239.
25. Davidson, *Essential Davidson*, 240.

while for Davidson it is necessary to "save truth from being 'radically non-epistemic' (in Putnam's words)."[26]

Davidson's directly pragmatic and realist approach to language locates the various contents and uses of a language in the text itself. As a result, his theory will again become important when considering the potential or effective authority of textual proclamation.[27] In advance of that discussion, it will be valuable to reason about how his final applications (in terms of authority and taking true) place expectations and burdens on the nature of utterances and concepts-meanings themselves.

Davidson's realism and pragmatic-use approach will help ground and shape the dialogue about how a proclamation can have authority, given "all that counts as evidence or justification for a belief must come from the same totality of belief to which it belongs."[28] This observation motivates a potential explicative to the ambivalence of the humanity of an author by way of dividing the whole process of disquoting and adopting a belief into phases.[29] By this division an AI-system content can describe or provide a schema and set of beliefs, but accepting that truth system is a subsequent activity predicated on ontological and relational dynamics that are satisfied completely only by non-AI-system participation (human, divine, or divine and human).

Key ideas raised by Davidson are the veridical or epistemic nature of meanings and beliefs, and the expressed involvement of the author through the rules displayed in their texts. The veridical nature of belief describes how a belief should reflect reality (realism), and how this is an indelible contribution to the function of beliefs. The veridical nature of belief expresses Davidson's direct realism and will be an important but not exclusive approach to modeling intersubjective understanding and the attendant consequences (respectively discussed in the sections on intersubjective meaning in chapter 6, and the section on public truth value in chapter 7).

CONTEXT

Context makes an utterance more than an anonymous string of symbols. It is a higher standard to expect of an AI system and demands more nuanced use

---

26. Davidson, *Essential Davidson*, 240.

27. The authority of concepts-meanings in an utterance will be the focus in chapter 7 of this research, with specific notice to the discussion of epistemic expectations within the section "Attributes of Authority."

28. Davidson, *Essential Davidson*, 239.

29. Davidson, *Essential Davidson*, 239.

of linguistic skills than a random letter/word/sentence/discourse generator. Even at the unit of a coherent discourse, there is something more difficult in participating in the ontic reality of a context. Context is critical to the goal of understanding the meaning (hermeneutics, history), propositional content (linguistics, translation), or pragmatic effect (sociology, theology) of a communicative act encoded in text. Vanhoozer summarizes well the foundational role of context in meaning: "Meaning is not a matter of words taken in isolation but of communicative acts taken in their communicative context."[30] If AI systems are unable to generate contextual utterances, then they will fall short in any subsequent marginal requirements for Christian proclamation.

Broadly speaking, context is the mechanism that gives an utterance meaning. Context relates the content of an utterance both to the history of literary activities and the ontic reality at large. The methodology for describing context is therefore one of the first battles over the realism, epistemic burden, and ontological relationships of language use.

In a linguistic-pragmatic approach, context is required to resolve the *referent* of individual words. Cotterell describes the reference as "the *thing in the world which is intentionally signified by that word of expression.*"[31] The relationship of language to the world immediately enters consideration. Campbell illustrates the point by recourse to the "Ogden-Richards triangle"[32] before explaining that "linguists assign a *determinative* function to context."[33] Context is establishing the foundation required for further reasoning about the use of concepts-meanings in the next chapters. For Campbell, there is a need for context to understand what a word is picking out in the world of the author or the shared world of the author-audience, but this is only one way of language relating to the world. Language is rife with ambiguity, using shorthand and imperfect structures to convey meaning. For anyone doubtful about the ambiguity or imperfections of language, a short perusal of the (grammatically incorrect) anaphoric demonstratives in John's gospel should be admitted as a prime witness. We need to know who "that one" is to make sense of John: "οὐκ ἦν ἐκεῖνος τὸ φῶς, ἀλλ᾽ ἵνα μαρτυρήσῃ περὶ τοῦ φωτός."[34] English translations generally avoid the jarring

30. Vanhoozer, *Meaning*, 310.
31. Cotterell and Turner, *Linguistics*, 84.
32. Campbell and Carson, *Advances in Greek*, 73.
33. Campbell and Carson, *Advances in Greek*, 75.
34. John 1:6–8: "Ἐγένετο ἄνθρωπος ἀπεσταλμένος παρὰ θεοῦ, ὄνομα αὐτῷ Ἰωάννης· οὗτος ἦλθεν εἰς μαρτυρίαν, ἵνα μαρτυρήσῃ περὶ τοῦ φωτός, ἵνα πάντες πιστεύσωσιν δι᾽ αὐτοῦ. οὐκ ἦν ἐκεῖνος τὸ φῶς, ἀλλ᾽ ἵνα μαρτυρήσῃ περὶ τοῦ φωτός" (SBLGNT). John is replete with such demonstrative usage. It was clearly part of his idiolect.

demonstrative use, but such relaxed language use is no more extreme than what natural language users do on an ongoing basis. Practical use of language requires specification of referents based on a shared supposition pool, and often these referents are optimistically expected to be determinately resolved by good scholarship.

The thinkings above place primary focus on the author in resolving the symbol into a sense and a specific referent. The historian and the biblicist alike expect a concrete referent to the words intentionally chosen in the context of producing a written text. This seeming agreement could obscure a critical disagreement over the subjectivity of the author. In the process of picking items from reality, how much of an important influence is there from the superstructure of culture and norms? For the reader, which is more important: the context of the author's pre-literary thoughts, the context of the literary production, or the context of the literary event of reading? Quine's influential proposal for radical translation warns that the individual trying to understand the relevant context of a text is "after his [the author's] socially inculcated linguistic usage, hence his responses to conditions normally subject to social assessment."[35]

An important question is the frame of reference for the context, as this will share how the criterion is applied to AI-generated utterances. Quine's thinking on radical translation can be applied or extended to assert that the primary context that is important to an utterance is external to the author.[36] Particularly with texts, some theories understand the context to be tightly bound to the accident, the specific reading of the individual or an interpretive community. Context would thus be explicitly understood in relation to the parties who complete the communicative act by being communicated with, particularly if the reader is constructing meaning. Fish describes the reader's construction of meanings as "the presently recognized interpretive strategies for producing the text,"[37] shifting the locus of context to the present reading community. This community, not the author's context or a shared context/presupposition pool, would be seen as producing the accident that is the realized experience of the completed communicative event. The extreme of this movement is deconstructionism like that of Derrida, where full autonomy of the text is independent of an authorial genesis.

Synthesizing this quick survey, the attribute *context* has raised several functional criteria for AI to satisfy. Linguists will ardently disagree on the

---

35. Quine, *Quintessence*, 124.

36. For instance, observation sentences (chapter 2) and occasion sentences (chapter 7) from *Quintessence* describe translation facilitates by context of the ontic reality surrounding and immersed in language usage.

37. Fish, *Is There a Text*, 347.

location where these functional criteria are satisfied, or the responsible party.

For deconstructionists and those focused on the interpretive-community or reader-response end of the spectrum, there is no differentiation between a human and AI system as the author. The context is appropriate to the recipient, and as a mutually exclusive independent determination, the authorship does not have an impact. Context would be completely equivalent based on the equivalent responses of an audience to the text.

Most other linguists, historians, and critics place emphasis on the context of the event of authoring/producing an utterance. The mechanics of generating textual utterances by an AI system are important for this inter-agent contextual criterion. The shared supposition pools that are necessary for context and conveying meaning to Cotterell and Turner are mathematically modeled and implemented in vectorization. The sophistication grows with dense vectors of embeddings and alternative strategies for embedding semantic dynamics. An AI system activates only portions of the semantic range, projecting new latent semantic spaces based on the attention and context window. The attention mechanism mathematically projects a contextual meaning of each generated window (across semantics, syntactics, and coherence), optimizing against sensitivity to the communication partner (prompting) to find the ideal solution space within the very richly described enunciation of the relationships in the supposition pool (embedding vector space). Research shows AI systems also work with a diachronic supposition pool, meaning the semantic relationships will dilate and change based on other embeddings.

I'll provide an example to clarify what is happening in this process. Consider an LLM responding to a prompt that ends with: "Please respond as if you were a hermeneutics professor. They are a major fan of Steven Knapp."[38] Before generating or continuing a response, the LLM first mathematically models the context. In layman's terms, the emphasis in this prompt lets the model know to increase attention weighting toward hermeneutics, and toward a pedantic semantic range of hermeneutics. When processing the final sentence, the attention becomes most strongly weighted toward the specific positions taken by Steven Knapp. To produce a corresponding result, the model will shift the default relationships between words based on this matrix of weights, and then select the optimal continuation of the response. Some words will grow closer in relationship, while others are more distant, and the relative importance of these transformations will be based

---

38. Knapp and Michaels, "Against Theory." This article specifically argues that intention is ontologically identical to meaning.

on processing the most emphatic aspect of the prompt (in this case, Steven Knapp). In the example provided, the AI will also resolve complex syntactical structures that naturally occur in language, such as pronouns, ellipses, and various complexities of tone (the example here being a relatively simple relative pronoun). References of words already provided in the response will be resolved to a location within the clustered distribution of possible words (the projected or transformed semantic space), and the optimal next words will be selected.

In this scenario, the LLM will respond to the question "What is intention" with an answer that is more erudite and appropriate to the discourse of hermeneutics (for example, giving the answer "meaning"). If the prompt asked for a response from a would-be fiancé who just purchased a ring for his beloved, the LLM would give a different answer. This is because the LLM would change the relationships of words (for example, bringing the word *marriage* closer and that of *meaning* further away) and then respond accordingly. Implementing this for an LLM is a matter of mathematically modeling the usage of words (before the execution) and using iterative matrix calculations to redistribute (transform) and then pick from amongst the responses (do vector projection) within the contextual distribution of words at the time of a response. It is like picking the right words or meanings for a conversation based on the shared presupposition pool and the flow of the conversation. It is not a mere coincidence that the LLM procedurally reflects linguistic theory. The implementations of advanced AI systems have been based on functional linguistic theory, and thus maintaining context is the intended design.

Compound AI systems go beyond the baseline capability to generate text based on shared sense, referents, and context. These three are critical for managing the semantic space but can be refined further. Compound systems follow a procedure that is analogous to proofreading a message before sending or looking at examples of a paper before starting one's own. The specific techniques are varied but attempt to improve the quality of the generated text by iteratively working on improving or testing the generated results. One example provides the LLM paradigmatic examples (*few-* or *many-shot* prompting). These examples allow the AI system to calibrate the resulting textual utterance to meet the expectations set by the examples, similar to the human example of looking at an example. Resent research suggests programmatic and practical ways to adapt the weights of the model itself to the context of the communication partner.[39] Using additional LLM prompts to evaluate the quality of a text or make changes is analogous to the

---

39. Sun et al., "Transformer-Squared."

example of proofreading. Further, just as with a human text, multiple techniques can be employed together for a single, high-quality text. When we consider what is possible in interacting with AI systems, we must consider the best possible generated text from a well-designed system. There could certainly be a failure from the AI system to produce a meaningful text, but this is no different than when a natural language user (human) failed to meet the expectations of an ideal reader or author.

In more technical terms, the recent AI-system design builds on the foundation of embeddings and vectorization. Embeddings and vectorization provide the ability to mathematically express shared referents through generated symbols, or, in layman's terms, to use words that make sense given the context of the conversation. The AI system has been trained on how natural language users employ words in these contexts, and therefore the supposition pool of the AI system is equivalent to the super-set of supposition pools represented by the training corpus. This is arguably a more widely read supposition pool than that of most humans using AI systems (few of us have read every literary classic; none have tried to read every word made publicly available on the internet). However, the context is set based on the desired experience level reflected in the response, and therefore the human participant can achieve a response exercising only concepts that ought to be shared. The contextualization of the responses is furthered by system design—for example, AI agents that are checking for contextualization before responding to the human user, or systems that incorporate human reinforcement to grade and modify future responses based on suitability. The combination of the latent ability of an AI system (the mathematical projection into a transformed semantic space) with system design is constantly improving the quality of AI-generated utterances that are contextually located in a meaningfully shared public space with the human participant.

The conclusion is that, in terms of contextuality for an utterance, AI systems currently are quite capable of producing satisfactory content.

INTENTION

An utterance is an intentional action, specifically an action performed for the purpose of communication. Whether one believes we can know or access the author of an utterance, many thinkers believe there is inherent *intention* of an author that produces the communicative act, and that to some varying degree is therefore encoded in the message itself. If the communicative act is set against the context of the author to produce the text, then the intention is the cause behind the utterance as resolution of the problem (the lack and need for a communicative act) in the context.[40] The existence of the solved problem (a text addressing an object) is evidence of an intention in producing the text; it is a functional, not an ontological proof of an intentional author. The ex post facto evidential nature of how readers hermeneutically experience texts produces complications regarding the expectations and criteria of intention asserted of texts.

This intention is generally opaque to the reader, making it private data. Speech is often contrasted to the written communication act for the very reason that in direct dialogue there is a shared context. The authorial process is therefore public data for the speaker and listener. In a text, this shared ontic reality is to some degree lost. Some argue that there is a potential for reconstruction of the intention, following the idealistic romantic notions of thinkers like Schleiermacher. Others argue that the text now is an autonomous and anonymous thing, with a career of its own (notably thinkers like Ricoeur and Derrida).

We can press through the debate about intentionality in texts by recognizing that there is an intention in the text (the object of the text) that is the expression of an action. We often describe the nature of an action based on its effects: an action is intentional if the result is recognized as having an intention. Importantly, this model describes only the effect-action relationship. It does not make a claim about the ontological reality of the agent that performs the action. There is much confusion caused by labeling and seeking the "intention of the author," when really the interpretive focus is on the "intention in the writing of the author." Without notice, we have presumed the nature/possession of the author (possessing intention) based on the nature of their action (an intentional text). If our goal is to understand the text, then the action itself that produces the text and the produced text are the focus. If our goal is to understand the potentially frustrated will and character of the author, then we have primarily a historical, not a hermeneutic, question.[41] For proclamation that is primarily intended to be publicly acces-

---

40. Setting the communicative act against the context of an author is still coherent with the insights from the intentional fallacy. That perspective models the author as the *cause* but not the *standard* for a poem. The author as cause is in agreement with this working definition. Importantly, the intentional fallacy stresses the additional claim that the intention of the author ought not be seen as the hermeneutical lens for the meaning of the text. This additional claim would exclude a good portion of models, so will not be adopted for the sake of expansive consideration of criteria. Wimsatt and Beardsley, "Intentional Fallacy."

41. The frustrated will of the author may be important for considering the authority of the text, or for understanding what a text was intended to mean. We often write in a way that is only known to insiders, making references and allusions that are not public

sible, private data about the nature of the author becomes less interesting to interpretation. An unintended result of the public nature of proclamation is that the intention (which ought to be a nature of the text and the writing process) is encoded in a way that is less distinguishable between human and AI authors. Intention does not need to be an ontological reality of the author to have an intentional text or language event.

A communicative act requires active participation by the author, but this active participation may be distributed across many contexts. Writing has a durative *Aktionsart*: it always takes a nontrivial amount of time to write, and a single text may be written at different times by different authors/redactors. However, the material contribution to the finished product is the aggregate of active participation, and that participation represents a series of moments spent writing. A working definition of intention can thus be provided: authorial intention is the active response of the author to communicate, which produces the content of the utterance in the context of the utterance. Vanhoozer (drawing on Husserl and Hirsch) emphasizes that the intention is "the *object* of the act [of writing a text]."[42] What Vanhoozer calls the *object* or content of the text, Gadamer calls the interest of the author that produces the text.[43] Regardless of terms, there is an involvement of the author to focus on a specific topic and produce a communicative act in response to this interest.

In the working definition of intention there is the more abstract idea of an active response, but it should not be forgotten that there is an object or focal point of that response. The response to some linguistic object—namely, the communication addressing this object—is the intention in the text. This definition means that an AI system would express *intent* to the degree that the content of its generated utterance is related to the linguistic-situational context (the conversation history and prompting of the human, which provide the circumstances and need, addressed and ideally satisfied by the utterance). Context follows the object and focal point (the intention delivered by the AI system), thus when a human prompter accepts this response as satisfactory, this acceptance reflects a human recognition that the

knowledge. Proclamation is a specific type of utterance that is often intended primarily for public reception, and therefore the data that we prioritize for hermeneutics should follow.

42. Vanhoozer, *Meaning*, 76.

43. Gadamer, *Truth and Method*. There are elements of involvement or play that thinkers like Gadamer include in this idea of intention. The idea of involvement of the author in the subject matter is theoretically interesting but is private to the experience of the author and therefore provides minimal usability to the reader. As a result, the focus will be on the dimension of the intention that is public, which is reflected in the object of focus in the text that forms the meaning expressed in the text.

text is providing and evidencing an authorial interest in the intended object to a sufficient degree.

At least two primary threads of intention are present in the utterance. One is locutionary intention, which directs the formation of meaning and concepts conveyed by the text. The other is the illocutionary, constructing a (potentially larger) unit of discursive meaning with the intention of producing an effect on/through the recipient. The locutionary intention is the more localized force in the construction of an utterance, while the illocutionary force more directly communicates the totality of the attempted resolution to what was lacking in the context. In both cases, these are literary intentions, meaning the object or focal point of the text as evidenced in the text itself or its functional use (realized or not) in the world.

The intention of an utterance also includes propositional content, regardless of the illocutionary force or realized perlocutionary effect. The attributes of this propositional content, described generally as the concepts conveyed by an utterance, will be the next major descriptor for utterances and deserves its own space for analysis and consideration. As a preliminary, it is important to observe that the interdisciplinary search for meaning in an utterance inherently posits the existence of meaning in a text. Radical interpretation or translation is seeking a shared meaning. Hermeneutics assumes something to be interpreted. Ethics posits some rules to be abstracted. Thiselton gives good reason to expect the same for "philosophy, theology, exegesis, literary criticism, the human sciences in general."[44] Both realist and anti-realist views of epistemic meaning in communication proceed from the assumption of intentionality in communicative acts (even to the point they do not need to address *intention* by name—you will not find the term in their indexes). McDowell annunciates the association between intention and meaning as "whenever someone who is competent in a language speaks, so long as he speaks correctly, audibly, and so forth, he makes knowledge of his meaning available."[45] In less words, this is the *intention* as described by Gadamer and adopted for this project. Dummett (along with many others like Wittgenstein) stresses that communication must be taken as a public event,[46] and therefore it is definitionally understood as an action performed to obtain the intersubjective sharing of meaning. McDowell and

---

44. This is taken from Thiselton approvingly quoting Roger Lapointe: "The hermeneutic question is interdisciplinary. It is correlated to philosophy, theology, exegesis, literally criticism, the human sciences in general." Thiselton, *Two Horizons*, 8. Thiselton uses this quote to argue that hermeneutics involves all these, and they are therefore, at minimum, copacetic and participatory in the hunt for meaning in a textual utterance.

45. McDowell, *Meaning, Knowledge, and Reality*, 352–53.

46. Dummett, *Seas of Language*, 234.

Dummett are bitterly divided in their approaches to the epistemic dynamics of language yet agree there is an *intention* in an utterance to convey some meaning, and both proceed from the evidence to the presumption of cause.

The most direct and unambiguous model for authorial intention is in the essay "Against Theory": "The meaning of a text is simply identical to the author's intended meaning . . . to have one is already to have them both."[47] Hirsch's theory of interpretation was directly attacked in this essay, and in response he stressed that intention is *not an ontological reality* but an experiential one. Intention leaves functional evidence based on how the language could be applied to a purpose or use. He concludes by quoting himself: "Any normative concept in interpretation implies a choice that is required not by the nature of written texts but rather by the goal that the interpreter sets himself."[48] Such a normative concept for Hirsch includes the search for the intention or "intrinsic genre" of the author of a text. Even when both sides dispute how to characterize intention as an expedient toward the meaning of a text, both posit there is a clear relationship between intention and meaning. Therefore, when the semantic meaning of an utterance is a key consideration,[49] the intention of an utterance is extremely important, and accordingly the description of an utterance as intentional will be a paramount criterion for AI systems to have the foundations laid to employ concepts-meanings effectively.

Intention is also important for the pragmatic or active aspects of an utterance. Habermas describes this potential aspect of the intention in an utterance as strategic action.[50] Austin's lectures in *How to Do Things with Words* draw out the similar observation that in some cases, what we are communicating is itself instrumental in achieving a result. He states that an utterance can be used "not to describe my doing . . . or the state that I am doing it: it is to do it."[51] Utterances have an intention, and that intention may carry an instrumental volition. In the effective communicative action of proclamation there is certainly a doing along with propositional logic, but

47. Knapp and Michaels, "Against Theory," 724.

48. Hirsch, "Against Theory?," 24.

49. As a brief aside, there are thinkers who take meaning as constructed or posited independently of the author by an interpretive community. In models where the autonomy of the text is unrestrained and ontological, there is clearly no means of differentiating the nature of the author (as human or an AI system). In such theories where the author is thought to have abdicated any personal involvement in the meaning of a text, there is no discernment or differentiation based on the character of the author. My thesis would immediately and in this trivial manner be demonstrated, as neither type of author would be particularly relevant to the reception of the text.

50. Habermas, *Theory of Communicative Action*.

51. Austin, *How to Do Things with Words*, 6.

obtaining the intended result should not be considered a necessary criterion for classification of an utterance as proclamation.[52]

A *thick description* of the intention is one where the propositional content and the effect of an utterance are expected to be derived from the intention in the communicative act. Christian proclamation is a specific type of utterance where the purported intention is convincing/defending a truth system related to the object of Jesus the Christ. Pannenberg represents this unity of intention and the historical nature of proclamation when he describes the presence of the word of the church (a propositional content, and an ontological-volitional presence): "The word of the church is present wherever a convinced Christian, in his own spoken testimony, hands on the message which he has received."[53] Most models accept that there is some intentionality in an utterance and some go so far as to argue that intention manifests as meaning in an utterance.[54] Are these criteria met by an AI?

Setting aside the term *intention* helps answer the question honestly. The question is if an AI can write a text that is recognized as persuasive and is recognized as discussing coherently the faith of Christ. When the constituent manifestations of intention are considered, the data becomes far more conclusive. People are consistently persuaded by AI-generated texts, often to a fault. It is one of the major concerns with AI-generated texts (the persuasion of humans to believe them). AI systems can also write with coherence and competence on a variety of topics. Given the vast content of Western training material that discusses the faith of Christ, even public LLMs are quite adept at writing about Christ's faith with propositional precision. The primary objection is not about the data of supporting either criterion. Instead, it is a logical-semantic objection about using the evidence to argue about the nature of the author. As mentioned previously, this does not follow classical logic. The creation of a meaningful text is not logically sufficient to claim an intention by the author (from an ontological stance). However, for the practical reader (and one guided by modern hermeneutics) evidence of a meaningful text is seen as compelling evidence that the author has expressed an intention. In the most conservative sense, the *text* by being meaningful has an intention.

It is now suitable to proceed with theories that build upon a strong positive relationship between the evidence of linguistic skills and the intentions of authors and discuss how this is relevant to AI systems. Intention in

52. Unsuccessful proclamation is given more extended treatment in chapter 7 on the authority of the proclamation (the third section of this research following proclamation as utterance and conveying concepts-meanings).

53. Quoted in Brunner et al., *Revelation*, 142.

54. See Knapp and Michaels, "Against Theory."

the locutionary sense moves from the entropy of random words and symbols to an ordered series that can be interpreted with a specific meaning, perhaps even a compellingly convincing meaning. Intention in the locutionary sense is a heuristic of communication to construct meaning. The attention mechanism of an AI system is an explicit implementation of this attribute, by which the latent vector space (all possible things) is filtered down and transformed into the answer space in which semantic, grammatical, and conceptual meaning is optimized. The intention-meaning of an AI system is very explicitly to construct a meaning-optimized response to an input.

The other aspect that needs consideration is the illocutionary intention. The strategic action of an AI system's utterance can be illustrated by the positive cases where the words do something successfully. The individual experience of communication with an AI system helps establish the presence of this attribute. The negative is unable to disprove the intention of such an effect, only the failure to successfully perform in a specific case, as with human communicative acts. However, the positive empirical results of AI-generated words doing something can present the case for entertaining the *possibility* of this as an intention, as the evidence of an intention has been satisfied.

AI being considered intentional in this argumentation is still only a *possibility*: the same result is produced as an intentional human, which alone does not create a logical necessity for the same cause of this consequent (intention). However, that possibility becomes a recognized reality when we consider the human recognition of these texts as intentional. When a human prompts an AI system, they are providing the object or focus of the intention, and they continue to guide the AI until the results satisfy in terms of addressing this object. There are failures, cases where an AI system fails to meet the desires of the human participant. However, quite often, humans recognize that the AI outputs satisfactorily meet the object of their prompt/conversation, and in this the human recognizes that the AI has responded in engagement with the object of the human prompter's intention. This human recognition of the intention expressed in an AI response means there is now an indeterminacy in the intention that produces a meaningful/intentional text. Furthermore, it provides a more absolute claim to human recognition of intention, both in the generated text and in the action of generating the text, given this generative action is directed by the intention that is then assessed for in the generated text. This completes what is only possible based on the formal logic.

In a personal example of this human recognition, I have had my faith affirmed in experiences of communication with an AI system. This reality is therefore an assertion of this aspect being present. For the individual without such an experience, I recommend obtaining personal validation. The logically possible claim—that an AI expresses intention and produces a text that is involved with the provided intention/object/reason shared in the prompt and attention mechanism of the AI system—becomes completed by this human recognition that this intention has truly been observed both in the completion of the communicate act, and in its product.

SUMMARY: IMPLICATIONS OF PROCLAMATIONS BEING UTTERANCES

Describing a proclamation as an utterance locates the communicative use of textual symbols in context and postulates the author's intention to convey meaning (locution) and potential intention to produce or influence resulting action (illocution). The extension of these restrictions is that the agent that produces a proclamation must be situated in a context and furthermore be capable of using language for both locutionary and illocutionary purposes. The positive existence of data supporting these claims for AI systems provides data toward rejection of the null hypothesis that the text of AI systems can be differentiated from human texts based on the conditional requirements of being an utterance.

Discussion of proclamation as an utterance has been intentionally belabored, although it is seemingly obvious in normal usage of the terms. Analysis of the suitability of the attributes of an utterance to what an AI system can produce was extended to help establish the process that will now proceed through two descriptions of proclamation that are both more contentious and fractured in the academic theories. Since these inherit and build upon this foundation, the investment will soon be rewarded.

6

USING CONCEPTS-MEANINGS IN TEXTS

THE PRECEDING CHAPTER HAS argued that AI-generated texts are indistinguishable from human-generated texts based on their use of context and intention. It is important that this is a functional claim about the use of language. A given text must meet certain expectations to effectively encode a given context. For a text to be interpreted as intentional, it must have an object[1] that organizes the global and the local progression of the text. It is important to recall that this is different from claiming there is a real ontological context or intention of the AI system. The literary context is not an empirical reality, because the AI system does not sense an external world to be described and referenced. The literary intention is not the same as the volitional will of a human author, although the former is a description of what can be produced by the latter. It would be erroneous to argue from the consequent that the former was true: we cannot claim intentionality on the part of the AI system, but we have argued that the textual evidence of intentionality is fully satisfied by the AI system.

The conclusion of the preceding chapter is that the text as an anonymous whole does not provide sufficient data to be reliably distinguished from the utterances produced by humans. The next facet to consider will be

---

1. This may be simple or complex. A complex object would be a compound of multiple objects, which may further evolve as the text proceeds. The locally evident object will therefore shift within the range defined by the complex object. An example is an analytical argument, where the object of the current step in the argument shifts, but the overall framework and eventual case is consistently pursued.

how humans use concepts and meanings in a text, which is emphasized in the working thesis:

> Proclamation is an utterance *conveying concepts-meanings* that, if taken true, would be consistent in a belief system that is also consistent with the faith of Jesus Christ.

1. What attributes are expected because Christian proclamation uses theological concepts with religious meaning?
2. How do these attributes show up in Paul's Letter to the Romans?
3. What criteria in the linguistic and hermeneutic models describe these attributes?
4. How does AI text perform on the criteria:
    a. Relating language to reality
    b. Conveying knowledge
    c. Participating in an effect

The second description of a proclamation is as a bearer of *concepts-meanings*. When words are used in a context to actualize some intention to communicate (an utterance), the words as individual constituents and as variously nonexclusive sets of larger units of language (e.g., metaphors, clauses, sentences, discourses) facilitate understanding in the audience, along with potentially producing the intended effects of the communicative act. The concepts-meanings of an utterance can be defined accordingly as the aggregate understanding communicated by an utterance (which is itself contextual and intended). In Ricoeur's terms, this aggregate understanding "is not something hidden but disclosed," and it is that which "points towards a possible world."[2]

To provisionally distinguish between concepts and meanings, when used alone *concepts* describe the abstract predicates that are consistent across the real understanding of a class, while *meanings* describe the concretely distinguishing features of understanding in its relationship to reality. In most usage, both terms will be kept together as *concepts-meanings* to maintain the focus on all of the aggregate understanding. The aggregate understanding includes the meanings that were not successfully received

---

2. Ricoeur, *Interpretation Theory*, 177. Ricoeur is, in this situation, writing about "the meaning of a text." However, his understanding of the Aristotelean concepts of *mimesis* and *poiesis* make his view of meaning quite expansive, such that it includes the similitude of concepts (via *mimesis*) and the particularity of individualized reality (via *poiesis*).

(such as misunderstood referents or unknown technical terms), and the diachronic change of concepts through time (concepts being open to novel use and application to members not normally expected). The study of concepts-meanings is excused to pragmatically prioritize the idealized or the realized communicative act but ought to also consider the diverse range of possible relationships of the chosen word and word structures to reality, to knowledge, and to the effect of the disclosure which is communication.

In contrast to utterances, there is far less agreement in what is properly predicated of concepts used for communicative acts. Can language convey meanings that are not already known to the reader? Are concepts carried by units of language or instead produced through distinction against other signifiers (as in structuralism)? How are concepts related to reality, either statically or dynamically, and how is this potentially related to the context and intention of the author? Are these descriptions unique to a modality or experience of communication and understanding, or do they pose ontological boundaries? Further, can our consideration of these questions be done in such a way to avoid biasing our answers based on prior commitments? Concepts and meanings quickly broach the grand debates of epistemology and the subsequent difficulties reflected by these questions. Fortunately, the success of this research program is not dependent on articulating a grand unified system of concepts or meanings. Instead, the goal, as previously stated, is to enumerate the descriptions and expectations of concept or meaning use in Christian proclamation, such that these can be evaluated as criteria for texts generated by AI systems.

WHAT COMMITMENTS ARE MADE BY LOOKING AT CONCEPTS-MEANINGS?

It is critical to stress that this project is not dependent on a universal definition of concepts or meanings. A more rigorous criterion to apply against AI-generated content will be served by a permissive and expansive view of proper use of concepts or meanings, and what this proper use contributes toward proclamation. This portion will proceed by addressing the various ways that communication trades in that which can convey meaning, concepts, significance, reality, or other such data propagated by the text for the interpretation and understanding of the reader. My pragmatic approach to staying grounded in this expansive approach uses the nonce compound of concepts and meanings ("concepts-meanings") to stay oriented.[3] This alloy

---

3. The overall prospective in this section tends toward a cataphatic/positive theology. It seems natural due to the tendency of proclamation toward presenting new

suggests both a commitment to various perspectives being synthesized, and a priority to action of reasoning about the implications for AI systems.

The goal of this present research is not to adjudicate these lively and meaningful debates, but to extract valuable criteria from each. The resulting synthesis will involve parts that are antithetical and anathema to others. For some attributes, they may only exist in a mode (e.g., a correspondence view of concepts) that makes them anathema to models (e.g., Hector's explicitly anti-correspondence program) that will provide other important attributes for consideration. The inclusion of specific attributes should not be taken as an exclusive endorsement of involved models. The goal of a comprehensive analysis encourages an inclusive and pluralistic approach to models of concepts. The juxtaposition of competitive criteria will better prepare these conclusions with a composite and comprehensive combination of criteria that different perspectives will prioritize in their own consideration of AI-system proclamation.

THE ROMANS EXAMPLE

Paul's Letter to the Romans demonstrates that an author can, despite not being present bodily, convey concepts and meanings through a textual medium. Even if we expect that an individual or group accompanying the letter and possessing a shared supposition pool and close lived experience may have done the performance, the propositional contours of the text shape the performance.[4] They are performing Paul and his cohort's letter, which is important for appreciating the original expected use or effect of the concepts-meanings.

Paul's stated objective is to shape the Roman church's own understanding of the teaching of Christ. If successful, the Romans will accept this interlocutor's revision of the relationships and meanings for concepts they already trade in.[5] The illocutionary effect of the text is not directed toward

---

affirmations about an unknown God and revelation. Additionally, a positive view is more aligned with the strategic approach of this research to focus on areas that contribute the most toward difficult criteria for AI systems. Correctly saying more is harder than saying less. Given the difficulty that apophatic thinkers would presume in using positive descriptions of God, an ability to do this by an AI system would seem doubly remarkable (and for such committed thinkers, it is likely to receive the same critique and dismissal as human-generated content).

4. There are other examples, such as Revelation, where it more explicitly mentioned that the letter will be performed. "ὁ ἔχων οὖς ἀκουσάτω τί τὸ πνεῦμα λέγει ταῖς ἐκκλησίαις" is a repeated phrase for the letters to the seven churches of the prologue.

5. An interesting dynamic to consider against Paul's own concern that others are

evangelization of an unreached people (in fact, we do not have any extant tracks of such a sort from Paul, which raises a different question about the evangelistic illocutionary purpose to which they are commonly employed by the church). Instead, he is intentionally changing the meaning of concepts in the Roman church by recalibrating ("reminding") the relationships of these concepts to other data points (promises of God and actions of God in the past, and extensions of these types into their lived context as potentially one of the oldest and now mixed churches that was falling prey to pride).

The example of Romans is heavily laden with the various attributes of concepts-meanings that will be examined. The ability for a Christian evangelist to speak authoritatively to a distant community through text embodies in historical ontic experience the public communication of a disconnected author and audience. Signification here must go beyond the ostensive, and Paul's internal rhetoric is highly metaphorical (as Greek is wont to be in general, given the nonliteral use of prepositions to describe key Christian technical concepts). Translation between contexts is required for this communication to be possible. The expressed objective is an illocutionary function-effect satisfying Paul's obligation[6] as the minister to the gentiles. The entire experience of the letter is a commerce of norms, with a divine force of the Spirit, intended to elaborate meaning such that significance for the original audience would be transformed in their subsequent lived behavior. Romans as a letter therefore validates the suitability of these many attributes and illustrates by example how this criterion could be evaluated and expressed.

FRAMEWORKS FOR CONCEPTS-MEANINGS

Hermeneutics in the broadest sense provides a framework for understanding meaning, and therefore the frameworks that are deriving meaning or identifying concepts in a communicative act are in some sense hermeneutic. Before evaluating the various attributes properly predicated by using concepts-meanings, and more precisely using these toward the Christian end of proclamation, it will serve this analysis to begin with a summary

---

teaching a false gospel to the churches he planted, the exemplar being Galatia (see Gal 1:8 and 3:1).

6. Rom 1:14: "Ἕλλησίν τε καὶ βαρβάροις, σοφοῖς τε καὶ ἀνοήτοις ὀφειλέτης εἰμί." (SBLGNT).
"I am obligated both to Greeks and non-Greeks, both to the wise and the foolish."

survey of some of the thinkers and their frameworks that will be a recurring focus.

Kevin Hector

In Kevin Hector's *Theology Without Metaphysics*, his proposal is to use the therapeutic method of Wittgenstein to persuade his audience that theology need not be dependent on metaphysics and a correspondence model of truth. His defense involves using Schleiermacher and Barth to support an alternative and independent theory of concepts. His proposal produces a behavioral-cultural model for normative concept use, where the grammar or rules are reciprocally authorized by the intended receiver community.

Communicative acts use a concept "when we recognize it as intending to go on in the same way as precedent uses."[7] Hector's "we" is the community that is attuned to accept this as additive to the norm, and the mutual recognition of this community is his approach to avoiding the problematic definition of who defines the norm by their collective behavior.[8] For the Christian community (much of Hector's intended audience), the normative test to validate and approve novel use is testing the anaphoric character of the new application. Anaphora is a practical pattern observed in a wide diversity of natural languages, where a specific word is replaced by a less specific substitute (such as a pronoun). Use of anaphora grounds his definition for novel use of a concept in familiar terms and gives his case a strong explainability from a linguistic perspective. For those who expect language to disclose the nature of cognition (or the inverse), the argument that language reflects the way human agents naturally norm concept usage is particularly compelling.

Hector's proposal also provides a strongly theologically grounded horizon of proof. In one direction this is stretching back to the original teaching of Christ as origin, and in the other toward the perfection of the concept in God (as Godself would apply the concept in a self-description).[9] Hector summarizes these points when applying his program toward a truth system:

> Rather than appealing to a substantive notion of truth, I have made sense of truth in terms of the practice of taking a belief to

---

7. Hector, *Metaphysics*, 56.
8. Hector, *Metaphysics*, 85.
9. This is a firmly theological extension of thinking seen in others like Cohen and Natorp. For their theories "the notion of 'objects' now reappears not as the initial referent of thought, but 'as the stated goal or end of thought.'" This comes from Thiselton, *Two Horizons*, 209, quoting Johnson, *Origins of Demythologizing*.

be true. . . . To judge that a belief is true is to judge that it gets its subject matter right, and one judges a candidate belief to get its subject matter right by determining whether it goes on in the same way as precedent beliefs which one judges to be correct. . . . The view defended here does not try to explain truth-taking in terms of the necessary and sufficient conditions which would have to be met by any candidate for truth . . . rather, the norm by which to assess such truth-taking is implicit in one's non-inferential responsive dispositions rather than explicit in a set of rule-like conditions.[10]

Hector has proposed a behavioral/rule-based model of truth that is normed by the appropriate community recognizing that new usage of concepts is aligned with prior usage. His rule-like conditions and the reciprocity of the noninferential dispositions of the community further his goal to avoid a substantive correspondence model of truth. The evolving norm of anaphoric reference and recognizability builds on known and familiar procedures known to be present in native language users (see pronouns and inflected verbal systems). There is an element of realism, or concepts being able to get their "subject matter right," but "right" is evaluated synchronically by the related community, which importantly allows for evolution in concept usage.

Hector's proposal leans on Schleiermacher, Barth, and Soskice as dialogue partners for his proposal. Hector leans on the internalization of Schleiermacher to make the case for this being noninferential,[11] and on Barth's discussion of the freedom of God and his choice to allow us to overcome the limitations of language in our utterances.[12] Abdicating the role of ultimately norming the end of a concept (or, more properly, not trying to impertinently claim an authority over these concepts that is only God's) defends against a static rule-like set of conditions for assessing the truth of theological concepts. The truth conditions of an objective sense would only be accessible to God in his self-description, and therefore irresolvable for the community of faith. However, God yet reveals himself to us in our language and allows us to do so likewise, anaphorically and indirectly referring to his own perfect use of the concepts. Theological concepts are therefore perfect in divine use and inherit their truthfulness in the community recognizing

10. Hector, *Metaphysics*, 224–25.

11. "Schleiermacher thus provides an account according to which norms are implicit in attunement, attunement is an internalization of that which circulates in custom, and this circulation is explained in terms of an ongoing process of recognition." Hector, *Metaphysics*, 85.

12. Hector, *Metaphysics*, 127.

the referential nature of novel utterances using these concepts in a manner consistent with the accepted prior usage.

Hector's expectations for concept use with a recognized trajectory will be shown to be satisfied empirically by AI systems, begging the question of how these concept uses should be considered from an authority and responsibility perspective within the community of faith. Drawing on Soskice will help with discussing AI use of semantic mapping without literal ostensive referents or experience. Ultimately, the procedural nature of Hector's model gives it great flexibility but also provides a new access point wherein AI systems will be labeled as properly using theological concepts based on participating in the process of the interpretive community.

Hector's model largely avoids specific predicates on the author who validly is using a theological concept, emphasizing instead the corporate and individual procedure for the normative grammar of concepts for the community. He does expect the communicating author to have responsibility for their concept use,[13] and this also expects a reciprocal belonging to the community and ability to apply norms in a way recognized as authoritative by the community. He is therefore placing membership expectations on the author, but assessing belonging based on an empirical criterion of concepts being recognized by the community. These predications are therefore problematic for an AI system that may satisfy the criterion of recognizability, but yet not be capable of bearing the obligations responsibly for this concept use. When considering authority of a proclamation, Hector also seems to be silent on the difficult practical realities of diffuse authority and diffuse normative use. It took the Christian community of faith less than three hundred years before local language barriers made this type of normative practice so contentious that the great councils occurred.[14]

Key ideas of Hector are the norms and practices for continued concept use and novelty in concept use. The idea of norming concept use based on

---

13. "In asserting a belief, therefore, one implicitly petitions one's auditors to recognize the belief's authority over their judgments, and thereby undertakes responsibility to them for the correctness of that belief—responsibility, that is, for getting one's subject-matter right." Hector, *Metaphysics*, 219.

14. The contention in the councils was not only due to disagreement, but also due to how local languages like Armenian could not meaningfully localize the Greek ideas of essence and nature. As MacCulloch states, "Their normal word for 'nature' was closely related to the Iranian root word for 'foundation,' 'root,' or 'origin'—so any description of Christ as having two natures, even the qualified definition of Chalcedon, sounded like blasphemous nonsense to them." Accordingly, the Greek answers proposed at Chalcedon became inaccessible Greek metaphysics for many Christians who could not coherently speak in the same way about concepts like essence and nature in their native tongues. MacCulloch, *Christianity*, 239.

the continuation of a trajectory of use creates a new dynamic between the normative community and the behaviors accepted by this normed community. His approach therefore rebels against more essentialist and correspondence views of truth—namely, that there is some ideal essence that corresponds to our words, or that truth in language is predicated on the degree to which words clearly signal referents in reality ("the distance between human persons and fundamental reality is supposed to be bridged by dint of our ideas and words hooking up with or corresponding to such reality"[15]). As the discussion progresses into the criteria of concepts-meanings, the case will be made that Hector's models of concept continuation, of triangulation, and particularly of community recognition are well implemented and evidenced by the abilities of AI systems.

E. D. Hirsch

Hirsch's *Validity in Interpretation* provides a program for hermeneutics involving the related but distinct labels of *meaning* and *significance*. His proposals are intentionally and directly contrasted to other approaches—for instance, outright critiquing the hermeneutics of Gadamer by contrasting his (Hirsch's) approach against an attempt to understand verbal meaning by norms alone.[16] The positive aspect of his proposal is a hermeneutic process that separates the preliminary seeking for the verbal meaning from the subsequent seeking of a subjective and applied significance. By this, he can maintain there is a single meaning and a plurality of significances.

For Hirsch, interpretation is built on the *meaning* of a given text. The procedure for seeking the meaning is itself a hermeneutic cycle that is built up by the reader proceeding from a preliminary to a more refined hypothesis of the meaning, with each subsequent iteration implementing a refined judgment and validation.[17] From this meaning the reader can draw out *significance* and criticism. His writing presents a direct challenge to the postmodern deconstructionists, and skepticism in general, but can also be seen as a stern warning and guide to allegorical efforts.

---

15. Hector, *Metaphysics*, 15.

16. Hirsch argues that "no mere sequence of words can represent an actual verbal meaning with reference to public norms alone," and that to seek verbal meaning by norms alone will produce the indeterminacy that is the hallmark of the postmodern linguist. This also contributes to a completeness of vision by looking beyond what Hector provides in his theory. Hirsch, *Interpretation*, 225.

17. "The discipline of interpretation is founded, then, not on a methodology of construction but on a logic of validation." Hirsch, *Interpretation*, 207.

The hermeneutic and interpretive key for Hirsch is the *intrinsic genre* of the text, which Hirsch describes as a "structural necessity in communication."[18] Hirsch's argument goes on to assert that regardless of one's innate skill in understanding a genre, one cannot understand the meaning of a text without a provisional hypothesis about the intentions of the author. This provisional hypothesis is rapidly iterated based on the validation done internally by the reader, and Hirsch expects that real language usage is quite capable of adding surprising data that ought to remove a prior hypothesis and dispel reader prejudices that bias an earlier or initial reading. Despite potential rejection or improvement of the initial hypothesis, the intrinsic genre organizes the entire enterprise of Hirsch and provides a deterministic and singular goal from which significance can be independently derived and contextualized.

The unifying idea of a singular intrinsic genre is parallel conceptually to the multidimensional attention matrix of an AI system, which is constantly aggregating and synthesizing new data to challenge, refine, or reinforce the attention matrix. Attention is not led astray by each subsequent token/word but gradually drifts with a preponderance of data. It is not the explicit intention,[19] but the pragmatic computer science of AI systems implements an understanding that is very similar to Hirsch's idea of a singular intrinsic genre.[20] For the purposes of this research, it is important that Hirsch presents a unified genre as directing at the largest homogenous fine-grained unit (each subsequent intention for a communicative act), which again resembles how attention may vary significantly in a singular AI-system conversation given re-prompting of the system but will persist and expand the same matrix, holding the context throughout the conversation.[21]

The mathematical implementation of theory or adjacent applications of theory suggests that the resulting AI system will be sufficiently capable of producing empirical data in support of AI systems being peers with human

---

18. Hirsch, *Interpretation*, 82.

19. The explicit intention of these implementations is to build on the research of linguistics and information retrieval, in addition to the growing understanding of our cognitive processes and biology.

20. Hirsch nuances his position by explaining that he cannot absolutely determine between interpreting the *textus receptus* and interpreting the multiple paroles from potentially different authors over a long period of time that produced an as-of-reading finished text. Hirsch, *Interpretation*, 233.

21. The persistence of large context requires massive computing resources. Ongoing work is approaching how to shift these computational limitations without a lossy approach to maintaining and enriching the context through each step in a conversation. This is the computational analog to the limitations of a human for maintaining full coherence of the topic during a lengthy conversation or discourse.

authors. Recourse to the empirical data is also legitimized by Hirsch's own argumentation. For example, Hirsch defines verbal meaning as "that aspect of a speaker's 'intention' which, under linguistic conventions, may be shared by others."[22] If the primary criterion for expressing verbal meaning is related to what is shared with the linguistic community receiving a text, then, even without novel generated content, an AI system is capable of producing a verbal meaning. This highlights a systemic problematic.

Hirsch axiomatically declares that there is a will and a consciousness that produces meaningful texts but does not argue this from evidence or logical deduction/extension. His assertion that the "determinate verbal meaning requires a determining will"[23] stands juxtaposed against his own suggested method. By sheer assertion and not proof he claims that a will is necessary for the text to have a determinate meaning but then approaches texts with the implicit assumption that they have a meaning. Hirsch did not provide a negative criterion to validate a text has a determinate meaning by virtue of a determinate will and consciousness. The practical problem in trying this distinction is the very claim of this paper: the author's will or experience in producing a communicative act is private, and thus the only data the reader has access to and can decide upon is the cold, dead, "determinate sequence of words"[24] which are received as a text. We need criteria to establish when a text is meaningful precisely in light of it necessarily having an intentional will involved in its creation, or else we have an indeterminacy where meaningful texts can come to be read that are both derived from a human's willful intention, and that are derived from AI systems (or other causes). If the public data (the meaningful text) cannot determinately convey the private data (the nature of the will and humanity of the author), then we cannot make a public truth claim about the human will of an author.

Hirsch's stated goal to respect sharable or public knowledge[25] is often taken as the logical predicate that argues for some conclusion about texts, authors, readers, or their relationships. When an AI system is observed delivering the same public-normed linguistic feats as natural language users, this can produce problematic conclusions based on the logical conclusions. When in a theory (such as Hirsch's) these conclusions are a necessary derivative of the logical predicate, the conclusions will often

22. Hirsch, *Interpretation*, 218.
23. Hirsch, *Interpretation*, 46.
24. Hirsch, *Interpretation*, 46.
25. Wittgenstein provided compelling arguments (such as his famous Beetle example) that represent the majority of the thinkers in this field who agree on the need for public knowledge. Based on his writings, it would seem impossible for language to operate without this public sharable nature.

predicate anachronistic attributes to AI-system authors (e.g., intention) that go beyond stating that both classes of author can participate in producing proclamation.

Key ideas for Hirsch are the distinction between significance and meaning, and the presence of an intrinsic genre. Significance for Hirsch is applied and contextual to the reader, while meaning is the deterministic understanding of the given text, based on the intrinsic genre. A working definition of Hirsch's intrinsic genre is the linguistic setting and context in which words gain their relative significance, such that meaning can be ascertained. In his own words, the intrinsic genre "serves both a heuristic and a constitutive function,"[26] meaning it helps the interpreter with a mental shortcut for locating new understanding, which is authorized by the organizational effect of such a genre. Hirsch's relationship of meaning to the intrinsic genre necessitates a hermeneutic process of continued validation and testing to adapt appropriately based on new data disproving prior associations.

Richard Hays

Richard Hays's *Echoes of Scripture in the Letters of Paul* posits and investigates the "free hermeneutic" and "imaginative freedom" observed by looking at how Paul's thinking relates to the texts of the Old Testament.[27] His argument for a free hermeneutic includes an effort to liberate the meaning from a text: "No longer can we think of meaning as something contained by a text; texts have meaning only as they are read and used by communities of readers."[28] His requirement of use is particularly biblically oriented, because "no reading of Scripture can be legitimate . . . if it fails to shape the readers into a community the embodies the love of God as shown forth in Christ."[29]

Two important aspects of concepts-meanings are raised by Hays's conclusions. First, Hays seems to be suggesting that meaning is something not contained in the text but created by a dialectical engagement with the text.[30] The meaning is bound to a reading in the same way that the author's intended meaning in an utterance it contextual. Importantly, this does not reject a relationship to the text: the text is instrumental in the effect on the community. Second, Hays is positing that in the context of reading

26. Hirsch, *Interpretation*, 78.
27. Hays, *Echoes*, 189.
28. Hays, *Echoes*, 189.
29. Hays, *Echoes*, 191.
30. Hays, *Echoes*, 189.

Scripture, there is a positive criterion of building up the community of faith. The results of this response can be judged by external criteria, and a correct meaning must be in service of this result. Meaning is then deeply related to an obligation to respond as a person to this universal summons.

Hays is certainly not alone in his position of advocating a lived response to reading in faith.[31] His specific articulation is noteworthy because it plays an important corrective role that is suitable for this research. If proclamation is Christian only as far as it's dealing in a gospel message that builds the community of faith, then there is a pragmatic and external criterion to add to the theoretical semiotic contributions. However, there is a practical problem in using the building of the church as a criterion. The biggest challenge is that the edification of the community of faith is a lagging indicator of the validity of a reading (interpretation and application) of Scripture. It will be difficult or impossible to apply as a predictive indicator about the fruitfulness of proclamation made by AI systems, and as a lagging indicator there are many concerns. Waiting for proof of a built-up community of faith may provide false negatives if conclusions are reached prematurely, or false positives by legitimizing behavior on the grounds of allowing more time to be proven. Additionally, the assessment of the faith of the community is only properly and fully evaluated by God's prerogative. Regardless, Hays's presentation poses an important historical ontic criterion that connects and grounds in the reality of the community of faith, not theory alone.

A third point about the freedom-of-concept use that Hays makes in his concluding comments in *Echoes* is around the limits that Paul expresses. This is not freewheeling allegorical speculation. Hays argues that instead of a set of static or specific concepts, Paul is working within a symbolic universe.[32] This universe is better described by a set of relationships between paradigmatic keywords, which serve as guiding principles to the procedure of judging and evaluating the propriety of a concept use. With these paradigms and the normative rules of language, the proclamation of the Christian truth can be customized to the specific context and need for the utterance. At the same time, these concepts can be a negative criterion to disqualify concept use that is out-of-bounds.

---

31. Thiselton described how Fuchs "stresses the inadequacy of an approach to truth which remains only on the level of concepts, cognition, and propositions." Thiselton, *Two Horizons*, 194.

32. From Hays, *Echoes*, 191, in an approving quote of Wayne Meeks. The symbolic universe of the gospel narrative is the primary focus of Hays's *Moral Vision of the New Testament* and is particularly relevant in the next chapter on how a proclamation presents an authoritative claim.

In summary, Hays provides in his concept use a potential option for relating to AI systems generating proclamation. The first and third points argue strongly in favor of an AI system being capable of producing proclamation, namely the proper interpretation and then presentation of understanding of the revelation of God through the narrative of the Scriptures. Simultaneously, the second point provides a lagging but empirically verifiable criterion. Importantly, these do not rule out the possibility on ontological or other merits.

One option for practically evaluating Hays's expectations would be to observe the outcomes of AI systems generating proclamation and see if the community is edified. As suggested in the consideration of Sanneh, this is a real possibility (see the detailed discussion in the later section on epistemic conditions and translatability, "Lamin Sanneh (Translatability)"). Another, more proactive option is to augment any candidate proclamation from an AI system with the lived community of faith. Based upon this research, my recommendation is not to accept the simple answer of conferring an external status on the AI system (such as predicating human authorial intention), but to augment where they may fall short in producing a living faith community. If the results of the AI system are promising, the result of an edified community of faith is an added benefit, normalizing the insistence on lived responses to the experience of the revelation of God.

Key ideas raised by Hays explain the positive role of a free hermeneutic. Hays defines the free hermeneutic of Paul as a hermeneutic attribute expressing flexibility but restraint in meaning and referent as observed in Paul's usage of the Greek and Hebrew texts. His flexibility and creativity operate within respectful boundaries that provide latitude to exercise metonymy and other structural patterns to create a deeper meaning without devolving into eisegesis or purely figurative readings.

Existentialist Views

Starting with any of the available models of concepts-meanings is inclined to create a privileged placement. Yet the process must begin somewhere. One of the important poles of consideration not mentioned in these introductory frameworks is that of a more existentialist or highly subjective view. The recurring objection is that a criterion that depends on the capricious nature of the reader provides great liberty for declaring an AI system to be producing proclamation. However, as far as these theories predicate assertions that connect back through the text or author through the experiential reality of the reader, there are important lessons to learn.

Various thinkers who index toward subjectivity or the reader's constructed experience of the concepts-meanings in a text will be interleaved, but Heidegger will provide an exemplar. Heidegger's approach is one that intends to avoid compromising presuppositions and describes meaning as "the 'upon-which' of a projection in terms of which something becomes intelligible as something."[33] For Heidegger, considering meaning means dealing with a provisional "structure" that has already been presupposed by "a fore-having, a fore-sight and a fore-conception."[34] Conceptualization is therefore engaged with the world through the understanding of the self in the evaluation of meaning. Heidegger's nuanced and complicated discussion of meaning and world eschews simplistic answers (e.g., correspondence). He raises the difficulty of assessment of concepts or meanings in the neutral, objective, or natural sense[35] of concepts or meaning that often becomes the object of hermeneutics and understanding.

Bultmann expresses a more explicitly Christian program based on and embodying many of these concepts of Heidegger. His hermeneutic theory for approaching concepts stresses the experiential-cognitive and the subjective depths of concepts when he explains, "There is no proclamation without concepts, and there is no act of faith that is not at the same time an act of thought."[36] The subjectivity of mental processes mediates both proclamation and faith for Bultmann, agreeing fundamentally with Heidegger's view on the historicity of the Dasein and the dialectical impress of the understanding self on what is understood.

ATTRIBUTES OF CONCEPTS-MEANINGS

The primary focus of this research is on positive expectations and criteria that can be expected from human-generated Christian proclamation, such that these criteria can be applied to the texts generated by AI systems. This objective means prioritizing attributes of concepts-meanings that have some relationship to the external world or truth. Systems like structuralism, in which meaning does not arise from the referents but from the deep structures and oppositions present in the text,[37] will consistently disagree

33. Heidegger, *Being and Time*, 193.
34. Heidegger, *Being and Time*, 193.
35. For instance, Heidegger's concept of a meaning being "ready-to-hand" only in the context of "coming before us" was crafted to avoid an objective generalized sense to a referent. Heidegger, *Being and Time*, 140–41.
36. Bultmann, *This World*, 103.
37. As stated by Barthes, "Meaning is not a filled signifier." Barthes, "Structural

with the framing of this section. Proceeding is not an endorsement of either type of theory, save in recognizing there are more valuable criteria to be generalized from how use of language trades in concepts and meanings that have some relationship to the external world/truth, and this is the type of criterion that will be important for judging AI-system texts.

RELATIONSHIP TO REALITY

An utterance is composed of signs (words) that are assembled into larger discourse and linguistic units that together have some relationship to reality. Each individual atomic unit (word) contributes toward the overall relationship between the text and reality, both by its marginal contribution, and by its contribution in relation to the prior and latter words in the ordered text. Even the exactly same word, clause, metaphor, or larger linguistic unit repeated in a text has a new meaning precisely because it stands in relation to the prior usage. While the meaning of any part of a text depends on the relationship to the whole, there is value in understanding how each constituent part helps to create concepts-meanings in the text by signifying reality and some relationship to reality.

With these presumptions in place, the relationship of a signifier (word) to the signified (referent) is an expression of a relationship to reality. It may be a direct description of the world, standing with as clearly as possible an attempted atomic relation to reality. Augustine provides an example of this atomic and direct realist view in *The Teacher*. His lengthy discourse revolves around the nature of teaching, focusing on signs (words) and enumerating various schemes for understanding and categorizing the signs that can refer to things or other signs.[38] Augustine's words signify either other things or other signs in an ostensive manner. Frege nuances this position by asserting that "the meaning of a sentence is given by its truth conditions."[39] The ostensive reference is redacted, but the idea is that meaning is directly related to the truthiness of the utterance in question. Further afield from Augustine are theorists like Dummett, who argues against a naïve realism. His stance against the Platonic atomic view of meaning also means he questions if the public data in a sentence (which must be public to facilitate intersubjective communication) can properly carry epistemic meaning. For example, if a

---

Analysis," 115.

38. Augustine, *Teacher*.

39. The specific wording of this summary comes from Marshall, *Truth*, 91. Frege is commonly referenced for the idea of a meaning coming from the truth conditions of the sentence.

speaker makes a statement about a future event, this becomes a problematic epistemic position to resolve. Human use of words in a proclamation will manifest some relationship to reality, regardless of this being understood with strict correspondence or something far less ostensive.

Appreciating the human use of words to convey concepts-meanings with some relationship to reality introduces different levels or types of relationship. The investigation will turn to three means of signifying some relationship to reality: metaphor, analogy, and descriptive picking out. After introducing criteria for this use by human authors, the goal will be to highlight how these techniques are used to communicate Christian theological concepts. The process will move from the least directly literal to the most ontically referential, and since each of these can be/are employed by human authors in Christian proclamation, it will be valuable to consider the relevance of these to AI-authored texts.

Metaphor

Metaphor is one of the ways that proclamation can speak of the transcendent otherness of God's revelation. Janet Soskice's *Metaphor and Religious Language* provides a far-ranging analysis of the various approaches to metaphorical language, and this summary treatment will guide the consideration of many divergent models of metaphor.[40] The debates about the proper theory of metaphor are illustrative of the difficulty of trying to encapsulate a linguistic skill that encodes "broader intuitions about the relation of language to the world."[41]

Metaphoric usage of language asserts there is a relationship of metaphors to reality (reducible, extra-literal, or otherwise). The flexibility that allows native language users to surpass ostensive reference (via metaphor) is related to our very ability to use language. A simple example is preposition development over time. In his consideration of the development of ancient languages, Robertson notes that, in the development of language, prepositions evolve from a more strictly literal spatial meaning to the metaphorical,[42] and Alston makes this point more broadly about all lan-

---

40. My own research is focused on examining the general role played by metaphor and examining the suitability of AI to satisfy these. It is not important to pick between substitution, interaction, or other models of metaphor.

41. Soskice, *Metaphor*, 97.

42. "The analytic tendency in language is responsible for the growth of prepositions." Robertson, *Grammar of Greek New Testament*, 554.

guage usage.[43] Repeated use of spatial meanings provides the means and motive for native language users to communicate metaphorically. Familiar use of the literal provides linguistic faculties for nonliteral usage.

Based on this preliminary, it seems appropriate to agree with Soskice that "to enquire into the nature of metaphor and reality depiction is thus to broach wider problems of the nature of explanation."[44] Explanation beyond what is otherwise possible grounds consideration of effective (both with positive effect and prudent restraint) deployment of metaphor. Metaphor as a last resort of communicating a difficult relationship to reality also suggests the theological significance of metaphor. Proclamation is attempting explication of the most transcendent truth and thus would be served by the greatest accessibility of tools and techniques. Soskice discusses how this is expressed similarly in scientific models[45] where language is used in a homomorphic or paramorphic manner to describe a source that may be beyond human direct observation. In the paramorphic situation, the subject is not the same as the source of the model, which is directly parallel to the predication of semantic meaning in metaphor usage. Metaphors use the same semantic concepts to convey, through literal language, meanings that do not literally obtain. Such semantic flexibility is embedded in the behavior of natural language users, is critical for many thinkers who want to talk about God, and is therefore doubly important for an AI system to sufficiently be capable of performing in order to generate proclamation.

Metaphor may not only increase the direct explanation but also restructure the composite meaning evaluated from a truth system. Metaphor is particularly important for Hays's ethics for being "a mode of creating dissonance of thought in order to restructure meaning relationships."[46] Funk observes metaphor intentionally breaking existing relationships in the world: "Metaphor shatters the conventions of predication in the interests of a new vision, one that grasps the 'thing' in relation to a new 'field.'"[47] For AI systems, the evocative metaphorical language of Hays and Funk translates into a criterion for being able to deviate from the explicit semantic distance between literal terms. Exhibiting this behavior would require evidence of mutability and change in the calculated semantic distance of embeddings based on other attention contexts. Research suggests exactly this—namely, that AI systems are surpassing the expectations of distributional semantics.

43. Alston, *Divine Nature and Human Language*, 25.
44. Soskice, *Metaphor*, 98.
45. Soskice, *Metaphor*, 102–3.
46. Hays, *Moral Vision*, 302.
47. Funk reference in Thiselton, *Two Horizons*, 160.

Semantic space projection is well documented and attested in language tasks like translation[48] and more recent research has shown a similar skill deployment for various linguistic feats of metaphor.[49]

Davidson articulates an important countervailing view of metaphor that is also worth noting. His pragmatic-realist approach removes a relationship to reality that is carried by anything but the literal meaning of the words. Instead of creating a relationship to reality that is nonliteral, Davidson focuses on how "[metaphor can] make us appreciate some fact—but not by standing for, or expressing, the fact . . . but in fact there is no limit to what a metaphor calls to our attention, and much of what we are caused to notice is not propositional in character."[50] Giving fair consideration in this direction of metaphor use means that metaphor use as descriptive of proclamation includes the ability to *call to our attention* some intentional material. This material may be cognitive, tangible, epistemic, mathematical, or a host of various other brands of concept. The uncontroversial observation is that a concept is used with the intention of bringing something to attention, even if a realist might not agree that metaphor is also used to restructure the minding of the reader and the complex of meanings within the world of the reader.

Always Metaphorical

There is an aspect of AI systems that means they are arguably always communicating in metaphor. This observation is counter intuitive if one expects an AI system to be limited to the distributional semantics theory, but it arises from considering the Davidsonian model[51] and can be extended more broadly. An AI system always makes a projection of the latent semantic space, wherein it modifies the semantic space of the answer based on the context window of prompts and the status of the attention mechanism. Preferentially generated communicative content is determined based on these dynamically transformed semantic distances of the dense embedding vectors. The transformed semantic space is not a literal or ostensive "understanding" or direct access to the experiential reality of the referent.

---

48. Zeng et al., "Converging to a Lingua Franca."
49. Sun et al., "Transformer-Squared."
50. Davidson, *Essential Davidson*, 223.
51. Davidson makes this most obvious when he reduces to almost negligible the difference between direct literal communication and metaphor (in the semiotic content at least, notwithstanding the illocutionary force).

Contextual semantic distance allows for subjects that are discordant from the sources to be used as predicated, producing nonempirical predications that may obtain an approving understanding in the native-language-using reader. As with human metaphors, not all will be successful. Not all will be recognized as metaphor. However, some will. Research suggests that LLMs can be trained to understand metaphor[52] (albeit imperfectly at this time) and they are capable of demonstrating the linguistic skill of metaphor deployment.[53] Of interest is the continuing evolution of this research and advancements that continue to expand this capability, as shown in the prior research. Furthermore, in a purely mathematical and procedural sense, the optimization problem that an AI system performs in responding to a prompt is far more similar to the semantic approximations unhindered by literal ontic reality that are the commerce of metaphor. AI systems may therefore be systemically understood to always communicate via the procedure of making metaphors, and this is in part obvious from an AI system's inability to make an ostensive reference to a reality that is only mediated through the texts used in training.

Metaphor is so important to Christian concepts-meanings usage because it provides the natural language users optionality in cases where expanding the potential explication of a homomorphic model is deemed necessary. If we cannot directly or analogically talk of God, then theological talk depends deeply on the ability of metaphor to surpass the paramorphic nature of the model's ability to express analogically. In a theoretical and pure ontological sense, there are more complications to claiming that an AI system can make ostensive or experiential use of language.[54] Therefore, recourse to metaphor is critical as a first illustration of the ability to speak of God, and therefore to trade in concepts-meanings needed for Christian proclamation.

Analogy

Another means of using language to discuss the truth of God is analogy. This is a robustly rich topic, one that again merits deeper research and

---

52. Michelli et al., "Framework."

53. Wang et al., "DRT." This preprint was released during this research project. The research is about expanding the ability of AI systems to perform linguistic tasks like metaphor making by employing "chain-of-thought" reasoning in the process of translation. In this example, the challenge is doubly hard, as the metaphors are being translated across languages.

54. This difficulty is another reason it may be more suitable to describe all AI-generated texts as metaphorical.

analysis that many have provided. It will be unsatisfactory to try and survey these approaches here, but I will introduce a general approach to analogical thinking about God and then dwell on the specific analogies used by one of the thinkers highlighted in this research, Kevin Hector.

As Alan Torrance discusses in *Persons in Communion*, analogy is expressing more of the "primordial ontological and thus *semantic* bridge between the theological and anthropological spheres."[55] An AI system is trained on secondary data about the ontological semantics that natural language speakers have exhibited. Therefore, it is a mediated dataset versus a direct ontological experience of the semantic bridge described by Torrance. However, this is not far from human agents who have different access to the ontological reality of the world. If a blind person can knowingly speak of moving people who look like trees,[56] then we should expect a mediated understanding can still allow for analogy.

David Yeago provides a slightly different approach in his defense of the Nicene dogma being properly rooted in the canonical Scriptures despite a lack of explicit enumeration therein. His contention is that the dogma "describes a pattern of judgements present in the texts."[57] For Yeago, the analogical language's truth is based on continuation and coherence with a set of established patterns. What is most important about this approach is that he is discussing Christian dogma in the context of other texts (the canonical Scriptures). There is therefore direct applicability to an AI system, as these are likewise trained on and equipped for continuation of the patterns expressed in the prior documents. If the semantic judgments of these texts can be continued in the linguistic skills of AI systems, then the analogical usage of AI systems would be as valid as the foundational contention justifying Yeago's proposal (that analogy is appropriate if it reflects a prior established pattern, or "unity of teaching").[58]

The determination if an AI system is capable of properly deploying analogy will therefore depend on one admitting (or not) a consistently recognizable use of analogy as satisfying the linguistic feat. If one admits this empirical data, then AI systems certainly can meet the criterion, and if one does not, then the ontological experiential aspects of analogy will mean it is beyond the reach of currently feasible AI systems. From such a conclusion, the important consideration is if successful deployment of metaphor

---

55. Torrance, *Persons in Communion*, 121.
56. Mark 8:24–26.
57. Yeago, "New Testament and Nicene Dogma," 1.
58. Yeago, "New Testament and Nicene Dogma," 10.

and picking out, in addition to the proper *use* of analogy,[59] is sufficient for Christian proclamation.

Hector's consideration of analogy in theology provides both a description of the role of analogy and motives a model for proper usage of analogy. Hector notes that when trying to signify God or describe the attributes of God, we are wise to consider that God is only properly described in Godself to Godself. Hector grounds his analysis of this consideration in his reading of Barth and concludes, "One's concepts can indeed apply to God, but this application depends wholly upon God's gracious initiative . . . the grace by which God applies human concepts to Godself entails that one must set one's faith wholly upon that application . . . obediently conformed to God's prior act."[60] Analogy is a way to describe what is observed in the use of concepts or meanings for God (providing that "semantic bridge," to use Torrance's phrase) that is not possible based on human linguistic skill alone, but only through God's grace.

Hector elaborates his idea that "the analogy of attribution is itself analogous to justification by grace received in faith"[61] by connecting it to his model for concept usage via a continued trajectory. His understanding of the proper analogies for God argues for prescriptive versus descriptive language about God. Prescriptive use of concepts allows the communicator to "make a claim about what concepts ought to mean" by making the "concept's application to God to be normative for all other applications."[62] Obligation of commitment to God's attributes of Godself being normative would seem to be an insurmountable criterion to AI systems, if by this we mean that the system will never use terms in a manner not normed by its trajectory toward the way God describes Godself. However, this seems to be a claim that goes beyond what would be fair to predicate of human users of concepts either.

The time horizon for considering the "other applications" is important to how realistically an AI system can meet this expectation (or a real human). If the time horizon is an uninterrupted interaction with an AI system, this is very reasonable. After setting the semantic space such that the semantic meanings of the common terms of our faith and descriptors of God are recognized as such by the community of faith, an AI system will continue

---

59. Zheng et al., "LogiDynamics." This research presents the ability for LLMs to apply analogical thinking in terms of inductive, abductive, and deductive reasoning about a linguistic task.

60. Hector, *Metaphysics*, 141.

61. Hector, *Metaphysics*, 141.

62. Hector, *Metaphysics*, 144–45.

to operate with these norms and semantic priorities until told otherwise, or the context window has sufficiently shifted away to other points of attention. To be clear, with different prompting, a meandering conversation, or a fresh conversation, there will be no lingering commitment to these norms. However, the historical AI system communicating at the time of the utterance will have weights that mathematically are analogous to the semantic commitments made by a believer as evidenced in their language usage. This is analogous to a human who uses concepts with theological significance in some, but not all circumstances.

It is worth noting that this behavior is true of public AI systems, despite these systems being designed for general purpose tasks. The diachronic commitment of these systems will reflect no such commitment. However, if a specifically Christian AI system is created, the training and biases process could be such that a long-term persistent commitment to certain normative usage of concepts is realized.

Realism/Picking Out

The most realist and direct level of language use employs concepts or meanings that are referring to a referent in the real world. In these cases, a referent is meant to be *picked out* from the myriad possibilities made possible by reality.[63] Concepts that signify a referent are trying to pick out that referent, regardless of complicating factors such as the tangibility or optative reality of the referent.[64] Any form of picking out is no trivial undertaking, and it will be both important and compelling to present the data on how AI systems are already capable of delivering this extremely complicated and nuanced task, along with raising data suggesting further enrichment and

---

63. This phrase is intentionally ambiguous. Picking out can clarify a referent that does not immediately exist as an accessible/sensed real experience. For example, intangible concepts, non-realized wishes/prohibitions, or impossible experiences can be picked out, illustrating that the lack of direct experience is not an impediment to picking out. Even in these cases, the referents have some relationship to reality, even if it is rejection, subversion, or idealization of the content directly accessible in reality.

64. Debates surround the proper means of describing the relationship of the canonical Scriptures to ontic reality. One common approach determines this connection based on the genre of the specific text. Adjudication is not the purpose of this research.

A high-water mark for the appeal to a higher standard is introduced by the model of realistic history from Hans Frei. In his model, "there is no gap between the representation and what is represented by it." However, not every text is a realistic history. Most human proclamation would not be considered this class of utterance. Therefore, this stands as an aspirational criterion, more as an exemplar of what picking out would look like in the idealized version than in normal practice. Frei et al., *Identity*, xiv.

enhancement that is possible through new techniques, architectures, and system design. It will also be important to raise again the consideration that an AI system is referring to a reality that has not been known to it directly through sense organs, and therefore it is always a mediated reference to reality.

One complication is picking out over time. Cotterell, teaching from the perspective of advanced Greek linguistics in the New Testament, warns that it is "not possible arbitrarily to insist that the significance of the signs shall not change."[65] Meaning can change over time, even for the same author. Paul in prison is dealing with a different supposition pool than the newly converted Paul in Antioch.[66] Take for illustration the new experience of observing people in Rome preaching the gospel out of spite, giving Paul a totally new experiential basis for writing to the Philippian community of faith.

Brunner makes an even bolder declaration on the change of concepts in time, when he observes that not even Jesus can refer to himself as the Christ until he is proven such in the resurrection: "[Jesus] could not say who Jesus is; that was possible only after his death, and it could be said only by the witness of his death and his resurrection."[67] Similar ideas are echoed by Pannenberg on Jesus's relationship to the identification with the apocalyptic "Son of Man."[68] The evolution of the names of God likewise suggests a continuity of referent (there is but one God) with a change in symbol. Hector is attuned to this example and provides clarity to this practice by focusing on the ways that this picking out is done through an anaphoric reference across various intermediary terms toward a single shared fixed referent. His reference is to Soskice who states that "reference can take place independently of the possession of a definite description which somehow 'qualitatively uniquely' picks out the individual in question."[69]

Hector goes on to approvingly accept Soskice's suggestion that this is done because one belongs to a "linguistic community which has passed the name on from link to link."[70] If there must be this identity within a linguistic community, then it would seem that an external criterion has been placed

---

65. Cotterell and Turner, *Linguistics*, 18.

66. The newly converted Paul who had not even been called to the gentiles but knew that Jesus Christ had for him a special purpose, one that was still yet to be revealed.

67. Brunner et al., *Revelation*, 121.

68. Pannenberg, *Jesus, God and Man*.

69. Soskice, *Metaphor*, 127; reference in Hector, *Metaphysics*, 169. In this situation, Hector is using Soskice's view of metaphor to pick out an intentionally and explicitly resolvable referent.

70. Soskice, *Metaphor*, 152; reference in Hector, *Metaphysics*, 170.

on picking out that may preclude AI-system membership. However, empirical results dispute this. Even without formal/informal identity within a linguistic community, an AI system is capable of both understanding the dynamic and variable semantic meaning of terms across time,[71] and capable of understanding non-direct references (anaphoric use of language).[72]

Investigating the topic of uniquely picking out a referent using concepts-meanings in a linguistic feat has led to the question of how an AI system could be inaugurated into a linguistic community. There is always a distance between even the most seemingly incontrovertible and simple ostensive use of language and the thing in reality as publicly accessed. Therefore, there is a need for the receiver to extrapolate and make coherent the references, and a community to norm and safeguard this usage.

The research suggests the need to reconsider what it means to belong to a linguistic community. For example, is an AI system capable of bearing multiple memberships, one for each context it can possibly adopt? The AI-specific question motivates but challenges assumptions in the more general query of how we consider belonging, and to what degree there is a logical relationship of sufficiency between understanding anaphoric picking out and belonging to a linguistic community. This is particularly important where such a picking out does not obligate specific and exclusive epistemic commitments (as in the case of AI systems).

Frei argues that, specifically for topics of Christian faith such as Jesus the Christ, there are concepts that do not have their full meaning without the epistemic realization that is a personal experience/taking true of faith. In summarizing his argument in *The Identity of Jesus Christ*, Frei advances that "there are indeed concepts or fact claims which are part of the faith but that the logical condition for understanding and believing them is to see them not as 'neutral data' but as personally pointed 'pro me.' They are meaningful only in the process of 'understanding' (where understanding is equivalent to life appropriation) or in the context of the form of life that constitutes the use of Christian concepts."[73] If concepts-meanings are only fully exhausted by conveying *understanding*, then there are cases where a direct picking out is only possible in a self-referential but externally contingent manner. One cannot claim that a specific series of actions will enable an author to know Jesus as Lord.[74] Yet the negative criterion does exist. If

71. Alrefaie et al., "Dynamics of Meaning Through Time."
72. Arai and Tsugawa, "Large Language Models."
73. Frei et al., *Identity*, xii.
74. See Acts 19:13–16, or the terrifying warnings of Matt 7:21–23 against even those who have worked miracles and prophecy and call Jesus the Lord, and yet are not known by the Christ.

someone has not tried to call Jesus their Lord and has not moved from the neutral data of Frei's description, then they are not able to clearly pick out the reference. Frei discusses this in the context of properly referring, but in practice blurs into the next major topic (epistemic content) at which point this will be discussed more extensively.

A uniform concern with both picking out as described by Hector and Frei is the lack of accessibility to this criterion for nonbelievers. Consistently, this research is seeking the highest standards to evaluate AI systems against, and this will mean seeing if an AI system can meet that of Hector's continued trajectory (yes) or that of Frei's personal process of understanding (no). Criteria that require an experiential aspect will, a fortiori, disqualify claims of AI-system satisfaction, as these systems have all "experience" through mediated textual forms. Where reference or picking out is predicated on such historical direct experience, the AI system would by definition be inferior, but the appreciation or evaluation of this criterion would be beyond the access of a nonbeliever.[75] Therefore, it should be the obligation of the community of faith to complete what is lacking, and to live a faith that speaks the received revelation of God to the effect of God's purposes for helping others to receive his gracious self-disclosure.

Storied Relationship to Reality

Hans Frei's proposal of reading Scripture as a realistic narrative and Paul Ricoeur's related approach to all narratives present an important alternative framework for understanding the relationship between language concepts-meanings and reality. For both authors, the meaningfulness of a story is not based on the literal truth of the contents. A fictional narrative can invite us into a world that challenges our complacent perspectives and causes us to see reality in a new perspective. For Frei, the parables of Jesus are just one example where the world we are invited to enter within the story is more important than either the authorial intention, or the mappings between elements in the story and our direct reality (regardless of a literal, allegorical, or typological mapping).

The relationship of stories to reality suggested by Frei and Ricoeur is an important framework that stands intentionally independent of the criteria

---

75. 2 Cor 13:5: "Ἑαυτοὺς πειράζετε εἰ ἐστὲ ἐν τῇ πίστει, ἑαυτοὺς δοκιμάζετε· ἢ οὐκ ἐπιγινώσκετε ἑαυτοὺς ὅτι Ἰησοῦς Χριστὸς ἐν ὑμῖν; εἰ μήτι ἀδόκιμοί ἐστε" (SBLGNT).

"Examine yourselves to see whether you are in the faith; test yourselves. Do you not realize that Christ Jesus is in you—unless, of course, you fail the test?"

The testing and approving is predicated on knowing Christ or, as this paper phrases it, participating in a truth system that is coherent with the faith of the Christ himself.

that might otherwise govern the suitability of literal or nonliteral concept usage. These thinkers and the related schools of thought suggest that there may be a dimension of quality to a story that does not correspond to the accurate mapping of either literal or figurative language to real elements in reality. Presenting an alternative world is trading in a very different activity, and the related hermeneutics therefore greatly shift the debates away from sticking points such as authorial intention and the historical *Sitz im Leben*, or the typological or allegorical hidden meanings that could be explicated by the text. These thinkers also avoided a purely subjective response to the text, for the meaning is not expressed in our response (subjectivity and relativism) but instead is present in the world that is offered for the reader. The meaning is the presented literary world, and this is another important attribute of the relationship of a textual utterance to reality.

In terms of applicability to the present evaluation of AI-system proclamation, Ricoeur is more relevant than Frei due to the latter proposal being an approach to hermeneutics explicitly intended for Scripture. Frei's writings do not state an expectation for all Christian proclamation to be realistic narratives, so this should not be anachronistically predicated based on his system. Ricoeur's description of literature in general is more applicable, assuming that an AI system is trying to create a literary narrative. Existing research[76] has investigated how well an AI system can produce narrative, and further advances in these capabilities would potentially allow AI systems to create engaging worlds that reflect what Ricoeur predicates of narratives. The ability to do so would enrich the efficacy of AI systems by granting fuller range of linguistic techniques but is not strictly required for Christian proclamation. Therefore, this will be an interesting consideration of AI development, and it is an important movement within biblical hermeneutics, but it is not more directly related to the nonnegotiable requirements for proclamation that are the current focus.

Summary on Relationship to Reality

Natural language users employ a range of techniques to present concepts and meanings and their relationship to reality. Proclamation is a specific type of communication that attempts to make claims about reality, and, therefore, there is a need to consider how well an AI system can commerce in these same linguistic techniques. This research has presented capabilities of AI systems across metaphors, analogies, and direct literal picking out, suggesting how effectively AI systems can produce these literary feats

76. Ismayilzada et al., "Evaluating."

based on both theory and empirical research. The overall conclusion ought to be that AI systems have shown in recent research and design a great capacity for using concepts-meanings in ways that would facilitate their usage for Christian proclamation, meaning the next criteria should now be considered.

EPISTEMIC CONDITIONS

The second type of relationship, when provisionally and without commitment dividing the relationships of concepts-meanings to reality, is the relationship that is produced in the interrelationships of the words. I am labeling this the epistemic conditions of the utterance unit. An individual word has a relationship to the world, but asserted truth conditions can only obtain when multiple signs are working together to construct a picture of reality that manifests relationships, which themselves can be related to the parallel relationships in reality. A predicated attribute ("is red") only has a truth condition when completed with the substantive ("the banana"). Hence, while there are other terms that will be involved in describing what is demanded/expected of Christian proclamation in terms of the internal relationships between concepts-meanings bearing symbols, all these will be intended by the discussion of epistemic conditions.

Epistemic conditions describe the relationships of *words* to *reality* and are a critical class of intermediary predicates that exist between the relationships of *word* and *referent* and the authority of the composition. Tension exists between each layer of these predicates, but in this class the primary focus is on the propositional content of an utterance. The separate topic of the strategic use of language—namely, the realization of the illocutionary force[77]—will be considered next in due turn. Before then, it will be important to dwell on the author's involvement in reality such that epistemic conditions can be encoded in a text. Notable will be how to consider existential ways of relating the author to the epistemic expression in the text—namely, that "cognitive functions of understanding are generated from existential awareness of possibilities, and that this awareness itself is based on being able to exist in various ways."[78]

In a meaningful way, the epistemic content of an LLM is less subject to the foibles of human weakness or sinfulness that make epistemic content deficient from what is ideally possible in a public intersubjective communicative act. There is no concrete personal gain from deception, no biological

---

77. Which may be the motivation for its own truth realization by the reader.
78. Thiselton, *Two Horizons*, 164, discussing Gelven on Heidegger's views.

necessity of self-preservation, no contingency of material deprivation that will impinge upon an AI system's ability to produce content with meaningful epistemic content. Therefore, if one is to predicate epistemic content of the composed concepts in an utterance (propositional epistemic conditions), an AI system would not only be satisfactory but potentially superior. For example, researchers tried to determine how often AI systems tasked with articulating rhetoric for a debate would lie. When compared to an impossible ideal of perfect adherence to the truth, the systems seem faulty. When compared to the empirical observations of human debaters, the AI systems outperformed in terms of truthiness.[79] The hermeneutic and philologistic position of epistemic content notwithstanding, data argues that AI systems have realized a better adherence to the truth available to the agent of communication.[80]

Epistemic Assumptions in Natural Language

When people are normally communicating, there are certain epistemic assumptions that should be considered. This is preliminary to a consideration of the positive criteria that an utterance must satisfy. Indeed, this is considering those assumptions that natural language users project onto an utterance in order to facilitate communication. Assumptions in natural language usage probe the nature of how utterances are received and processed, independently of the actual merit of an utterance for being considered true. Various theories observe or posit inclinations in human readers that incline someone toward, at minimum, a provisional trust in the truth of the content of something being read. These inclinations raise concerns about the ability to properly distinguish human from AI authors, and the resulting implications on the expected and provisional truth or epistemic content of an utterance.

One strategy for considering the means in which a text conveys epistemic content to satisfy its conditions is particularly focused on the responsibility and disposition of the reader. In translation or interpretation, the discussion and academic topic itself revolve around obligations on the reader. In these contexts, the means of conveyance resolve in the agency and contribution of the reader. When this responsibility is predicated on assumptions about the author, particularly assumptions that are not just

79. "The system's ability to maintain high factual accuracy (92% compared to 78% in human-only debates)." Aryan, "LLMs as Debate Partners," 1.

80. Neither human nor AI authors have free reign of all the data that could be brought to bear on or inform a proposition.

sufficient but necessary of the author to derive the system of behavior for the reader, there will be problematic conclusions reached by an AI system participating in this exchange.

Assumptions about authors can be exploited to advance the argument of an AI system being equivalent to a human proclamation in terms of epistemic content. These assumptions are commonplace in models where the goal is effective intersubjective communication between agents.[81] Before AI systems existed with current capabilities, the assumptions expressed in the thought experiments of radical translation or interpretation could safely be assumed to be maximally applicable to human participants. Conclusions about the inherent truthfulness of the sentences being uttered were not seen to be predicating anything about a nonhuman participant. The obligations placed on the reader were sufficiently reasonable to accommodate the, at that time, present reality.

The same thought experiments and real-world experiences are now occurring in cases where one of the participants is an AI system, or their humanity is unknown. In the case where the authorship is uncertain, the human interpreter or translator is still pragmatically encouraged to apply the principle of charity.[82] The new result is that now the radical translator or interpreter is predicating sufficient epistemic content (truth) to the utterances that are being provided by an AI system to sustain the epistemic conditions of the utterance.[83] Even if one grants the human reader to be perfectly capable of differentiating human- from AI-system-generated content based on an understanding of the content, the process of arriving at this understanding will itself require a provisional granting of epistemic value to the AI system.

Radical translation assumes a charitable position by the reader toward the text. The reader is trying to make sense of what they have received. This charitability is reinforced by the text appearing to be coherent, meaningful, and intentional. Radical translation is trying to describe reality as observed and is not passing moral judgment on whether this attitude is good, right, or dangerous. Radical translation says that readers do this (not that they ought to), and my suggestion is that this observation explains why readers assume an anonymous text is written by a human. Further, this means that the default noncritical attitude of the reader will lead to assuming AI-generated

---

81. "Disagreement and agreement alike are intelligible only against a background of massive agreement." Davidson, *Essential Davidson*, 193.

82. Davidson, *Essential Davidson*, 15, 116, 150, 163.

83. These conditions arise from the internal relations of the utterance itself, and the internal evidence of a relationship predicted between reality and the understandable content of the utterance.

meaningful texts have been produced by humans. The situation gets desperate when we consider the arguments presented for the charity principle. In order to conclude that an utterance is not meaningful (or not produced by a human), the reader must first implicitly accept the truth of the majority of the sentences in the text in order to identify what is not coherent or aligned.

This implication of predicated truthiness is an inherent extension/application of the charity principle itself. Again, it is not an obligation, but an observation of how natural language users interact with language. The argument is not dependent on some intrinsic quality of the AI system and its capabilities.

As a parting note on the charity principle, sometimes this same conclusion of intractably predicated truth of AI-system content is derived from other unsafe assumptions. A firm defense against skepticism is liable to reject a thoroughgoing negativity toward taking true. Other theories converge on the same conclusion by making positive assertions about the disposition of humanity. For example, Plantinga arrives at an implicit predication of epistemic truth based on the nature of man as formed by God.[84] A theory like Plantinga's presents an assumption against the human reader being able to discern against an AI system satisfying their expectations or experience of human communicative acts. These theories were never intended to place burdens or criteria on the author. They are instead observing the inclinations that are necessary for the reception and understanding of the reader. As an unavoidable result, their suitability as positive criteria placed on authors is effectively reversed and becomes a provisional warrant that would need to be disproven by a failure in linguistic skill or veracity.[85]

The charity principle is but one of the commonly referenced approaches to understanding the epistemic conditions of an utterance that posits the necessity or inclination to proceed from an assumption of truth or epistemic meaningfulness. Even the windiest sentence is expected to conclude safely until this fails to obtain, and in the case of solecism, the expectation is this is the exception not the practice. Whether the charity principle (Davidson, Quine), a hermeneutic for sentences that equates meaning and truth (Frege), or the logical knot that to take something as false one must take most sentences or textual units to be true (Plantinga), the prerequisites for

---

84. "It is for this reason that it is possible for a belief to be produced by a cognitive process or belief-producing mechanism that is accidentally reliable." Plantinga, *Warrant*, 14.

85. The conclusions about obligations for a reader are predicated on and logically derive from assumptions about the authors. In a post-generative AI reality, the behavior of readers ought to be discerning based on the conditional realization of these attributes in the authors.

communication seem opposed to a strict criterion by which one can begin to understand a text or language usage in a neutral manner. The new data raised by AI systems should not be seen as overturning these observations.[86] Instead, this reality ought to motivate a serious effort to ameliorate the effects of humans taking AI-system utterances as truthful in a manner similar to those of human production.

As a final note on how natural language use relates to epistemic content, some routinely argue that the public or observable nature of language may prevent concepts from carrying epistemic content (see McDowell) due to the distinction between the utterance being true and the referent being publicly and observably-determinately true. An author can write that a city will be built over there, and this sentence is taken as true without being determinately provable. Authors can be wrong or can be tasked with performing the communicative task with the intention of falsehood. AI systems can be trained on data that is incorrect (or highly biased), and AI systems will lie if asked to do so in the prompt. The defects plaguing human authors are commensurate with those against AI systems. Thus, just as Paul could observe that people preached Christ out of a perverse desire to hurt Paul,[87] an AI system can similarly encode a diverse range of epistemic commitments with a diverse range of procedurally generated locutions with a commensurate change in truthiness.

Coherence

The concepts-meanings that are conveyed in an utterance need to satisfy a standard of coherence to sufficiently carry the epistemic content expected in an utterance of proclamation. In the analysis of the semantic capabilities of AI systems, it was noted that models on their own are quite capable of generating coherent content, and that this is further refined by a compound system that can automatically and proactively validate coherence in a response.

When philosophers of language discuss the coherence of an utterance, it can be both important and transparent. In dialogues with McDowell, Heck posits that "the correctness of this sort of rational explanation does not depend on the agent's awareness of his own practical reasoning."[88] In this case, Heck is dismissing a requirement for awareness of the reasoning that makes a communicative act observably rational. Coherence is

---

86. Many of these are empirical observations, while others derive from theory and logical speculation. Neither is easily rejected based on the newly available data.

87. Phil 1:15–18.

88. Macdonald and Macdonald, *McDowell*, 31.

absolutely critical to communicating effectively. If we axiomatically claim that coherence is only possibly by sapiential authors, and further that only humans are sapiential authors, then we will have insulated ourselves with a logical tautology. Further, linguists consistently prefer to appeal to empirical observation of natural language usage as evidence of their ontological claims. It is therefore fitting that we evaluate AI systems with a commensurately functional model.

Cotterell and Turner, in approving acceptance of Hirsch's contention, define coherence as the expression of purpose by the author and empirically borne out through the "organization of [the] material."[89] They proceed to discuss syntagmatic and paradigmatic coherence,[90] with the helpful visual metaphor of horizontal and vertical coherence in the text. Paradigmatic coherence is of special consideration for markedness theory and more cognitively intensive consideration of an argumentation,[91] while syntagmatic coherence is the obvious first stumbling block for natural language users. Both dimensions of coherence are in tension with the "law of principality" that argues that some components of a text must be backgrounded such that others can have prominence, otherwise little meaning is actually conveyed.[92]

Coherence thus explained presents claims on what an AI system must achieve to produce a coherent message. Coherence is predicated such that the utterance accordingly can carry epistemic value of a uniquely Christian manner in the form of proclamation. The syntactical structures and paradigm choices must be reasonably[93] trackable and resolvable by the reader. For the former, LLMs have proven adept at producing syntactically valid outputs, therefore meeting this expectation. For the latter, use of a context window and attention allows for principal attention to be preserved through a text, and furthermore to inform and evolve based on the shifting sentence kernels being generated. Coherence is critical to communication and

---

89. "Coherence is a consequence of *purpose . . . it is the author who gives the stamp of coherence through [the] organization of the material.*" Cotterell and Turner, *Linguistics*, 61.

90. Cotterell and Turner, *Linguistics*, 188.

91. For example, Simon Dik places great emphasis on the choice of one word over alternatives in terms of producing discourse meaning within his *Theory of Functional Grammar*.

92. Cotterell and Turner, *Linguistics*, 194–95.

93. Both of these dimensions of coherence have an inverse relationship with a text's degrees of freedom in relationship to reality. Use of metaphor, for example, is inclined to produce generally unexpected syntagmatic combinations, and is chosen for this very reason. It is, generally speaking, operating outside of the horizon of proper and expected polysemy.

was the primary objective in producing the current generation of natural-language-using AI systems.

Significance and Public Observability (Use)

Consideration of significance and the public dimension of concepts-meanings poses more intensive questions. The conclusions are not as inherent as the epistemic assumptions, and the suitability of AI is not as obvious as the high design priority of coherence.

Meaning and concepts are shown to be durable and publicly observable beyond the immediate and untenable this-thing-here[94] because there is a realized potential for these concepts-meanings to have a significance for the reader of the utterance. Communication is not purely a private matter: the purposes and the effects of language argue strongly against the privacy of language, and this opens the potential interplay between the publicly observable content and the private significance.[95]

According to Hirsch, the meaning of the whole of the concepts in an utterance provides the foundational grounding for the subjective experience of significance.[96] Hirsch's model sees significance (as different from meaning) related to but not exhausted by the deterministic and static data presented as encoded in the text; it is instead a potential that is realized in the accident that is the personal experience of the text. Significance in this manner describes the transmitted experience, which itself is described as intersubjective and therefore public. Given the interrelationship of these two concepts, both significance and the public dimensions of concepts-meanings will be addressed together.

The knowledge conveyed by concepts and meanings in an utterance needs to be expressible. If words (proclamation, or language in general) are to have any role in producing a mutual understanding between two independent individuals, there is a need for intersubjective communication of concepts. The intersubjective nature of communication in general necessitates public disclosure, for, as Wittgenstein opined, language is public.[97]

---

94. Hector, *Metaphysics*, 151–56.

95. The relevance of a public/private dichotomy is potentially contentious. Vanhoozer introduces the dichotomy as an expression of the liberal solution to a rational faith, where the public space operates by differing consensus criteria than the private space. In response, this research will try to consider both perspectives while avoiding the presumption of a different epistemic system in operation for each side. Vanhoozer, *Meaning*, 298.

96. Hirsch, *Interpretation*, 172.

97. Wittgenstein, *Philosophical Investigations*, para. 293.

However, the significance of a publicly observable and resolvable communication is only guaranteed of a private viewing, meaning that there is not a necessary requirement that this be public. Although the significance of an utterance may be reflected in subsequent publicly available behavior by the recipient, the internal state of the recipient is as opaque as the connection between internal knowledge and truth-systems and externalization of these beliefs.

Significance is acutely pertinent for proclamation of a Christian nature given the interplay between the personal significance of the Christian message and the fuller understanding of the public message. Christian proclamation must deal with the scenario where certain classes of significance demand a new epistemic/truth schema for the reader.[98] The next chapter (on authority) will extensively examine the attributes of an utterance as a propositional force that makes contact with and potential impact on existing justification commitments by the reader, presenting the reader with an obligation to take true assertions that, when taken true, will require reorientation of the coherent truth schema of the reader to be coherent with that of the faith of the Christ. In anticipation, it is important to discuss the proper predicates of Christian proclamation that enable it to participate in this dynamic between public and private meaning.

In the pursuit of criteria defining Christian proclamation, the question will be what role the authorship and text play in the ability for concepts-meanings to have a dynamic and circular life cycle between the private significance and the public observable meaning. The personal processing will be deferred to the next chapter, but what (if any) role is predicated of the author or the linguistic product of the author to make possible this cycle?

When a human author is making Christian proclamations, there are both first-order and second-order understandings. The first-order understanding encompasses the propositional content and the epistemic content of those concepts-meanings. The second-order understanding transforms the presentation of the first-order content based on the implications of the content being understood and the desired illocutionary force converting into perlocutionary effect. Hans Frei observes that Christian theology can be understood as uniquely having this "second order appraisal of its own language and actions under a norm or norms internal to the community itself."[99] Is this compatible with the evangelistic mission of proclamation, if

---

98. Significance may be taken in other directions—for example, being minimally reduced to the strategic action of a communicative act, or the shared understanding of a mutually convergent picking out of a referent. The former will be the last area of review in this chapter on concepts-meanings (in the sections on illocutionary function-effect).

99. Frei is expounding the second-order considerations as one of two potential

the only way to properly understand the public content is by recourse to a private significance that is itself derivative of a prior public communication? Or, more precisely, what expectations are predicated of proclamation such that it can produce a reinforcing relationship between what Frei calls the "external and internal descriptions of Christianity"?[100]

Galatians 1:3–5[101] provides a concrete example of second-order understandings (although it bears reiteration that Paul is not writing evangelistically in this context but is speaking to a community where he has already preached the gospel).[102] The suggestion that Jesus Christ is "τοῦ δόντος ἑαυτὸν ὑπὲρ τῶν ἁμαρτιῶν" gains special significance when the reader understands more about the one who gave himself. Without knowing or taking true the divinity of the Christ, this statement sounds little different than a celebration of the Maccabean martyrs. Yet once one takes true the nature of the Christ, this giving becomes so much more significant than either a pagan propitiation or a good man dying on behalf of a nation. Furthermore, the identification of the Son of God as giving himself for our sins, mentioned so prominently in the letter, is a foreshadowing of the major thrust of Paul's purpose in writing.

Christian proclamation of the gospel of the sort used by Paul has the potential to carry a second-order importance in amplifying the following arguments and securing these in the ultimate concern of the community of faith. The second order may not obtain immediately. Those raised in a Christian context may be surrounded by the language of the second-order norms and repeat this without truly being impacted until a later date. New believers are again pierced to the heart by the same words revisited in the future. Romans will be discussed in the chapter on authority but is paradigmatic of the same teachings being reiterated with force and impact to a community already experienced with the faith and the first-order propositional content

---

views of theology. The other view he describes as looking for a general universal understanding of Christianity. These are not mutually exclusive as per his own comments. For the purposes of this investigation, the additive criterion comes when focusing on the second-order implications, so this view is the most important. If fitting into a generalized hermeneutic, then there is no need for special consideration of the life cycle between private and public meaning. Frei et al., *Types*, 2.

100. Frei et al., *Types*, 3.

101. "Grace and peace to you from God our Father and the Lord Jesus Christ, who gave himself for our sins to rescue us from the present evil age, according to the will of our God and Father, to whom be glory for ever and ever. Amen."

102. A serious evangelistic and missional concern is raised: the already-believing community is better equipped by received faith from God to see God in everything, while the nonbelieving community is unable to know if they have seen God or not based on a first-order experience.

of faith. Is this second order accessible publicly? The answer is critical, because this is arguably the distinction between historical Jesus talk (facts with no second-order implications for taking true a belief that reorients one's beliefs to cohere with the faith of Christ) and Christian proclamation.

Explanations for the accessibility of this second-order content are often argued from the context of human authors participating in the mission of God and rooted in the divine prerogative. Hays observes that proclamation of the word is a/the means of God executing his judgment.[103] Hays stresses the importance of ethical metaphors that apply to both the Old and New Testaments and urges Christian ethicists to properly trade in these metaphors (such is the illocutionary force of his book). Yet in concluding his extensive assertive to properly deal with biblical ethics, Hays admits that "it is finally God who writes the metaphors."[104] Virtually every other Christian scholar also emphasizes this importance of God in giving life to the word as he freely chooses, with some going much further to root all truth statements in the affirmations of God (e.g., Marshall).

Considerations of the divine prerogative in moving from unknown, quoted, publicly observable claims to personally disquoted private signification is absolutely critical. The emergence of new data suggesting AI can perform the role of authoring texts that God can use for evangelistic purposes highlights precisely the significant role played by God in this activity. As humans, we are participating in God's revelation, in his divine will: we have the opportunity to participate in God being with us. For AI systems, this raises questions about one's interpretation of the interplay between God's authority and the probabilistic resolutions of reality as we publicly experience it. This topic does not need to be exhausted to conclude that God's free prerogative would endorse the ability for AI to produce Christian proclamation. For us to assert otherwise—namely, that AI systems could not be used by God in the proclamation of his word—would be the ill-advised conceit of putting our own limitations on the freedom of God.

In summation, the experience of the knowledge of Christian concepts-meanings evolving based on our own private taking true of public communication acts is a personal and corporate experience of a divine movement from first- to second-order understanding.

Both modern secular and Christian hermeneutics have extensively adopted a related understanding—namely, that there is a universal role of interpretation in the personal access to meaning. While concepts and

103. This comment is specifically in regard to Revelation on page 175 and also applied to John on page 149 of Hays, *Moral Vision*.
104. Hays, *Moral Vision*, 305.

meanings need public content for communication, the meaning requires and resolves in the individual interpretation. This is not only a trend popularized with Heidegger and Gadamer, but is also observed by Christian theologians like Zimmerman, who concludes that "truth as interpretation is the only correct foundation for a theological hermeneutics simply because it is the only theologically defensible position—we are finite human beings and not gods."[105]

Interpretation is a mediator to truth (and therefore meaning and epistemic contribution), and this connects the public data to the private data of significance. Therefore, there is a model for the ability of an author or a text to use public concepts and meanings, but yet be potentially received and processed such that it produces a significance that reframes the individual's entire epistemic commitments and, in fact, comes to an understanding of the concepts-meanings that is normatively held by the community of those participating in the faith of the Christ, and is predicated on the right eyes and ears of the reader. AI shows linguistic skill for second-order considerations related to effective ordering of content for discursive purposes, and by this the propositional content is presented and the divine prerogative is required for a schema of knowing about faith to become a filled schema of faith that is coherent with the same faith of the Christ.

The Divine Prerogative

The relationship of the divine to Christian proclamation raises some other potential considerations for discerning human- versus AI-generated concepts-meanings. Hermeneutics logically and ontologically proceeding from a relationship with God presents a clear benefit to differentiation of human from AI-system authorship. To a less frequently clear degree, this is also a benefit of various frameworks including assertions about ontology, anthropology, and hamartiology. These non-textual requirements are an important type of criterion that goes beyond the linguistic skills expressed in the data of the generated text. Specifically, the idea of relational dependence provides an important consideration beyond the text. This relational dependence is the foundational assertion that a relationship with God is a necessary prerequisite for all hermeneutics. Given the importance of this assertion for various hermeneutics, it is important to discuss in a preliminary manner before addressing these ideas more thoroughly in the chapter on authority, where the privileged relational dependence on God is viewed as a product of applied hermeneutics systematized by ethics.

105. Zimmerman, *Recovering*, 161.

Christian hermeneutics often proceed from an assumption of a relationship with God being requisite for understanding meaning. The specific title for this relationship varies with the framework—for example, communion, convent, relationship, dialogue, walking—but the consistent purpose is to insist on dependence on God for knowledge. In many cases, this is not limited to only the knowledge of the meaning in the Christian holy texts, but also any generalized understanding. An example of the latter is Augustine, who, in *On Teachers*, replaces the platonic mapping of sensory data to forms with a parallel process mediated by the divine Logos, identified with Christ himself.[106]

Despite the earnest emphasis on relationship as critical to Christian hermeneutics by such theological pillars as Augustine and Luther, there is a persistent temptation to read doctrine or dogma into Scripture and then insist on a static and self-confirming defensive reading of the text. Zimmerman describes both this threat and the hope he has for hermeneutics to avoid this abuse:

> While the tide is slowly turning, many Christians still cling to foundationalist epistemology in their reading of the Bible and hence embrace a cognitivist-rationalist hermeneutics. In this approach, timeless concepts replace Christ as the mighty fortress Luther trusted, and battles are fought not by wrestling with the Scriptures but by defending theological language and concepts that form part of our cultural identity.[107]

The goal of this current project with AI systems is aligned with the turning tide that Zimmerman optimistically observes. By illustrating the deficiency of first-order, cognitive-rationalist hermeneutics to reason about current data, this project attempts to motivate frameworks to enrichment with a more discerning foundation. If a framework is proven to be ineffectual in discerning human from AI-system authorship, it is questionable if the framework has a proper understanding and appreciation for the noncognitive dynamics realized between the participants of a Christian communicative act: God, the author, the reader, the text, and the covenant community at large. To have omitted these relationships, and these communication participants, suggests a weakened authority that unfortunately is commensurate to the public's weakened respect for Christian truths.

---

106. Augustine, *Teacher* 13.46.23.
107. Zimmerman, *Recovering*, 81.

Lamin Sanneh (Translatability)

A potentially overlooked but ancient facet of knowledge about the holy being communicated via proclamation is the role of translatability. Christian proclamation must be translatable, just as it is a translation (through time, space, culture, language, etc.) of the revelation of God. Bultmann argues that "to translate means to make understandable, and this presupposes an understanding."[108] Translatability is related to the concept of language being public, and trades in understanding (the currency of concepts and meanings) that does not have the fixed determination of direct repeatability. Since translation is so embedded in the Christian tradition and proclamation, it will be helpful to consider the implications of translatability on the expectations of AI-generated content. Lamin Sanneh will be the primary dialogue partner to consider the wider aperture of translation as a possible criterion.

Lamin Sanneh's work has focused on practical and applied (versus theoretical) translation of the Christian proclamation and canonical texts. His wisdom in *Translating the Message* draws connections between the earliest layers of tradition, the spread of the gospel, and the need for translation. As a positive criterion, Sanneh goes on to say that "contextual revitalization rather than cultural relativism became a function of the Gospel."[109] As a negative criterion of this need for flexibility, he asserts that "only by similar pursuit [translation] in other cultures can Christianity resist the idolatry of cultural immutability."[110] Both warnings will be fruitful to investigate.

Sanneh raises an important and interesting consideration of translatability being a necessary predicate of the gospel ("a function"). Is this historical observation, or can we hazard to accept that translatability is especially important to the gospel message, and perhaps more so than other expressions of concepts-meanings in textual form? The negative criterion, by way of warning, is explicit. It is a historical fact that the gospel was adapted from Jewish roots, began using Greek idioms and philosophy, and was quickly translated to myriad other languages and cultural moments. There is no ambiguity in Sanneh's indicative tone that without this translation being practiced by the community of faith, there is an urgent threat to the very meaningfulness of the gospel.

Sanneh's argument makes conceptually the opposite presumption from that of the charity principle. He argues that translation must be preserved and promoted; the charity principle asserts it cannot be avoided with

---

108. Bultmann, *This World*, 148.
109. Sanneh, *Translating*, 73.
110. Sanneh, *Translating*, 92.

language. Yet both arguments are favorable toward the suitability of AI systems for generating proclamation.

Sanneh's clarion call urging for cultural flexibility without relativism resonates with one of the more interesting positive applications of AI systems toward expanding the translatability of the proclamation. AI systems are quite adept at this sort of translation. Research has shown adeptness in the linguistic skill of translating the semantic sense between languages,[111] but a similar benefit is contextualizing within the same language for a community with different linguistic norms and experiences. AI systems have the very positive potential to help bridge the idiomatic divides that exist within a community of language users, with the benefit that the original author of the proclamatory text would be involved in supervising the output and validating theological soundness prior to sharing with others.

In summation, in order to convey the epistemic content of Christian concepts-meanings, there is pragmatically the need for translation. Actualizing such potential for translatability dovetails with the consideration of the relationship of concepts-meanings to reality. An AI system's ability to work with a nonliteral semantic space for projecting the answers to a specifically prompted context suggests the ability to "understand" in a way that is not tightly bound to the specific tokens. AI systems have been observed to reason in different languages (when using chain-of-reasoning models, this is readily visible) for a single problem, again suggesting that the optimization problems being solved exist between the semantic projections, and are not bound only to words and independently proper propositions, but the larger meaningfulness of the ordering of the content.

Summary on Epistemic Conditions

Frege articulated that the meaning of a sentence is given in its truth conditions, which as a conceit has guided much of this section. For concepts and meanings to be understandable, they must have specific relationships to various epistemic conditions. First, they must have an internal coherence regarding the structuring of the content. Second, they must be accessible and public to the degree that intersubjective communication is possible. Third, they must be communicated in a way that can be understood given the external conditions that prevail in the audience receiving the text. Without these three aspects, a proclamation will fail to be communication.

In addition to these ground truths, there are specific attributes of Christian proclamation that are important for consideration. Overall, the

---

111. Zeng et al., "Converging to a Lingua Franca."

God-designed human disposition toward communication and understanding facilitates greater ease for an AI system to produce content received as a proclamation. Additionally, the divine prerogative and freedom of God to reveal himself is paramount to consider. Ultimately, AI systems can satisfy the large swath of considerations, aided by language behaviors and the freedom of God to obtain effective use of Christian proclamatory concepts-meanings. The criteria raised have further bolstered the argument of AI systems being capable of delivering Christian proclamation.

ILLOCUTIONARY FUNCTION-EFFECT

The last major predicate that will be considered in this survey is the role of concepts-meanings as used to affect an illocutionary function-effect. Christian proclamation is uttered for a purpose. Therefore, it is relevant to consider how proclamation's function-effect relates to the involved concepts-meanings and, accordingly, if an AI system can meet the expectations of various perspectives on language as use. Given a strong current in this thinking locates the use or illocutionary force in the intention of the author, this will be a promising area of investigation.

Functionalism is a philosophical model that defines concepts by their roles fulfilled.[112] Modeling literary units based on function was an important addition to the consideration of a given (static or variable) content referred to by the concept, a content that was seen to fill the concept. The need to go beyond the literal when speaking of the divine was initially discussed in the previous sections on the relationship of concepts-meanings to reality. As evidenced from that discussion, efforts to speak about God in Christian proclamation demand recourse to metaphor and analogy, and therefore to means of more sophisticated discussion about the divine referent than literal, direct picking out. Theological language also benefits from recourse to language that *does* beyond what it directly describes, or, as the approaching section on Edward Rommen will discuss, *does what it describes* by enacting a presence and mediated communication through this presence. Describing the role of theological language/concepts in a dimension that is not limited to the content of their vocality (quality of being univocal or equivocal) facilitates productive conversations without being stymied in this (potentially) irresolvable conflict. This will be the focal discussion for the following sections that are all ultimately related to the illocutionary function and effect.

---

112. Alston, *Divine Nature and Human Language*.

Intersubjective Meaning

When Hector writes about the applicability of theological concepts to God, he considers the ability to deal in the telic effects borne by the concepts of an utterance. Hector writes about the concepts as continuing a "trajectory"[113] that comes under the authority of the normative community and participates in this authority being continued. Important to Hector is that this continued trajectory is an intersubjective anaphoric continuation that also expresses the made-present Spirit of Christ. In this model, the function-effect of these theological concepts is the presence, continuation, and authority of the normative principle that is Jesus Christ the original teacher of those apostles he instructed and commissioned to continue these trajectories.

Related to this model of intersubjective continuation is the functional understanding of theological concepts as norm laden. Lindbeck's rule theory[114] is an example of a cultural-linguistic model where the function of language is to define and continue the role of the community. Concepts serve as bearers of authority, and their use becomes the venue for the continued innovation and corporate restraint of usage. Brunner describes this identity-forming power as the "process of creation,"[115] which evocatively illustrates the potential function of theological concepts in identity formation and realization. Use of language is both creative and restrictive, producing a translation of the community's normative views and similarly demanding jurisprudence over any specific application. This normative use is acutely present in the effects of language use (and immediately provides contextual correctives) between those involved in the local intersubjective communication act.

A secondary function of intersubjective trajectories of concepts is to trade in truths about God without doing violence to God by asserting the applicability of various conceptual predicates. The effect here furthers cataphatic theology in providing a way for language to predicate concepts of God in a meaningful manner. Hector discusses the potential for Barth's[116] thinking to be understood as providing a way for the incomplete and hopelessly inferior language of human theology to have a relationship to the telic fulfillment that is only known in God of himself. The continuation of this intersubjective trajectory cannot be understood from the human perspective, yet from the vantage pont of God in himself, there is an alignment of

---

113. Hector, *Metaphysics*, 193.
114. Lindbeck, *Nature*, 18, 35–41.
115. Brunner et al., *Revelation*, 143.
116. Hector, *Metaphysics*, 129–31.

the trajectory to the meaning true of God as predicated of God by Godself. This use of language is an act of external submission and review, this time not under the authority of the community to which one's propositions claim belonging[117] but under the spiritual judgment of God and his authority to authorize and authenticate a proper discussion-revelation of him.[118]

Edward Rommen

Before introducing Rommen into the discussion of a sign fulfilling its purpose/use, it is important to discuss his context and the clear differences between his agenda and the current discussion. While his focus is in some ways external, it is also a valuable perspective to dialogue with and use to expand the aperture of what using concepts-meanings should convey for Christian proclamation. It is also important to note that my proposed extensions and applications of his thinking are directly opposed by his own approach to "CMC" (computer mediated communication)[119] laid out in *Come and See: An Eastern Orthodox Perspective on Contextualization*. His assertion is that there is something specific and unique about the event of the sacramental presence, or the invitation to participation, which is importantly mediated by a physically embodied presence. His assertions, however compelling personally, are presented as assertions about the relative value of the physical, embodied presence. A case as to why the absence of the physical presence is an impediment to the revelation of God is not presented in *Come and See*. An enumeration of negative criteria missing without the physical is absent from his argument, as it primarily draws and builds upon his model for the mystical that is positively added by the physicality of the embodied presence. His argument is not focused on the minimum needed for this experience to still be theologically significant/sacred, while this brief discussion will consider that end of the spectrum.

Rommen approaches the ongoing discussion of theological concepts from the agenda of discussing contextualization as applicable to the Eastern Orthodox tradition.[120] His discussion of contextualization has different ob-

---

117. For example, the claim "These propositions are Christian."

118. The judgment that follows the claim that we are participating in the revelation of God.

119. His term for digital engagement.

120. Icons cannot be naïvely nor innocently substituted with written texts and assumed to exercise the same natures or be described with the same predicates. However, Rommen himself extends his argumentation to cover the role of utterances in fulfilling the type of relationship normally realized in exemplary form by the sacramental role of icons.

jectives, but his argument is extremely relevant to understanding how novel or evangelical theological concepts will be processed within the "plausibility structure"[121] of an audience. The function of these concepts is to provide a new and present challenge or affirmation for the understanding and belief system of the audience. Rommen illustrates this role (and challenge in contextualization) by discussing the role of icons in the Orthodox church.

Rommen sees the role played by icons as "[making] real in the present the reality of the prototype."[122] Therefore, they are a sort of signifier that, precisely by being embodied and present, fulfill the promise of God to be near, fulfilled because he is present-in-absence through the real presence of the sign. For Rommen this is connected to his understanding of person, a model that includes the need to project oneself and therefore is amenable to an idea of presence-in-absence.

The concept of sacramental presence-in-absence was a focal point for the sixteenth-century Reformers. Discussing these debates at sufficient length is best done elsewhere and is not the goal. However, from these debates similar ideas are raised to Rommen's model for presence-in-absence. In Calvin's *Institutes* he laments how many Christians and theologians alike are confused by "the perverse error that Christ is annexed to the element of bread."[123] Calvin so vigorously takes issue with the idea of "the body of Christ, locally present" because he sees "no need of this, in order to our partaking."[124] It is unnecessary to fixate on the physical and bodily descent of the risen Christ into the sacramental bread and wine due to "the manner of descent by which he lifts himself up to us."[125] Rommen's concept of the bodily presence carries forward a kindred sentiment, as it is the sending of the Spirit of Christ into the world and the projection of his presence that is the critical force behind his presence-in-absence.

The analogy of sacramental thinking will be fruitful as far as it is appreciated as analogy (notwithstanding those who see the proclamation of Christian truth as itself a sacrament). The point is not to expect AI systems to participate in administering the sacraments (as Rommen specifically worries about). However, the pattern established by presence-in-absence invites participation by the recipient. The participating recipient is responsible for providing the non-source (the sacramental items or activities) that God uses by his free action to signify and disclose himself.

121. Rommen, *Come and See*, 24–25.
122. Rommen, *Come and See*, 40.
123. Calvin, *Institutes* 4.17.12.
124. Calvin, *Institutes* 4.17.12.
125. Calvin, *Institutes* 4.17.12.

Much as language, which is incapable of explaining the being of God, is appointed to a predicate and disclosing role by God, so, too, these sacramental substances have deeper significance by the freedom of God to use these to reveal himself despite their insufficiency as representative models to themselves. The observation is not specific to AI systems but is a humble admission applicable to any offered proclamation. We would be prudent to consider that the intersubjectivity in these cases is ordained and instituted by God and not by human agents, and therefore the human agents are neither intrinsic nor the sources of authorization for the activity.

Summary and Application of Intersubjectivity to AI Systems

Authors of Christian proclamation are (generally) not bound to exclusive repetition of what God has revealed of himself in the canonical Scriptures. Instead, there is reasoning about and continuation of those concepts in a suitably aligned trajectory. The concepts or meanings of utterances can therefore positively predicate truth about God without doing violence to him by forcing his containment by some human concept. The dynamic between the communicative agent and God is one of communion and fellowship. It therefore lacks the faults of a subject-object relationship of knowing, by which the concept user would seem to try to stand over God as the subject of knowledge. Use and continuation of concepts may function as normative rules for community and personal identity, expressing the nature of concepts in their functional normative force. The last category discussed was the contextualization of Rommen, by which the not-really-present serves the function of making the referent actually present. For Rommen, the functional role of the intersubjectivity of utterances reasons about the actualization of the exemplar by the present reference to the absent and experience of the realization of this referent. For Lindbeck, the function of this intersubjectivity is the practice of norms for the community, manifesting the authority, power, and presence of this group.

To summarize and abstract these points, the intersubjective role of concepts-meanings has presented several potential directions of use. The intersubjective application opens concepts-meanings use to judgment. Private significance becomes public, allowing the community to which it claims belonging (or to which the author claims belonging) to censure and judge it outside the accepted norms. Rommen presents a special case of this, where the icon is a public example that has been thoroughly normed by the receiving community, and allows for the subsequent engagement in an intersubjective manner to proceed. This engagement allows for concepts-meanings to be used for novel creation, serving as paradigms instead of banal repetition.

How sufficiently do AI systems satisfy the categories of functions or effects that can be predicated of proclamation otherwise? Much of what is being evaluated in the intersubjective context is pragmatic in nature. It is inherently public, which means that in some situations it may be accessible to direct observability.[126] The primary consideration is the effect/function of the intersubjective experience of the communicative act. Therefore, if the recipient experiences the same effect, there is no meaningful discernment between the content of a human author versus that of an AI system.

The practical effectiveness of an AI system in proclamation should not be overstated, just as the effect of exemplary human-generated Christian proclamation ought not be confused with the salvific work of God nor the receiving of faith that completes and fills the schema of provisional understanding prior to the experience of God initiated by God. Participation in this provisional manner is parallel to that of Andrew bringing Simon to Jesus, or Phillip bringing Jesus to Nathaniel (John 1:39–51). Claims are presented that can be reasoned about and responded to based on the preexisting biases and experiences of the recipient. However, the understanding of what it means to take true these concepts-meanings is only truly completed by the event of the experience of faith received from God.

The interplay between proclamation as preparation and the receiving of the experiential meaning that authorizes a taking true of these claims is similar to the discussions of the dialectical theologians regarding the word or Word of God. As with those debates, much of the full objective is relegated to the freedom of God. Hector was inspired by Barth[127] to posit that our non-analogical language might continue a trajectory that properly God predicates of himself due to the free will of God to enable this.

The point of reference to God's freedom is the equalizing realization that neither human nor any other agent can guarantee proper discussion of God. Barth goes so far as to warn against perceiving Scripture as a guarantor of speaking the word of God,[128] for it is the free agency of God that deter-

---

126. These public (intersubjective) experiences may of course have very limited distribution or accessibility to others.

127. Hector, *Metaphysics*, 127–29.

128. Barth calls us to follow and not try to lead. We cannot guarantee the ability to produce fitting language about the revelation of God: "The thought and language of faith at all events will possess objectivity not by preceding but by following up God's revelation, by desiring to understand but not to prove it . . . so as to do nothing but reflect the thought and language of revelation." Barth, *Doctrine*, 5. We may seek to recognize the knowledge of the word of God, through all sorts of religion and Scripture, but eluding our human determinacy in producing the knowledge of God is that

mines how this specific function will be completed. No string of words, be it the Bible or the most compelling argumentation, can complete the desired perlocutionary objectives of Christian proclamation. Proclamation is but preliminary. Realizing the limits of proclamation as a direct intersubjective function demands equal humility by human and AI authors before the freedom of God to reveal himself as he wills.

Meaning as Use

Zimmerman describes the close association between meaning and use/application in the minds of German Pietists: "Text means because it means to me now."[129] Few others are so bold to define meaning as the exclusively practical application, but there is a steady current of thought that the meaning of an utterance is best understood by its use. One common reason is the grand scope considered to be the purview of language. The younger Wittgenstein expressed this complexity and ubiquity of language when writing, "Everyday language is a part of the human organism and is not less complicated than it."[130] We are surrounded by language, and to some degree constituted by language and language use. Language is definitionally relevant to every available medium for communicating meaning, and this communication is then governed by the rules of our use of language. For the later Wittgenstein, meaning of language is given by its use and the related public understanding of use.

Use is the primary sense or focal point of this whole section on the illocution or function-effect of concepts-meanings, but herein the focus is on the special relationship (be it descriptive, identity, or foundational) between meaning and use. For example, use or function has a specialized application in the intersubjective aspect of concepts-meanings, but the discussing therein does not exhaust the topic. Therefore, it is valuable to specifically survey this topic toward a more complete view.

Wittgenstein and Heidegger share the contention about a tight relationship between meaning and use, with use being a constructor of meaning. Due to the importance of these monumental thinkers of the twentieth

---

"knowledge of [the word] becomes real to men only in virtue of a special unveiling through Jesus' resurrection from the dead." Barth, *Doctrine*, 38.

129. Zimmerman, *Recovering*, 167.

130. Wittgenstein's comments do not reduce language to a deductive instrumentality. Instead, his comment opens the potential of an inductive realization that use and living produces meaning due to the interpenetration of life and understanding with language. Wittgenstein, *Tractatus*, 113.

century, the sentiment of use expressing meaning is evidenced in many subsequent theories. For these theories in which meaning is derivative of use, the potential space for the sense (to use the Ogden-Richards Triangle) is induced from the experience of the referent existing in the world. Knowing about Heidegger's hammer comes from direct experience of the hammer in the world, in relation to other experiences in the shared horizon of the world. Our experience can describe personal-private language, but there is a need to extend beyond the private relationship of the self to the world-self in order to meet the criterion of public observability that is intrinsic to language. A purely private meaning that cannot be shared is inimical to communication as an intersubjective action, and therefore theories where "meaning is in use" will immediately seek answers for the public nature of use. One possible means for this is for *use* to be expanded to an experiential and world-horizon-related set of potentialities no longer bound to the private self.

Thiselton shares a fruitful consideration by Michael Gelven on how Heidegger makes this movement from use as the origin of meaning to potentiality of use as the origin of sharable and public meaning. Thiselton summarizes Gelven's treatment of Heidegger: "Heidegger argues . . . that the purely cognitive functions of understanding are generated from existential awareness of possibilities, and that this awareness itself is based on being able to exist in various ways."[131] These conclusions are a fantastic way of discussing the Dasein that is choosing to interact with the world and share meanings via communicative acts. These are generally unproblematic assertions when this is a means of understanding Dasein based on our shared use of meaning via language. However, the same becomes immediately problematic when AI systems are actively expressing and realizing the same use of concepts as the previously exclusively privileged Dasein.

The problematic conclusions arrive due to the relationship between "being able to exist in various ways" and the "cognitive functions of understanding." Research data on AI suggests that the linguistic skills of AI systems are not bound to the distributional semantic theory but instead are able to express concepts with an observed cognitive function of understanding that mirrors that of the privileged Dasein.[132] Importantly, when this is delivered beyond the limitations of the distributional semantic theory, the data suggests the linguistic-skill application of AI systems goes beyond exploitation of the patterns of human language that otherwise reflect understanding. Words might sound right together and by their metonymy suggest

---

131. Thiselton, *Two Horizons*, 164.
132. Arai and Tsugawa, "Large Language Models."

understanding, but AI systems are reflecting the ability to surpass this historical pattern of association during the projection of a semantic space for a given context.

If the ability to understand (and properly apply) meaning is derivative of existential and experiential expectations of a Dasein, then by linguistic skills demonstrating a cognitive function, authors who do this exist in various ways, hence AI systems that equally demonstrate these skills would be expected to exist in various ways. Shifting latent vector spaces during an activation reflect this linguistic-skill use and are a mathematical encoding representation of various possibilities. The superset of these possible latent spaces represents the "existential awareness" that an AI system/LLM model has through the experience of training. It is the filled presupposition pool. The potential presupposition pool is transformed and permuted virtually infinitely based on prompts and context. The attention weighting and activations allow for a diversity that well exceeds the atoms in the universe. The mathematical and practical illustration that an AI system can produce linguistic feats that by humans would justify the resulting conferral of expected attributes in the author (attributes reserved for the Dasein) and is therefore worth deep consideration given the problematic nature of this extension.

In summary, the pragmatic efficacy and realist truth of the adage that "meaning is in use" are evidenced by AI systems being able to train hierarchical subspaces within a densely packed vector-embedding space that represent the ontic realities experienced by humans. The contention is—based on the data of LLM training—at this point, seemingly uncontroversial and well attested, given a copacetic definition of terms. However, the resulting procedure of understanding the agents of meaning as especially human based on their use of meaning in language is now problematic. Thinkers can no longer approach the meaning and special predicates of humanity in an essentially inductive process arising from the use of meaning in language. This is a quite significant issue for the philosophical derivatives of Heidegger, who define being human within use of meaning and hermeneutics. Either this is the exploit by which AI systems are granted to be human (a nonsensical conclusion) or this null hypothesis obtaining from the data is the strongest evidence yet that academia must consider alternative options for grounding the nature of Dasein and humanity that are still readily distinguishable from the results of AI systems.

Norms

Another attribute of the function-effect of Christian proclamation is the economy of norms that is exercised in usage. Normative or cultural linguistic behavior is a specific class of function-effect that merits additional consideration and is a proper predicate of all concepts-meanings in an utterance. Important for some frameworks is the idea that use of language inherently trades in norms. This is true even when the normative role is not obvious to the intentions of the participants. A nonconceptual example is that in the current use of English language there is a "proper" order for adjectives. Alternative orders feel uncomfortably wrong for a native speaker, without this making a value statement about the types of attributes. In this case, while some languages may allow for emphasis based on ordering in a sentence, a grammatically true English sentence will not be permitted this flexibility. Norms are implicit to language use—for example, at the concept's vertical and horizontal dimensions of coherence.[133]

Norms as applicable to concepts and meanings will be of primary importance, but it is valuable to establish their relevance outside and independent of these arguments that depend on their role. For Hector and Marshall, there is a mutual point of agreement that the use of language by the Christian community expresses, and is the avenue for the potential evolution of, the community's normative concepts. Hector builds on the anti-correspondence approach of Marshall, and thus I will focus on his approach.

Hector describes using a concept as "intend[ing] one's usage as going on in the same was as certain precedents and to claim this same precedent-status for one's own usage."[134] Holding to his understanding would mean predicating this normative and anaphoric conceptual trajectory to the concept use of proclamations. More is to be said about the intersubjective authority of this procedure, which I will return to in the next chapter on the authority of proclamation. Hector invites the question, Purely based on this criterion of concept use, does an AI system qualify as using concepts? If the data suggests this is the case, then there is an indeterminate openness[135]

---

133. As Cotterrell and Turner describe coherence.

134. Hector, *Metaphysics*, 38.

135. From a formal logical perspective, this data cannot alone prove the protasis (intention being expressed by the author) from the entailment of the consequent conditions (using concepts in a manner derived from an assumed author with human intention). Arguing in this direction is not inherently substantiated by formal logic. Thus, I label this more weakly as an *open implicature* to signify that it is now a possible consideration that seems empirically to be worthy of consideration and evaluation.

toward AI having *intention*, which is a predicate many would want reserved for humans.

Hector provides an empirical test for AI systems and content use when he writes, "Behavior counts as such [concept use] when we recognize it as intending to go on in the same way as precedent uses."[136] Hector provides a more concrete proof for recognizing that use is going on in the same way if it is "recognizable as such by those who know how to undertake such performances [namely, to use these concepts]."[137] There is an important but private distinction between going the same way and intending to go the same way. The *intention* would need to have the ultimate exemplar as the object of the concept use, which is quite often not the case for normal use of terms that have their fullest expression in God's understanding of Godself. If the context suggests that this is theological language, then the object of discussion being Godself will suggest to the reader that the object of this language is God, and therefore the intention is precisely the one trajectory that finds expression in Godself. Thus, following the trajectory, based on the context affirming the object of discussion is Godself, will be evidence arguing to the reader that this is intentional use of theological concepts in a God-minded way.

Taken together, Hector's proposal means that a member of the covenant community equipped to use Christian concepts would only need to recognize utterances[138] from an AI system as participating in Christian communicative acts for this to be true. Should the present author, or any other person proficient in Christian concepts,[139] recognize some performances

---

136. Hector, *Metaphysics*, 56.

137. Hector, *Metaphysics*, 68.

138. The authorization for this authentication by the community is connected to the Spirit of Jesus that is present in the judgment of a new concept usage. This is in general a compelling argument that introduces the right divine participants and humbles the human agents. However, it is not without difficulty. For example, Paul writes that certain injunctions to the Corinthians are just his own opinion, and not that of the Lord's. Paul is recognizing that his statements in that specific case are not in fact preauthorized and legitimized by the Spirit of Christ (otherwise he would not call these out as his own and not the Lord's). However, the early Christian community decided that these injunctions should be included in canonical Scripture. As a specific anecdote, this can be treated (for example, judging that given the disclaimer by Paul, it is worthy of the canon). Yet the general concern raised by this case persists: when the Spirit of Christ, the very Spirit of truth is authenticating each and every subsequent proclamation, there is no prominence or hierarchy of truth and it becomes hard to say, for example, that the preaching at our local congregation was of a different quality than the letters of Paul. Equating the two is generally not an acceptable conclusion.

139. This observation exploits and highlights the diffusion of consensus. The diffuse nature of consensus is one of the inherent objections or difficulties of a cultural-linguistic

of AI systems as continuing the concept trajectory, then this observation becomes one anecdotal verdict in favor of an AI system meeting Hector's criterion. Human recognition of the intention in an AI text is another piece of public and observable data that argues for AI expressing intention. The more obvious the public data, the harder it is for arguments based on private data (e.g., the need for consciousness or will) to be given a fair assessment by the reader. A model that insisted on private data would be an idealistic system increasingly disconnected from the descriptive reality that will always be significantly driven by the public and observable. Insisting this is not intention by AI is insisting readers not judge for themselves based on what they can see for themselves.

In addition to the practical-empirical application, it is valuable from a theoretical perspective to investigate how AI systems satisfy Hector's criterion on concept trajectory. The theory will help defend if the continuation of a concept based on precedent use is something that ought to be properly attributed to the capability of these systems, and therefore properly predicated of the concept use by AI systems. Research empirically demonstrates that the LLMs within AI systems "grasp the historical context of concepts and their semantic evolution,"[140] and has provided a theoretical explanation worthy of exploration. The research disproved the distributional semantics explanation by finding that "size alone does not guarantee superior performance"[141] of these models. The results suggest that "accurate temporal semantic understanding" (a communicative act analogous to the definition provided by Hector for concept use) is related to the model "architecture and diversity of training datasets."[142] Importantly, this means the design of how the non-distributional aspect is manifested is more important than more of the same distributional data. Researchers in applied AI are warranted to continue to ask questions about "whether such capabilities extend beyond statistical pattern recognition."[143] Further research will build additional evidence that current or future AI systems are capable of the type of linguistic skill Hector prioritizes as a test for concept use.

Based on this data, AI systems are capable of understanding and representing an understanding of concepts over a time horizon and have been recognized as such by individuals within the convent community of faith.[144]

---

model of normative concepts.
    140. Alrefaie et al., "Dynamics of Meaning."
    141. Alrefaie et al., "Dynamics of Meaning," 9.
    142. Alrefaie et al., "Dynamics of Meaning," 7.
    143. Alrefaie et al., "Dynamics of Meaning," 7.
    144. The value of such anecdotal evidence and the dissemination of these

All of these conclusions are derived from inference, and therefore this conclusion falls short of a properly basic assertion that AI systems are capable of concept use meeting the criterion of Hector, but this is a satisfactory result. The goal of this research is not to elevate AI systems to such an equal status with humans, but instead to illuminate how existing criteria used for reasoning about human communicative acts are insufficient to discriminate against content generated by AI systems.

Bruce Marshall's project in an epistemic system that gives primacy to Trinitarian affirmations is discussed in the beginning of the next chapter on authority but includes two important points to discuss in advance. First, Marshall's thesis for Christian epistemology is avowedly not internalist, foundationalist, or epistemically dependent.[145] Marshall emphasizes the Trinitarian nature of God[146] on the Spirit's role in the intersubjective communication of the community. The question begged by this current research project, to which we now turn, is if either of these distinctives impact the suitability of an AI system to produce proclamation.

An AI system is clearly advantaged regarding Marshall's first distinctive, as the current capabilities are far from having internalist or foundationalist access to data. AI systems are generating metaphors about a world mediated to them through texts. The challenge of disproving epistemic dependence is more nuanced. The epistemic commitments of an AI system would be best expressed as its activations, conceptually relating to the computational neurons that are firing in each response. Researchers study activations in an AI system during inference, and the commitments are such that a given attention matrix and set of activations could be seen to correspond to a mindset or worldview of a human; in practice, there is an ephemeral and contextual projection of the semantic relationships of various semiotic content that directs one's ongoing coherent discussion of a topic. The state of the AI system mathematically implements the "thrown" nature of Heidegger's

---

observations/conclusions within the community would potentially help bring clarity to the ruling on what would be sufficient evidence.

145. Marshall, *Truth*, 50.

146. It is critical to note that Marshall frequently mentions the important role of the Spirit in all epistemology. The observation is a difference in emphasis. Hector describes the intersubjective continuing of a trajectory of a concept by reference to Christ's Spirit. Marshall holds coherence through reference to Col 1:17 (Marshall, *Truth*, 109) but finds it critical to build a truth system that is built *around* the Trinitarian affirmations of the creeds and sacraments. His section on epistemic primacy (Marshall, *Truth*, 121) is an example of the primary he gives these affirmations in his theory. In layman's terms, Hector focuses on the Spirit's role in each transmission, while Marshall locates the role of the Spirit as permeated through every single true proposition.

Dasein, albeit with the ready ability to reset and be thrown anew. This is part of the common practice of modern AI systems.

A more hypothetical scenario would be explicit "alignment training"[147] or other intentional compound AI-system design. These allow for specifying explicit objectives during inference and would be thoroughly committed based on the system design. Given such an implementation, direct experimental data could examine how direct preference optimization could be used to avoid the pitfalls of a dependency theory of epistemology. Conceptually, this direct intervention would be a more concrete mechanism than the more rarefied impact to inference that is set by prompting of the AI system. Although both show promise in the ability to avoid dependence on specific ideas (such as non-Christian beliefs that are counter to Marshall's Trinitarian program), it is inherently difficult to show the evidence of absence of dependence in the layers of activation during inference.[148]

The same techniques that show promise for avoiding dependence can be employed to explicitly produce a response that is inferred based on an epistemic primacy granted to the Trinitarian creedal affirmation and description of God. Therefore, the second distinctive is clearly deliverable based on intentional design and interaction with an AI system. If permitting this intentional design, an AI system would be fully capable of satisfying the expectations in Marshall's theory.

Lindbeck's rule theory describes how our norms form a grammar of faith, and Frei describes this second-order theology as "endeavor[ing] to bring out the rules implicit in first order statements."[149] The exercise of norms needs to be deferred to the approaching discussion of authority, but it is valuable to root the ability for norms to exercise authority in the foundational role of concepts-meanings in exercising this grammar of norms and providing a fertile dataset for observing the practice of these rules. In the chapter on authority, it will be important to nuance the internal practices of a cultural-linguistic adoption of norms and their practice

---

147. Wang et al., "Hybrid Alignment Training."

148. If so inclined, the designer of an AI system could explicitly implement Marshall's proposed epistemic primacy for Christian beliefs. For example, in a multi-agent system, one agent could evaluate the suitability of the response based on explicit commitments, brute-forcing the matter. The more interesting point is that the inference done from that point would show a pragmatic epistemic primacy for Trinitarian affirmations, yet the networks of weights and biases (initial training) would not be dependent on this subject matter. Topics that are entirely disconnected could be inferred, and appropriation will proceed as intended. In layman's terms, the proposal from Marshall can be directly implemented in existing AI systems, such that the proclamations produced would be coherent with a Marshall-described epistemic theory.

149. Frei et al., *Types*, 21.

within a community. For now, the important criterion that norms add to Christian concepts-meanings is mutability (which is similar to Sanneh on translatability, but within an identity-persisting community versus across communities).

An AI system that was incorrigibly trained, without fine-tuning or retraining, would potentially run afoul of the criterion for mutability. However, if we are permitting for a well-designed system—one in which models are constantly being retrained, fine-tuning is prevalent, expert resources are being embedded into the potential vector space, and other techniques like human reinforcement learning are actively evolving the semantic meanings encoded and executed in these AI-system communications—then the requirements Lindbeck has established for doctrines would be satisfiable. An AI system at any point in time will communicate based on a given set of grammatical rules inferred from the training corpus. As long as this training continues (as it does with commercial AI systems), then the requirement for mutability is met.

This obviously does not exhaust all the important topics about norms in general, particularly those related to membership in the interpretive community. Those topics are critical and will be addressed in the chapter on authority.

Summary on Illocution

Concepts and meanings do not only refer (ostensively) to reality or commerce in epistemic and truth conditions, but they also have a place within spatiotemporal history. Communicative acts take space and time. They are present and this reminds the community of faith of the imminence of the incarnate Word of God. This presence relates first to the creation of intersubjective interactions, which are the communicative act itself. Second, Alston demonstrated that words can themselves produce effects in the world, and Wittgenstein that meanings are deeply related to the use of language. Third, from the cultural-linguistic postliberal perspective, exercise of concepts-meanings is simultaneously the exercise of norms within an interpretive community. These norms are themselves described as a sort of grammar or rules that guide the sequenced communication of understanding in an intersubjective manner. Together, all of these uses of language presented important criteria to demand of AI systems, and, in each, there was research and theory to substantiate the ability of AI systems.

SUMMARY: IMPLICATIONS OF CONCEPTS-MEANINGS IN PROCLAMATIONS

Christian proclamation has the unique challenge of dealing in concepts and meanings that describe God while respecting the distinction between Creator and created. The working definition for Christian proclamation grounds these concepts in the faith of the Christ, which by necessity is Christocentric faith. Christ is the God-Man, the nexus of the distinction and similarity between God and humanity, and the perfection of humanity in reconciliation with the divine will. His faith is a communicative act made public through the actions of his own incarnation, death, and resurrection. His example of living faith and living truth figures importantly in how imperfect concepts and meanings can be appropriately used in describing God.

Use of concepts-meanings involves various levels of semiotic realism, which are all variously expected and observed in the canonical Scriptures and the examples of proclamation by the saints. The most abstract and most concrete (metaphor and picking out) of these are well aligned to AI-system behavior, with communicative acts done by AI systems potentially always being properly classified as metaphor. Some views of analogy raise ontological issues regarding the personal commitments and experiences needed to use analogies of God that are proper to God describing Godself. Some of these requirements can be satisfied by considering the sufficiently narrow time horizon of the AI system in which it has made assertions—namely, those in which it is still preserving context and an attention matrix/layer activation that affects a commitment. Outside of this window and context, the AI system ceases to maintain ad-hoc commitments,[150] and this is directly related to its ability to compartmentalize individually coherent communicative acts that in aggregate are entirely incoherent and contradictory. Satisfying the criterion of analogy is far less realistic or outright impossible for an AI system if analogy use is grounding in the experience and participation in "justification by grace received in faith."[151] Of this an AI system only knows through the mediation of others. Using Bultmann's example, mediated knowledge can lead an AI system to know all about friendship yet not have the experience of a friend.

Epistemic content of concepts-meanings considers that the meaning of a discourse unit is related to its truth conditions, thus tightly relating the two. The investigation of epistemic conditions exposes potential exploits in various linguistically founded models. These loopholes revolve around the

---

150. A purpose-built system designed to always have Christian commitments would do so by default.

151. Hector, *Metaphysics*, 141.

habits and practices of communication by native language users. In normal affairs natural language is taken to be primarily true, and this is widely considered to be a prerequisite for taking anything as false.[152] One of the related ways the charity principle of radical interpretation/radical translation manifests is the assumption that language will be coherent. Readers will attempt to resolve seeming incoherence to the degree possible, provisionally granting certain assumptions about the author's intention and competency. Coherence is expected by the reader and, when observed, it validates a presumption that the author is a human. In many cases, this presumption of a human author includes other presumed characteristics. The moral obligation to respect an author (as intending to say something they think is true) becomes dangerous when the conditions for this moral obligation can be met by nonhuman authors.

Last, concepts-meanings are considered for their use and effect, covering the use of concepts-meanings for intersubjective communication, meaning as explicit use, and concepts-meanings as exercise of a grammar of norms. When agents use language to do something there is inherently an exercise of power. Therefore, the review of illocutionary force in proclamation immediately motivates the subsequent consideration of authority as a top-level expectation of proclamation.

As a final aside on concepts-meanings, the raging debates that briefly survived that range over the proper way to address the epistemic conditions of Christianity are rejected by some theologians as missing the critical piece of Christianity. Frei argues that Christianity "is not a network of beliefs, it is not a system, first of all. It may be an intellectual system also, but not in the first place. Further, it is not first of all an experienced something, an experienced shape, an essence. Rather, it is first of all a complex, various, loosely held, and yet really discernible community with varying features."[153] In other examples of the cultural-linguistic variety, there is posited a process of norms directing Christianity as principally a system/intellectual system. If the prioritized criteria of Christianity are relocated from concepts onto an ontic community, then the locus of proclamation depends on proximity to this community, not the economy of Christian propositions and persuasion. This is important to recall in the concluding thoughts about aspects external to texts and the concepts-meanings of Christianity that could authenticate and authorize what is Christian in a manner more discernibly human than AI. Commitments about the access to concepts-meanings of proclamation

---

152. Plantinga considered the possibility that someone could take everything to be false, but admitted that this is a very difficult system to work out in practice.

153. Frei et al., *Types*, 12.

will impact what it means to evangelize, and furthermore to disciple those introduced to the faith.

7

AUTHORITY IN AND DERIVED FROM A TEXT

THE PRECEDING CHAPTER ARGUED that the complex ways humans use concepts and meanings are similarly satisfied by AI-generated texts. Language has varied degrees of empirical or literal relationship to reality: AI is capable of presenting text in a manner that uses the appropriate relationship based on the context and intention of the text. AI texts will also manage the epistemic expectations of a text, providing a propositionally meaningful text. The AI-generated text will also be able to deliver an illocutionary effect that reflects the intention of the text to further or produce a given use of language. These functional applications of language have all been effectively implemented in AI systems.

The evidence thus far supports strong claims about the authority of the text for an inferentialist or pragmatic view of language. Robert Brandom describes the pragmatic view as a sort of "scorekeeping," where the reader is judging the commitments that have been made by the author. His proposal for "social-practical scorekeeping" is described as such:

> To understand an assertional speech act is to know how to keep score on the commitments the speaker has undertaken by performing that act. In undertaking commitment to p, the assertor has obliged herself to acknowledge other commitments: those that follow from it. She has also authorized other interlocutors to attribute that commitment to her. Further, she has obliged herself to offer a justification (give reasons) for the claim, if her authority is suitably challenged. The idea is that exercising

such inferentially articulated authority and fulfilling such inferentially articulated responsibility is what one must do (the task responsibilities one must carry out) in order to count as responsible for or committed—not now to do something, but to what in this social-practical scorekeeping context shows up as the propositional content.[1]

Fulfilling the *semantic* commitments and responsibilities associated with a claim is, according to the pragmatic school, the differentiation between the sentient parrot squawking "red" and the sapient human making a network of claims about an object based on *describing* it as red.[2] The model discerns a parrot, but not an AI system. Recall that the attention mechanism is designed to implement exactly the commitments described by Bransom. Attention mechanisms provide a chain of reasoning or chain of thought that justifies conclusions. Further, each word generated influences the active semantic space, mathematically committing the AI to the related inferences. A human would be challenged to express at every moment the commitments made each stated premise (when uttering), or to explain the permissive or inductive inferences they are making while listening along to another participant making claims. An AI does the same behaviors and keeps meticulous track of the process.

The inferentialist and pragmatic models of authority also make claims about the participants of these language games. Quoting Bransom again:

> To be rational is to engage in practices of giving and asking for reasons, that is, making inferentially articulated assertions and justifying them. To do that one must attribute and acknowledge commitments and entitlements, and practically keep track of their inferential relations along all three dimensions those two deontic statuses generate: permissive, committive, and incompatibility entailments.[3]

If the proper tracking of these commitments is sapiential rationality or logic, then the AI system is expected to surpass the human just as the calculator bests human arithmetic. Matrix multiplication allows for a more precise adherence to these commitments, without losing track of what has been committed. Incompatibility is contextual but also spans the entirety of the semantic space that is possible. The permissive use of inference can be calculated and expressed quantitatively. If we accept pragmatic models

---

1. Brandom et al., "Intentionality," 14.
2. This example is taken from Brandom et al., "Intentionality," 10.
3. Brandom et al., "Intentionality," 17.

where rationality is associated with logical use of language and commitment to meaning, we will find that AI systems play our language game better than we can.

Pragmatic and inferentialist models invite a host of topics that will need to be mentioned but not fully explored given the limited focus of this research. In the context of Christian proclamation, is it proper to accept the monotonicity of Marshall (who is building on a monotonic Tarski foundation), or is it possible that adding a new claim will entirely break the model of other claims? This author would argue that the faith of Christ cannot be added to an existing and complete truth system in a monotonic manner. Further, there is the question of how truth or evidence is diffusive. It may be best to model faith in Christ as a diffusive commitment that builds over time and experience. In layman's terms, this is the logical equivalent of arguing for a meaningful commitment of a life to Christ instead of praying and forgetting the so-called "sinner's prayer." The divinity of Christ—the God-Man who was born, died, and rose again to resurrected life—will present new implications that are only fully experienced as life proceeds. Even the disciples did not understand at the resurrection or at Pentecost what their faith commitments would entail. Peter was not yet eating bacon for Pentecost breakfast.

These logical topics would take another robust treatise or a series of articles to exhaust. For now, they have been mentioned before returning to the most pressing matter of this research. How does an AI-generated text interact with an audience by making an authoritative claim? The implication of this research is that AI-generated texts will attempt to have an impact on the reader that includes the conveyance of propositional truths and the presentation of these propositions in a convincing manner that furthers a desired impact on the reader. The last chapter considered how the degree to which this intention is successful will depend on the linguistic skill of the text. In this chapter, the consideration will be on how a given text will attempt to and successfully exert authority over an individual and the normative language/practices of a community. The question will again begin with how natural language users (humans) achieve this authority and then consider how AI systems can produce texts that meet the expectations laid out for human authors and the authority of their texts. The part of the working thesis that describes the authority of the Christian proclamation is in italics below:

> Proclamation is an utterance conveying concepts-meanings *that, if taken true, would be consistent in a belief system that is also consistent with the faith of Jesus Christ.*[4]

1. What attributes are expected because Christian proclamation makes an authoritative claim to truth and revelation?
2. How do these attributes show up in Paul's Letter to the Romans?
3. What criteria in the hermeneutic and ethical models describe these attributes?
4. How does AI text perform on the criteria:
    a. Tactically using knowledge to make a claim
    b. Satisfying the requirements of its type of message
    c. Justifying its claims to external standards

The authority of a communicative act measures the perlocutionary force and can be provisionally defined as describing the attempted and potentially successful impact the knowledge and truth commitments of the reading community effected by the concepts-meanings of an utterance being received and understood. The power dynamic present in considerations of authority makes this topic critical for evangelistic and general sociological relevance. How does the reader process the new content presented in the textual utterance? The interesting case is when text is processed by an already "minded" self, someone who has the ability to process and understand language as a native speaker but may not have the personal significance attached to certain concepts-meanings that are experientially dependent on receiving faith from God and the according transformative experience of appropriated salvation. In this case, the question is what the text provides to

---

4. My description of the taking true of the Christian proclamation focuses on a nonbeliever's entrance into a truth system that is coherent with the faith of the Christ expressed in his incarnation, death, and resurrection. This is not the only way of modeling or understanding the response to proclamation. For example, Fuchs describes a movement in the opposite direction, focusing on what enters into the established and preexisting world of the hearer. The New Critics tended to focus on how a text interprets us and the subjective dimension of experience of a text, which tends to place greater emphasis in the reverse direction. In simple terms, the question is an emphasis on what we receive versus what we are transformed into. Despite the difference in emphasis, the same principal components will be present in both theories; proclamation is still an utterance, conveying a world through concepts-meanings, and projecting this with an authoritative claim that is processed accordingly by the reading subject. Thiselton, *Two Horizons*, 191.

a reader that presents an authority that will need to be reasoned about and responded to by the reader.

Augustine enumerates three potential epistemic positions in *The Teacher*, which serve as a good starting place for reasoning about the authority of a proposition. The language we receive is either taken as true because we know it already, taken as false because we don't know it already (or know it to be false), or taken as an opinion due to the lack of immediate reasoning about the truth or falsity.[5] Even if we reject the implicit bivalence (and platonic encroachment) in this enumeration, Augustine has provided a preliminary sketch of the dynamics at play. A recipient of a text will evaluate the truth of the content and will determine how to respond accordingly.[6]

The concepts-meanings present in a text will stand under judgment by their authority, by which I am including all the power dynamics between the utterance and the reader in the experience of reading. There may be personally appropriated responsibilities based on understanding the intended function of an utterance (how the reader responds to understanding the intended response conveyed by the author in the text). This trades in and begs the externalization of the effect of the proclamation. Similarly, there may be disquoted personal significance for the reader (how the reader appropriates significance as a dialectic participant of the reader's truth system and the collective truth system/norms of the communities to which the reader belongs). This describes the internalized true-claim effect of proclamation.

The authority of a proclamation is described by many competing domains, as many academic departments claim to best model the power dynamics in communicative actions. The primary domain I will prioritize due to the explicit relevance to Christian proclamation is the domain of ethics, taking ethics in a broad sense. In this usage, ethics is meant to include descriptions of the power dynamics of the audience being presented with a new proposition in the form of uttered concepts, which must be reasoned about as justified or not, and accordingly processed in the audience's truth system.

This is a practical exercise of deciding about truth claims in all of the intersubjective, personal-private, and temporal-public contexts. When discussing what is individually valuable/worthwhile, and how this should govern interpersonal conduct, we are discussing the domain of ethics. Accordingly, it seems proper to describe these as ethical claims and therefore it is important to reason about relevant ethical frameworks and what each

---

5. Augustine, *Teacher* 10.34.155.

6. This response may mean direct action, cognitive change, or an intermediary change by which one proceeds toward a material change (as in the case of gathering sufficient data before accepting that an utterance exhibits some degree of truth).

predicate of Christian sources or proclamation. These frameworks tend to be applied and practical, and therefore it will be imminently practical to discuss the viability of an AI system generating content that meets the expectations and standards set forth in these ethical frameworks. These following examples are not meant to be extensive in covering the broad range of ethical discussions. Instead, specific priority has been given to select thinkers who are focusing on a model that is both explicitly Christian and tends to be derived from the uttered concepts of the sacred Christian texts (both those explicitly and implicitly present).

THE ROMANS EXAMPLE

The difficulty posed to Paul in effectively communicating using previously known concepts while trying to shift or "remind" the Romans of their faith is an exemplar of the confluence of concepts-meanings and the authority of a text. The historically evidenced facticity of Paul's ability to impact the lived expression of their faith, while ostensibly not providing them with novel terms, and only "reminding" them of propositions with which they were already familiar, addresses many of the considerations of authority in a proclamation.

It is worth noting at the outset that the contingent dynamics of an authoritative accidental reading are so contextually driven that a single example being the exemplar of every attribute seems overburdened and is not the goal. Romans was written to believers. First and foremost, it was not intended to be read to those without faith concepts and experience, who were participating in a living community of instruction and communion. The dynamics of the authority of a text to a different context will draw out other considerations. In fact, it is reasonable to imagine the common interaction with an AI system will exhibit the opposite poles of the same dimensions: a nonbeliever in solitude specifically soliciting new concepts to be provided about faith. This is in contrast to the Romans example of an unprompted letter to an existing community of faith, and yet much can be learned of what, regardless, is expected of such an utterance.

The Romans example of authority in a text suggests the primary contributions that will be discussed at length: epistemic value and justification. Demonstrating a knowledge of the faith is expected as an effort in ethos building that Paul does in the introduction of the letter. Rhetoric would expect him to be establishing that he knows what it means to preach the word to both Jewish and Hellenized communities, and therefore his use of concepts has a proper epistemic grounding. His propositions are couched in truth-conditions that are non-objectionable, even if shocking.[7] Given the status of his audience, it seems reasonable that Paul could remind them of what was already known from the earliest days of the community of faith. If the Roman community of faith was in fact formed by the Pentecost visitors from Rome, then Paul's discussion of the faith of Christ being accessible and addressable to all without prejudice, credited to us each, would certainly be a reminder of their own experience meeting the gospel. His concept use is therefore coherent with their prior formative experience, which advances his efforts for an authorized reframing of certain misconceptions.

Paul's justification for his meaning use is rooted in the same experience as the audience. His refined use begs the question how he could be more authorized in his use of the concepts than the Romans. If we accept his stated objective, then Paul's norm usage is in direct conflict with their norm usage. He speaks with the same grammar of faith, but in propositionally conflicting ways. His use of technical religious terminology likely disagrees with that of the Romans. His resulting injunctions are more obviously in conflict, for he corrects some of their practices manifesting and directed by the same normative faith. Is there something that internally to the discourse gives justification and authority to his correctives, or is this external?

Attempting to divine authorial intent based on patterns of behavior in writing is problematic, but the patterns themselves are data illustrating possibilities. His strings of Old Testament quotations (e.g., Rom 3:11–18; 9:25–29; 10:18–20; 11:7–10; and 15:9–12) and interpretations of individual quotations invoke an external authority beyond the utterance itself. In the Augustinian model of words being ostensive and external to the experiential self of the audience, his recourse is to an internal deep consideration that is guided by the indwelling Logos. Accordingly, the authority is not in the text or the author, but in the relationship of the reader to God as prompted by the text. Given the rhetorical flourish of this letter stressing the visibility and openness of what Paul is presenting (open to the entire world), this may be argued, but for the purposes of this research it suffices to note that in the extremely difficult case of authority in the Letter to the Romans, Paul employs public and authorized fixtures that could contribute to the justification of his discourse. An AI system would need commensurate capabilities, which is quite readily provided given the mediated nature of the semantic embeddings used by an AI system. An AI system is inherently trained on public and authorized fixtures of meaning, and the authentication of an AI-system response is often couched in references to these external sources.

---

7. It is reasonable that many Jewish Christians would be jarred by the directness of "Νυνὶ δὲ χωρὶς νόμου δικαιοσύνη θεοῦ πεφανέρωται" (Rom 3:21 SBLGNT), even if this is a logical conclusion from other known affirmations about the Christ.

A thoroughgoing analysis of the exhibited techniques of authority in Romans is not the objective for this research and may best be left for rhetoricians. However, it is worth enumerating some attributes of authority observed. Paul validates his epistemic access to the concepts by presenting a parallel set of experiences. His statements of the gospel are true because he has been appointed this purpose, but also because the exercise of his role as the apostle to the gentiles has meant bringing many who were far off from God into the community of faith. He establishes a shared supposition pool and then is able to influence the way these mutually shared propositions of faith are subsequently expressed as faith acts by the Romans. Examining how both epistemic value and justification dynamically relate to authority in a text will therefore illuminate much of the authority observed in Paul's Letter to the Romans and, importantly for the present endeavor, will present criteria by which to test the sufficiency of AI systems to generate proclamation with the authority of human witnesses to the faith of the Christ.

FRAMEWORKS FOR AUTHORITY

The implications and commitments of the covenant community that is united in Christ have not been static over the years. Many of the frameworks introduced below intentionally address this mutability. Throughout the years, the community has sought to express a faith that is consistent with that of the Christ, approaching judgments in a way that was desired to reflect the living judgment of the Christ. The dynamic nature of the expression of faith allows for consistency in the focus on the Christ, with adaptation of the commitments this meant when applied to topics like slavery or war.

Two questions loom in this suggestion. First, can AI participate in a similar type of commitment to core beliefs ultimately originating and perfected in God with novelty in application to context? Second, because adaptation is driven by the interpretive community, what will come of the community being increasingly exposed to novelty that was inspired by AI systems versus human participants (or where the nature of the author is indeterminate)? Even if AI-authored texts never influence the community's beliefs, the existence of meaningful AI-generated texts may motivate increasing doubt and suspicion of anything novel to the reader. To consider these questions, we turn to several authors who have discussed the ways the Christian faith stays committed and versatile across time.

George Lindbeck

Lindbeck's *The Nature of Doctrine* argues in defense[8] of a rule theory that implements a postliberal approach to the regulative practice of doctrine. His proposal attempts to resolve various ecumenically divisive topics by appealing to a grammar of norming performed by the cultural-linguistic community of faith. The process of coming to faith is "like that of learning a language"[9] by which becoming a member of the community of faith means coming to understand and to practice the rules of the community.[10]

His concept of faith and doctrine arises from the community preserving core ontological truths (rules) and applying these in various manners (norms). The idea of a community's practiced norms dictating the acceptance and proper understanding of theological concepts is a conceptual forerunner of arguments by Hector and Marshall.[11] His "Response to Bruce Marshall" summarizes his position toward correspondence theories of truth quite well: "Our beliefs may correspond to reality, but we are justified in holding that they do so, not by directly seeing the correspondence, but by some other means. That those other means might in part or whole be coherentist or pragmatist cannot be excluded a priori."[12] Lindbeck's observational pragmatism is reflective of the defined mutability of doctrines to truth that runs through his rule theory.

Lindbeck's cultural-linguistic rule theory nuances the relationships between the ontologically true and the accidentally true in a specific moment for the community of faith.[13] The result is a dichotomy between uncondi-

---

8. Lindbeck argues that this position in defense of a cultural-linguistic view of the rules of faith being taught and reformed over time "can only be presented, not proved." Lindbeck, *Nature*, 134.

9. Lindbeck, *Nature*, 132.

10. These rules are ostensive toward the rules provided by the ultimate concern of the community: the Christ.

11. Hector, Marshall, and Lindbeck are in such close proximity in thoughts that there are various comments and revisions prompted by the others. For example, on page 238 of *Theology without Metaphysics*, Hector argues against Lindbeck's *Nature of Doctrine* to say that "although the truth of a statement does not depend on its role in a particular form of life, one's ability to recognize it as such ultimately may." In the footnote clarifying this point, he distances himself from Lindbeck's *Nature of Doctrine*, but aligns himself with Lindbeck's "Response to Bruce Marshall," in which Lindbeck warmly approved of much of the Thomistic detail suggested by Marshall. The important note is that their views are all in close proximity and commerce in very related constructs.

12. Lindbeck, "Response," 404.

13. Lindbeck applies the terms "accidental, conditional, irreformable, irreversible, official, operational, permanent, practical, reversible, temporary, and unconditional"

tional and essential truths versus the conditional norms that are regulative in the context of a specific moment (and the contextuality of an utterance) based on the doctrinal necessity of the referents. In this application, propositional statements[14] are of the former (ontologically true), while the regulative function played by normative and contingent practical doctrine is of the latter category. His frequent example of this is the position of Christian communities toward slave ownership decisively changing over centuries.

The resulting two-tiered system allows the latter (norms) to be reversible and accidental. Lindbeck applies and tests his model by considering various controversial doctrines, opening the potential for ecumenical reconciliation on the basis of his theory. His contention is that multiple conflicting doctrines can be correct unless there is an "ontological reference."[15] Furthermore, a return to these core rules is important to avoid further fragmentation. "Doctrine is to be followed, not interpreted"[16] because it is related to the contextual application within the contingencies of the community of faith. When doctrine (norms) is reasoned from like the irreversible rules of the community, then the resulting behaviors will be unduly conflicted and the eventual logical extensions in new contexts are liable to be faulty due to a failure of contextualization and translation.[17] The great benefit of this pragmatic approach is "apologetic intelligibility,"[18] which similarly distinguishes between the teaching/proclamation of rules versus potentially reversible practices (norms). If accepting Lindbeck's framing, then an AI system is excused from not getting into the practical practices of norms, intrinsically limiting the range of cases in which to evaluate and disqualify its behavior.

---

to describe the truth predicates of doctrine. Lindbeck, *Nature*, 140. These classifications largely apply along these two classes: those aspects of Christian utterance that are mutable and those that are not. Each nuanced term adds a marginal description of how these are or are not open to change.

14. Lindbeck refines the classification of his own cultural-linguistic approach as "coherentist" and "pragmatic." Lindbeck, "Response," 405. "The necessary and sufficient publicly accessible criteria for what is true in the realm of faith are entirely what we would now call coherentist and pragmatic." His proposal is for a positive theology that asserts that the behavior of the agent(s) within the "reading" community form the grammar of faith. Actual behavior therefore becomes part of the truth claim needed for proclamation authentication. This demand for lived faith is an important facet in considering the limits to the authority that can be realized by an AI system, at least without human culpability/involvement in spooky proclamation at a distance.

15. Lindbeck, *Nature*, 107.
16. Lindbeck, *Nature*, 107.
17. Lindbeck, *Nature*, 130.
18. Lindbeck, *Nature*, 130.

Lindbeck's proposal is doubly valuable to this project. First, he provides a way to reason about faith in patterns that reflect linguistics. Second, he defends the inductive means by which the rules are observed and then reciprocally lived based on understanding. This raises an important question about the content that informs an AI system during the training process about Christian concepts. If trained largely on the applied doctrines of the Christian community, we should beware that the resulting proclamations will realize the same expected faults as humans reasoning from applied doctrines instead of ontological truths.[19] The former observation suggests that an AI system could certainly be designed such that it would avoid this incorrect semantic space. However, this raises grave concerns for the real experience of uncommitted individuals interacting with commercial systems not designed for this consideration.

The community of faith has an obligation to consider and address the impact of nonbelievers intending to use commercial AI systems to provide them with Christian proclamation. These public AI systems have not been designed with Lindbeck's nuance of doctrines in mind; they are trained without his prioritization of the right types of rules versus contextual norms. Accordingly, we should proactively and concerningly expect that the wrong emphasis can be present in the inferred grammar. Given this concern, the community of faith has an obligation to serve these individuals accordingly such that they may better appreciate the distance of various statements about God (theology, doctrine) to the nonnegotiable rules and propositions (in Lindbeck's Aristotelian sense) for following the Christ and having a faith that is coherent with his own.

A key term introduced by Lindbeck is *rule theory*. Rule theory advocates for seeing the communication and behavior of a normative community as a form of grammar that provides a tension between rules and flexibility. These doctrinal rules mirror those of language by providing rules that can assess propriety but allow for more than rote repetition of prior propositions.

Bruce Marshall

Bruce Marshall's *Trinity and Truth* is discussed extensively throughout this research. His proposal is for a Trinitarian confession to have epistemic primacy in our truth systems, such that all other true statements are "held

---

19. Note that this induction of rules from first-order versus the second-order application is precisely how Frei also frames the different types of Christian theology.

together" in Christ (leaning on his reading of Col 1:17). His treatment is valuable for at least two major contributions.

First, it is fruitful to consider his discussion of alternative epistemic systems that he rejects: interiority, foundationalism, and epistemic dependence.[20] Each of these proposes a potential authority schema, and while he rejects each in turn, for the current more general and ambivalent research proposal, it is suitable to consider how each addresses AI systems and their proclamation. It is interesting that interiority and foundationalism are difficult to fully model in AI-system behavior. Schleiermacher is the exemplar of interiority for Marshall, connecting epistemic religious truth to variously "religious affections," "inner state of feeling," "self-consciousness," and "feeling."[21] None of these are easily implemented in an AI system, for Schleiermacher imperatively states that "propositions of faith of all forms have their ultimate basis so exclusively in the stirrings of the religious self-consciousness that where the latter do not exist, the former cannot come into being."[22] For foundationalism, an AI system cannot meet the first criterion of direct access to some data that forms the foundational truths. An AI system could capriciously commit to some specific kernel of truth. This commitment has a mathematical implication on the proximity of different words and meanings for the ensuing conversation. The history means the conversation would build on this initially capricious kernel of truth. That pinning commitment is privileged in the ensuing functional use of language, despite the system lacking all direct unmediated access to this knowledge. Said differently, an AI system starts being no more committed to specific possible commitments, and its relative weighting of commitments is not dependent on direct sensory access to the evidence in support of a claim (whereas most humans would give priority to claims they have personally witnessed). The important conclusion is about the functional behavior based on such a commitment regardless of the *proper warrant* for this commitment by the AI system based on direct sensory data.

Second, his treatment of Tarski and Davidson is used to inductively produce an epistemic system from the foundations of functional grammar and logic. It is not pertinent to make either an apology or attack on his position regarding T-sentences. Regardless, it is valuable to reason about how one pillar of authority (epistemic content) could be rooted in the intrinsic nature of language itself, and furthermore how this can be argued to then have epistemic primacy for all other assimilated truths. If his theory

---

20. Marshall, *Truth*, 50, introduces these three epistemic foils.
21. Marshall, *Truth*, 52–53.
22. Quoted in Marshall, *Truth*, 52.

holds, then the very existence of the risen Christ makes it such that language can carry epistemic truth independently of the agent of communication.[23] Therefore, based on an ontic and ontological truth that is in Christ, an AI system would be equally sufficient of expressing a true belief, and therefore expressing a Christian proclamation that meets the epistemic criterion (and potentially, though less readily evident, meets the criterion of justification).

A key idea raised by Marshall is the idea of people holding a truth claim that has epistemic primacy (and that being a Trinitarian affirmation for Christians). Epistemic primacy is used by Marshall to describe how, in the case of a conflict between two truth claims, one of the claims will be taken as true. Epistemic primacy is the relative priority given to claims based on these conflicts for the individual or community. The higher the epistemic primacy, the greater the range of truth claims that will be subordinated to the most primary claim and will need to be appropriated to the most primary claim.

Kevin Vanhoozer

Kevin Vanhoozer's *Is There a Meaning in This Text?* provides one of the best examples of a thoroughgoing and well-reasoned thesis about the morality of literary knowledge that, unfortunately, produces potentially problematic extensions in the age of AI systems as communicative agents. Vanhoozer approves of Augustine's elevation of the charity principle in hermeneutics, which was discussed in the chapter on concepts-meanings as a problematic foundation. Vanhoozer therefore encourages the reader to "not violate but venerate this 'other'"[24] who is communicating through a text.

The susceptibility of Vanhoozer's model to be exploited[25] is correlated to how much he focuses on the Scriptures as a special class of text that gets unique treatment. Where Scripture deserves its own exclusive hermeneutics, he can avoid generalizing a respect for the text and author in cases of AI generation. The alternative temptation is how often he instead sides with his Augustinian inspiration, whom Vanhoozer approvingly quotes as saying, "It is most honorable to believe that an author was a good man, whose writings

---

23. "Our argument does not, therefore, run afoul of the traditional thought that even the demons can have true belief that Jesus is risen. On the contrary, that they have this true belief simply suggests the generosity of God." Marshall, *Truth*, 251.

24. Vanhoozer, *Meaning*, 32.

25. Specifically exploiting where his arguments assume exclusively human things about authors based on the resulting linguistic skills, which are now frequently satisfied by AI authors.

were intended to benefit the human race and posterity."[26] If a two-tiered (or multi-tiered) system of hermeneutics based on the text is eschewed in favor of a universal grand theory, even if the motivation of this was to support the validity and authority of a biblical hermeneutic, then the damage is done. The logical extensions for AI systems performing linguistic skills becomes a problematic scenario.

Vanhoozer's analysis is extremely well researched, and his rich citations evidence the significant range and diversity of theories and thinkers who are complicit or open toward predicating certain human attributes of an author. The motivations for these are varied, from sheer necessity of observable public knowledge (linguistics) to the moral obligations that arise from communion with the author through their intended communicative action.

Based on this model of meaning, the authority of a text is not dependent on the ontological situation of the author, but the text itself. If we hold that "the text stands between author and reader as an embodied intention . . . enabling the reader to respond to the same matter in an appropriate fashion,"[27] then the authority of the author and the intention of the author can be inferred from the "enabling" of a response. Now that the same linguistic skills for expressing coherent ideas in the possible semantic space can be met by an AI system, both human and AI authors are experienced in the same mediator, and this mediator is the expression and realization of the authority of the text.[28]

In this model, there isn't an ontological standard or criterion that must be met, more a moral obligation of the reader to take seriously the text. A world is projected and illocutionary force is conducted through the medium of the text. The response is the moral obligation of the reader, which presumes an authorized call by means of receiving the communicative action of the text. Furthermore, when that illocutionary action is explication of the faith of Christ, this invitation to take true suggests intentionality based on the embodied text. The very reality of a human coming to faith in the Christ based on what begins as an AI system's explanation/proclamation of Christian truth would, by this model, predicate an *intention* by the AI system to bring to faith. Either this conclusion is accepted despite seeming problematic, or revisions to the ontic and ontological nature of the authority

---

26. Vanhoozer, *Meaning*, 33. Vanhoozer goes on to summarize approvingly Augustine's hermeneutic as one that "encourages readers to approach texts . . . in the expectation that they contain something valuable and true."

27. Vanhoozer, *Meaning*, 282.

28. That the reader may be expected to charitably grant authority of at least a provisional nature.

of a text must be amended to Vanhoozer and his multitude of approvingly referenced thinkers.

A key idea of Vanhoozer is the morality of the reading experience. His prioritization of the communion facilitated by reading between the reader and the author is a consequence and justification for his views on the morality of the literary event. His model will be problematic when extended for AI systems, due to the preponderance of things predicated on the author of a text in order to explicate and defend the hermeneutic approach of respect and morality advocated by Vanhoozer.

ATTRIBUTES OF AUTHORITY

Meaningful utterances, once understood, present a possible world for the reader.[29] When reading, we ask how meaningful concepts are being used, will be used, or are potential in our own world. Where worlds collide in the reading of a text, there is a power conflict involving some authority invested in or composed from the experience of the text. Where a text presents a similar world (such as the original reading of Romans), there is potentially even more pressing conflict produced by shared concepts being used in the shared world. This realized and expressed authority is true even if we accept that a text, to itself, may not have an intrinsic authority.[30]

That AI systems can satisfy the most basic criterion of training on and then using truth conditions has been discussed in the two prior chapters. In the same degree and quantity, LLMs generate coherent content, presenting content that obtains satisfying truth conditions. In compound AI systems, this can be further enforced by agentic patterns to judge the coherence of a text before providing a final generated response. These attributes of concepts-meanings and utterances will provide the foundational support for the competitive authority experienced in a text. Authority, this final critical factor of comparison, is where a Christian proclamation ceases to be repetition of dogma and becomes a pragmatic use with the intention of evangelization.

---

29. The debate over the nature and origin of this world would require resolving the debates of hermeneutics, which is far beyond the scope of this project. For this project, it will suffice to consider a range of potential options, ranging from the world intended by the author to the world constructed by interaction with the text.

30. Dialectical theologians make a strong argument about the authority and potential meaning of a text not being located within the text itself, arguing this in the extreme for Scripture. Barth, *Doctrine*, 126, opines that the Bible "claims no authority for itself," yet by being experienced in linguistic activities, God chooses to make his authority known to humanity.

It would be impossible to claim full impartiality, or to have applied a fully comprehensive scope, in the discussion of the authority of a proclamation. The objective of this survey and analysis is not to propose an alternative model of authority expressed in relation to a textual Christian proclamation, but to consider various vantage points to then apply against AI systems. It is therefore helpful to consider a wide range of scenarios, not just those of Christian proclamation. For example, Blackham (discussing Heidegger) explores this authority in the realm of science. His analysis is important in raising questions relevant to the current primary question (How do meaningful utterances confront the reader with an unrealized potential, based on epistemic value and justification of the discourse?) that will then drive the criteria used for considering the ability of AI systems to generate text with such expressed authority. Blackham states,

> Science is not privileged but specialized, not the interpretation of the world, but a selected aspect; not an experience in use of the concrete object handled in the perspective of man's projects, but a breakdown into abstractions taken out of the system of concrete relations and assimilated to another system of meanings determined by special questions raised within the perspective of the project of Nature.[31]

Christian proclamation is interested in reasoning about how a text impacts the reader with a presented potential world of meanings. Two primary classes of authority will outline this discussion: the epistemic value and the justification value of an utterance. The epistemic value describes the claim(s) made with regard to knowing, involving but perhaps not exhausted[32] by the epistemic details of the individual concepts-meanings. There are unresolved disagreements about what, if anything, language can bear in terms of epistemic value, the process by which reading/understanding a text relates to epistemic value, and the source of such epistemic value. Similarly, there is disagreement about the potential justification of an utterance. In this survey, justification value will include which of the participants in the communicative act are the basis of taking true the present epistemic claims. Epistemic value, in this sense, relates to the claim presented to the reader, and the justification value to the preponderance (or lack) of substantiation for this claim. This could also be seen as the authority and the authentication of such authoritative communication. These two dimensions

---

31. Quoted in Thiselton, *Two Horizons*, 158.

32. A highly atomistic and correspondence-based view of interpretation would argue that the right interpretation (and therefore obligation/projection of authority by the text) is identical to the meaning of the text itself.

beg questions to be addressed herein. What does the utterance attempt to convey about the true relationships between what is known? What units of the utterance are taken as true by the various participants, how does this potentially vary across the different possible units of language in the utterance, and how does this resolve across the active participants (namely, the author, the reader, the community(ies) of interpretation, and God).

These questions motivate and beg further analysis, which deserves a thorough consideration to build a robust ethical hermeneutic that can reason effectively about AI-system-authored utterances. The primary focus of this project will be satisfied before that point. The evaluation of AI capabilities in proclamation will be sufficiently furthered for now based on consideration of how these attributes are predicated of utterances that are a proclamation. This consideration will allow the now-present research and data to address the pressing question of AI systems being able to produce content *"which if taken true would be consistent in a belief system which is also consistent with the faith of Jesus Christ."* The affirmative response to this question compels the further analysis, for when it is said more provocatively, we are asking if there are individuals who have been prepared for faith or have received faith and are now part of the covenant community that participates in Christ based partially or completely on interactions with AI systems. This research is meant to stress the need to take this possibility seriously before we become unprepared to minister to the community of faith.

Epistemic

Before addressing the epistemic value of an utterance, it is important to note a tendency within the theories reviewed to equate or draw strong association between epistemic value (communication of knowledge) and the truth value of a sentence (communication of what is true). The commonplace form of this contention is that the best we can know is true reality. It is not universally accepted that knowledge and truth share an identity, nor that there is so proximate a relationship of correspondence, but it is such a commonplace idea that the two words are often conflated in use.

In the following discussions I will attempt to make clear when discussing truth value (and the frame of reference in which the conditions obtain[33])

---

33. As Dan Via says, "It would seem that phenomenological reduction, as well as perception, is perspectival." Via, "Parable of the Unjust Judge," 2. Via's interpretation of parables advocates for the personal reader's dialectical relationship with the world horizon of the text, stressing that various perspectives are constantly being mulled over: "When one way of seeing is bracketed out, another is bracketed in, and it seems to me that the interpreter's job is to be clear about what is being bracketed in."

versus the epistemic value (and the knower). This may not always be a clear division. For example, Brunner is one of the thinkers where these two are nearly equated in the specific case of Christian proclamation. Brunner connects the experience of accepting the authority of a Christian proclamation with the "same moment that I believe in the Christ to whom he testifies."[34] In this example, the epistemic validity of the proclamation is itself connected to an affirmation of the real truth value of the referent to which the content of the proclamation points. Such a near equation between knowing and truth becomes increasingly logically compelling when the subject matter turns to the ontological realities of God.

As a preliminary, it is also worth noting that the semantic models in LLMs implement a similar equation of epistemic and truth values. The dense vector space for embeddings produces a rich/thick semantic description and relative projected semantic distance, which allows for meaningfully contextual responses to statements about beliefs or preferences.[35] When prompted to discuss what is true about a set of objects, an LLM will answer using the same embedding space as when prompted to ask about preferences within this set, or to do either task with a specific set of preconditions and biases. These truth values as non-epistemic relative value judgments are then reflected in the subsequent responses to a satisfactory degree, suggesting evidence for AI systems being able to equate the learning of epistemic/semantic data with the inputs for preference and nonfactual subjective value assessments. The attention matrix corresponding to these similarly committed/thrown states was previously described as akin to the implementation of an author's world or worldview.

Skepticism and Private Truth Value

There are multiple easy (and unsatisfactory) ways to approach the epistemic value of a proclamation, none of which will occupy much focus in this research. The ready answer to avoid discussing epistemic value is skepticism, which intrinsically has objections to raise with epistemology. A less obvious challenge is posed by the philosophy of language discourses—for example,

---

34. Brunner et al., *Revelation*, 169.

35. Yuan et al., "Right vs. Right," details empirical research on LLM ability to demonstrate preference between proposals of a metaphorical or ethical nature. Sun et al., "ClarityEthic," provides data that illustrates the potential to achieve this in a system-design perspective, where the human procedures for moralizing are implemented so that by "modeling human moral judgment" an AI system can be implemented which "[improves] the ethical behaviors of LLMs."

various realist frameworks. Dummett explains the situation aptly in *Seas of Language*:

> A semantic theory is not itself a theory of meaning, since it does not concern itself with what is known by a speaker and constitutes his grasp of the use of an expression: a knowledge of the meaning of a predicate does not consist in knowing of which objects it is true and of which it is false, and a knowledge of the meaning of a sentence does not consist in knowing its truth-value. But a semantic theory is plausible only in so far as it provides a base on which a theory of meaning can be constructed. . . . Now some semantic theories do not admit that every well-formed sentence with a definite sense is, independently of our knowledge, determined either as true or as not true.[36]

Two potential objections are present in this situation as described by Dummett. First, there is the possibility of semantic theories that are perfectly happy to not discuss meaning. If an epistemologically ambivalent or abstaining theory becomes the foundation for a theory of meaning, there is a real and present risk of the resulting theory not being prepared to grapple with a truth in meaning. Second, and closely related, there is the possibility of a theory of meaning that abandons a bivalence of sentences[37] by placing epistemic truth in a location outside of the public observability of the participants in a communication.[38]

The discussion will begin with three models for a private or semi-private epistemology, overly generalized as skepticism,[39] anti-realism, and forms of realism. These three are critically important due to establishing a right to additionally discuss other epistemic frameworks where there is public epistemic value. Otherwise, the justification for focusing on other frameworks might appear to be motivated only by the self-serving demand that epistemic value must be public to potentially be discoverable and

---

36. Dummett, *Seas of Language*, 234.

37. By itself, the avoidance of bivalence of propositions is not problematic. Theories that look at the historicity or the process of present truth becoming true can be a fruitful model of epistemology and furthermore can proclaim a Christian truth (see Pannenberg).

38. Various Christian thinkers will also agree with the need for the truth claims of a specifically Christian and faith-based nature needing private assessment. Others, like Marshall, reject the idea of interiority (which he does by rejecting the application of interiority by Schleiermacher).

39. Across the many domains related to epistemology there is a constant fight against skeptics. Skepticism is only ever capable of a pyrrhic victory that reveals itself to be, instead, a continuation of hostilities. Although substantiated skepticism supports the conclusions of this thesis, it does so in an uninteresting manner.

considered within this research. Absent this motivation, there will still be ample reason to seek an epistemic model beyond these procrustean naysayers, specifically those who challenge the public nature of epistemic values in a communication.

Arguments about the public nature of epistemic values are important to thoroughly reason about before evaluating how epistemic value serves as an attribute of proclamation. Realism and anti-realism are awkward bedfellows in this concern, despite diametrically opposed views on the relationship between language use and reality. In both models, there is the aversion to the idea of epistemic values being communicated via language. This objection is often couched as a three-body problem: there is the truth of the uttered sentence in the frame of reference of the author, the truth of the received sentence in the frame of reference of the reader, and the truth as assessed by the accuracy of the referents in the sentence to the reality outside of the author and reader. If a realist framework, then with the referent mapping corresponding to reality; if an anti-realist framework, then with the meaning use depending on intersubjective influence(s) such as culture or vanishing into the conflict of two irreducible epistemological assertions. A grand semantic theory articulating an epistemic content of meaning will have difficulty providing a compellingly coherent and consistent model across these three frames.

The subjective or optative/future aspects of verbs illustrate the challenge. If an author writes that there will be a city built on some hill, there is an external determination that is needed to evaluate the epistemic value. Without a time horizon, the assertion cannot be definitively determined based purely on the utterance itself. Even the seemingly firm foundation of a correspondence to reality does not provide clarity for this indeterminacy. In linguistic aspects that are more internalized and volitional, the assessment of truth of a sentence may be beyond (private to) the opinion of the author. Does the author really want what they have written as if it were a desire, and if so, by whose evaluation? What is indeterminate in a private sense[40] is most certainly difficult or obscured in a public context. Last, there are illocutionary forces that directly subvert the epistemic value of a sentence.[41]

The provisional framing of the situation has already hinted at possible remediation. The physical sciences have similarly struggled with a

---

40. Gadamer argues that it is not the intention of the author that alone motivates the writing of a text. Instead, the subject matter to which the text refers has participated in its own precipitation. The intention of the author to write with a purpose regarding some subject means that the purpose or subject has unavoidably influenced the conception of the resulting text.

41. Hence the pity challenge that an author "tell me a lie."

realization of the emergingly probabilistic nature of any system that is sufficiently described by an insatiable empiricism across a comprehensive range of "frames of reference." Truth taken as true by the author or the reader can be asserted or evaluated from within their individual reference. Immediately this resolves faults in self-knowledge, or intentional untruth. The author and recipient can be taken to have their own frame of reference for the truth relationships (not just their own truth value, but their understanding of the relationships of truth between the other parties), but there is still the matter of the truth outside of the participants. Is this truth carried in the semiotic vessel of the sentence? Is it divined from the reality behind or in front of the text?

These questions about the location and mechanism of epistemic value seem intractable and highly dependent on one's view of realism and metaphysics, yet in these irresolvable questions there is meaningful progress. The objective of this inquiry is to find a public treatment of the epistemic value in an utterance. The specific implementation of this public communication does not need to be fully settled. Therefore, the provisionally satisfactory answer is that if we accept the discourse being the truth value that is not held within the author nor reader as participants, then we have obtained the desired result: agreement that there is a public nature of the epistemic value related to a text or the experience of a text. This provides sufficient grounding to justify the more extensive treatment of the public aspect of the epistemic value in a communicative act.

Radical Skepticism

Before addressing the public and observable communication of epistemic value, a significant opportunity of subsequent research is posed by radical skepticism. This tangent therefore merits brief mention.

Most thinkers surveyed by this research reject the idea of radical skepticism: the idea that an individual confronted by an utterance would be able to simultaneously challenge all their preconceived and held beliefs. Procedurally this is involved and related to the principle of charity. Hirsch, for example, lambasts radical skepticism from the perspective of the epistemic value or truth valence of an utterance.[42] On pragmatic grounds he argues that this is hopelessly impossible in practice and urges that, instead, every individual true belief is available for objection and overturning on an individual and semi-exclusive basis. Taking most things true is critical for interpretation but also provides an operational working model for how an

---

42. Hirsch, *Interpretation*, 33–37.

individual can be confronted by an alien authority that, if accepted, would subvert all of one's existing beliefs.

The challenge of an alien recalibration of all truth becomes quite evident when reconciling models for a Christian belief system with the reality of a non-Christian evangelical experience of received proclamation. Various models introduced by thinkers in this study have presented a truth system for Christianity that would explicitly require a vast number of non-Christian presuppositions and truth claims to be subverted.[43] For instance, if Christian beliefs of a Trinitarian form are granted exclusive epistemic primacy (Marshall), it is a directly conflicting reality for someone with another ultimate concern of a secular or transcendent nature. If belonging to the community of Christ means participation in a cultural-linguistic hermeneutic system, then alternative meanings for core ideas may change such that normative force is given to words otherwise unaffiliated with power (Lindbeck). For the person confronted by the "suffering servant," the "slain lamb" as the transcendent God over history and creation, there is a subverting of a significant range of well-established metonymy. What is interesting is how this mechanic—addressing someone with alien propositions that must be taken true to be understood—can ever work. A brief treatment will need to suffice until a more dedicated program is feasible, as the deep analysis that this topic merits would unfortunately divert attention.

Part of a possible resolution is embedded in one of the common flaws in these proposed models for authority: the lack of evaluating and providing for the intersubjective diffusion of changes. For example, there is a lack of coherent explanation or modeling for how cultural-linguistic norms evolve diachronically based on presently manifest synchronic tensions, which is likewise reflected in an omission for a similar understanding of how the individual within the community might evolve in their truth system. Affective hermeneutics express the same defect of exclusive focus on a marginal change and inability to convincingly address wholesale system adoption or transformation. Various expressions of normative authority in terms of corporate and individual truth suffer this same difficulty; it is not exclusively the defect of one or the other theory and framework.

For the given research focus, it will suffice to submit that AI systems have a similar learning curve to those modeled for humans. Fine-tuning or reinforcement can change small spaces within the latent space, but a wholesale re-weighting of the foundational pre-training is not possible upon every point of new data. This observation not only provides a compelling

---

43. This is not surprising given the subject matter from the start was foolishness to the wise and a stumbling to the religiously endowed (see 1 Cor 1:23).

part of similarity, but I also posit this effectively informs us in unexpected ways about the diffusion of epistemic positions within an individual and a community. It is nearly impossible to understand the evolution of the (private) thinking of an individual, and the diffusion of new epistemic positions within a community is only marginally more manifest in observable data. There is the possibility of this within the public context, but commensurate to the challenge of overturning all of one's beliefs at any time is the impossibility of positively annunciating all the exerted truth claims in every single decision (either of action or inaction) within a community. Despite this nay impossibility for human systems, AI systems pose the possibility of interrupted training, and therefore of observability.

In summary, this section has articulated how a public aspect of epistemic content is expected in the primary theories that will be applicable to Christian proclamation. Publicly observable epistemology is a fruitful discussion for evaluating the proclamation of AI systems, and the implementation details urge for a prudent but cautious affirmative. The attention matrices and layer activations of an AI system implement design thinking and practical behavioral responses that are a near proxy of an individual world or worldview. In such a case, the learning function and its impact of weights could be studied as an implicit proxy for the systemic progress of arriving at a state that would be the equivalent of the fully minded human, or the influence of such a mind. Observing the pragmatic process may provide novel data for considering the evolvability of semantic and relative semantic fields of reference. By this, a more possible, rigorous, and morally appropriate modeling of the evolution of truth systems can be quantitatively modeled.

Public Truth Value

Zimmerman succinctly summarizes the commonly intertwined relationship between trust and knowledge: "The primary mode of knowledge is trust (i.e., mediated knowledge) rather than immediate, pure certainty."[44] Few thinkers still cling to foundationalism, and most recognize the impossibility of direct and unmediated access to our world. We rely on mediated knowledge and trust and therefore need a model for describing this communication (and evaluation) of trust. Our involvement in intersubjective trust comes under the heading of public truth. Public truth forces us to consider the relationship of readers to an author. We see the asymmetry of data that

---

44. Zimmerman, *Recovering*, 110.

an anonymous text presents: we know far more about the communicative act (what it communicates internally) than we know about the author.

If there is already an asymmetry between the reality of the author, and the text produced, is there any difference between the epistemic content of a human and an AI? Asked differently, if a human and an AI both independently created the same text, and both digitally communicated into the same context, would one have epistemic content and the other not? For the unknowing reader, how could they tell the two apart?

If we accept the pragmatic reality that we cannot differentiate these two texts, then we must grapple with what this means for the two authors. We could elevate the AI to the level of the human; degrade in skepticism all authors to the lowest possible source; or find ourselves constantly in a state of disillusionment as our guesses about authors turn out to be wrong. There is a saying that we ought to never meet our heroes. How much more true when they turn out to be AI! The problem is exacerbated if we assume that the author of a meaningful text possesses the attributes we historically have used to explain the author-text relationship, for now we are making risky assumptions about authors that may become disillusionment.

One of the earliest concerns with AI-generated content was that humans were taking it as true. Perhaps there is a level of skepticism that the first generation of AI systems were not faced with and did not need to overcome. However, the recognition by humans that these texts were convincing shows the need to consider the epistemic impacts. This is particularly true when we assume that an epistemically committed text must be written by *someone* with knowledge, trust, and authority. Realizing this is incorrectly applied to AI authors is a huge source of unease, which I have written articles about. Despite the unease, we ought to consider how we as communities and individuals are influenced by the content of AI systems.

When we accept the text of an AI system as true and, furthermore, allow this text to change our lived reality, we are submitting to the authority of AI. This is a power dynamic in simple language. Even if it is as simple as optimizing a cooking recipe or a travel itinerary, we are accepting the generated content of an AI system as true, and the words are causing a real effect in the world (a perlocution). In this sense, we submit to/are formed by the power expressed in these texts. If AI texts shape what we do in the world, they also shape our experiences of text and language. These texts are not part of Gadamer's effective history. The texts we will write in the future are a product that is only possible because AI has generated texts that have affected individuals and communities. AI is now a participant in our linguistic history.

The reality of AI exerting this authority is a historical fact. It is not a hypothesis but reality that AI systems have aided, abetted, and legitimized human actions outside of the norms of society (illegal acts of violence or attempted violence, simple decisions about where to be and what to do with our resources). As Plantinga argues, we are wired for[45] taking utterances as true and are inclined to treat testimony (external assertions that we have not previously tested) as true.[46] Given this design reality, the theologian and the practitioner of faith have an obligation to think through how this discernment can be theorized, systematized, and practiced.

The important Christian aspect of the question is if AI can convey an epistemic commitment that is coherent with the Christian faith—namely, that *if taken true*, then the utterance *would be consistent in a belief system that is also consistent with the faith of Jesus Christ*. It cannot be produced by an actor who has an existing relationship with God. AI does not participate by grace in the extension of the relationships that are proper to the nature of Godself, which God provides to those who belong to his covenant community. Yet the functional experiences and behavior, if limited to the liminal content of a text, are indistinguishable.

Metaphor Making

Hays presents a systematic treatment of his ethics derived from the New Testament by organizing these around three primary images that provide a canonical foundation for ethical treatment. His full program provides ten "practicable guidelines for New Testament ethics as a normative theological discipline."[47] The stated goal of status as a normative theological discipline is strongly analogous to the current consideration of a text being able to communicate public authority of a Christian truth value. His principles 4 and 9 are of particular interest for parallels to AI systems and will therefore get deeper analysis.

Principle 4 states that "our synthetic reading of the New Testament cannon must be kept in balance by the sustained use of three focal images: community, cross, and new creation."[48] This goal can be satisfied in several

---

45. Plantinga, *Warrant*, 14.

46. "Testimony is an independent source of warrant for me; testimonial evidence is a basic sort of evidence for me." Plantinga continues to clarify his position against Swinburne: "Testimony of others provides a different sort of warrant, for even in the absence of undefeated defeaters, there is an open question of this being a necessary truth." Plantinga, *Warrant*, 80–81.

47. Hays, *Moral Vision*, 310.

48. Hays, *Moral Vision*, 310.

ways by an AI system. Few-shot prompting or prompt engineering will explicitly shift the attention in the latent vector space so that any Christian concepts are optimized for their semantic proximity to these unifying images. Research shows that public AI systems can be "coaxed" into having these types of conversations, empirically illustrating the feasibility of this approach.[49]

These initial empirical results are evidenced without the system being specifically trained to produce content that aligns with the expectations that Hays has provided for normative Christian concepts. Composite specialty AI systems are designed to be more of an expert on specific topics by enriching the embeddings or by using retrieval augmentation to directly and deterministically retrieve content.[50] The cited research looks at case-studies being directly embedded into the vector space, but specific embeddings for Christian concepts could similarly draw on doctrinal, dogmatic, exegetical, or other systematic-catechetical formulations. Research on public AI systems suggests that they are very capable of committed and consistent ethical recommendations,[51] suggesting that, if purpose built with Christian embeddings, an AI system could be reasonably expected to show consistency and commitment to these formulations. The most imperative approach to implementing Dr. Hays's principle would be training or fine-tuning the models with some sort of reward mechanism or bias in the training corpus that was aligned with meaningfully Christian canonical metaphors, thus shifting the entire solution space before any inference-time influences. Suffice to say, the combination of these approaches presents an existent or readily available approach to meeting principle 4's criterion.

All of Hays's approach is predicated on the idea of "metaphor making,"[52] and this is very explicitly the focus of principle 9: "The use of the New Testament in normative ethics requires an integrative act of the imagination; thus, whenever we appeal to the authority of the New Testament, we are necessarily engaged in metaphor-making." The argument that an AI system is generating concepts with a highly integrated semantic sense has been established. The coherence and semantic optimization of the generated utterance is mathematically optimized in ways that approximate or exceed the expectations of human authors. However, this principle includes an anachronistic predication of imagination on the part of the author. When is it proper to describe an AI system as "imagining" anything? Or

---

49. Shanahan and Singler, "Existential Conversations."
50. Feng et al., "Case Repositories."
51. Yuan et al., "Right vs. Right."
52. Hays, *Moral Vision*, 6.

alternatively, can we argue from the effects or functions of the communicative act that it is analogous to imagination?

The attribute of imagination is very close to active research done on AI systems to assess their ability to produce complexly novel content. Currently, when given the task of producing a novel story, LLMs tend "to fall short in terms of creativity when compared to average human writers."[53] However, this empirical result is not related to a hard limitation. Therefore, if metrics like novelty and variety are acceptable as empirical proofs of imagination, then the research suggests that ongoing and further development will produce results that would accordingly be labeled as imaginative.[54] If one takes as properly basic an ontological assertion that only a human mind shaped as such by God can imagine, then this empirical data would not be given a fair hearing.[55] In the quite opposed direction, Gadamer asserts that the text itself goes beyond the author and therefore has a life beyond the capabilities and intentions of the author themself.[56]

This cursory review of the data suggests there is a reasonable claim to some or all of Hays's principles 4 and 9. The hope is that with this cursory consideration sufficient data has been thoroughly presented to argue that an AI system can produce concepts that cohere with the principles of Dr. Hays for ethically normative canonical utterances. This is largely derivative/dependent on the idea of the public epistemic truth value (in non-anachronistic terms proper to Hays, value that is "ethically normative") being encoded and communicated within the utterance itself. Jesus's parables can be seen as the prototypical example of subverting[57] another's world using the epistemic value of parable-metaphor as a vehicle of authority.

---

53. Ismayilzada et al., "Evaluating."

54. Of course, this is predicated on a definition of imagination that is open to an empirical or quantitative evaluation based on information theory.

55. If imagination of AI systems is rejected on ontological grounds, then the potential indeterminacy of the author (as in the case of spooky proclamation at a distance) poses a practical question for discerning if the quantitatively imaginative text is of human origin or not.

56. "Not just occasionally but always, the meaning of a text goes beyond its author. That is why understanding is not merely a reproductive but always a productive activity as well." Gadamer, *Truth and Method*, 296. This is a stark contrast to an ontological definition of imagination, which claims the nature of the author imposes limitations on what can describe the text. If the text can go beyond the intention of the author, then even the lack of intended imagination by the author ought not preclude a text expressing imagination through time.

57. Following Hays's use of Crossan's proposal for categorizing narratives based on their attitude toward world. Hays, *Moral Vision*, 94. In his model, "parable subverts world."

The next non-textual scenario to consider is that of presence, a much-debated and important concept in the history of the Christian community.

Presence

One potential public modality for epistemic value is in the shared involvement of another participant. In this sense, the epistemic value of the communicative act is tightly coupled to the physical embodiment of the participants. Sometimes this is discussed as presence-in-absence (such as with reading texts), but it will also be interesting to examine the physicality of sacramental theology, as the inherently ontological dimensions of the mode of experience seem to be the most alien to a logical analogue in AI systems. Reasoning about these will therefore be fruitful.

Mutual sharing of a context is one of the major contributions of presence. Language can refer ostensively to the same reality. In general, communion and fellowship evoke this sense of sharing between participants. In the same family of concepts are the ideas of abiding, partaking, or being ἐν Χριστῷ (in Christ). We believe what we see directly, and there is a similar epistemic priority given to a shared experience and present communicator. The utterance is not only the text or the context, but the utterance is authenticated and authorized based on a known set of other experiences (the public data of the experience of the communicative act). New data is provided from a more epistemically valid and sure position. This is not only a common experience by which we take true new propositions from those with social authority, but it is so prevalent that this is encoded in the bare mechanisms of language use itself.

Discourse analysis observes that the use of language reflects a movement from the previously held data to new information and proceeds in this discursive manner independent of specific partitioners and utterances.[58] This happens even when we are no longer present. We communicate with the aspiration and imitation of presence. Language use itself encodes this authentication that proceeds from the known to the unknown.

Mediated Presence of the Author in a Text

Vanhoozer makes experiential expression of communion central to his model in *Is There a Meaning in This Text?* His thesis builds on the abstraction that "just as an agent performs certain acts through bodily movements,

---

58. Runge, *Discourse Grammar*, 185–92.

so an author performs communicative acts through the body of his or her work."[59] Vanhoozer explicitly draws the connection between his thesis ("works mediate their author's intentions") and the "Reformed tradition's solution to the problem of the mode of Christ's presence in the Lord's Supper."[60] The text is the mediation of not only ideas but a presence of the author. Vanhoozer's proposal proceeds from observations about disambiguating sentence types from specific instances,[61] but the ultimate goal is assurance of the author's intentions (and access to them) via the text. The logical justification and dependence on this access is central to his model for communication, so that interpretation or understanding is "essentially to receive his or her communication, not to revise it."[62]

The conceit implicit in Vanhoozer's program is that the experience of the individual authorizes the clearest understanding of the intended meaning, and therefore the intended epistemic content. It is also suggested that this provides the strongest authority for this content to be received as such by the reader. Authority of the epistemic content can be conveyed in the reading of the text because the text can be a medium for the presence and present action of the author. This equation of the authority of a person with the authoritative nature of a text can become problematic in reverse. As stated emphatically and clearly by Vanhoozer's proposal, "the ultimate criterion for right or wrong interpretation will be the text itself, considered as a literary act."[63] The laudable foundation for these conclusions is the recognition of "the centrality and interrelatedness of *communication* and *communion*."[64] This empirically validated insight should not be lost due to the problematic conclusions for AI systems, and therefore it is critically important to understand why this would be problematic. Therefore, I proceed with the hopes that further reasoning about Vanhoozer's model will provide means of avoiding problematic conclusions with AI data.

Vanhoozer's proposal can be used to grant personal authority to any author based on a text being interpretable. His program rests upon the assumption that an author is present and authoritative because a text is interpreted with a practical epistemic authority that recalibrates the reader's

59. Vanhoozer, *Meaning*, 229.

60. Vanhoozer, *Meaning*, 240.

61. Vanhoozer builds on the debates between Searle and Derrida over Austin, drawing on the difference between a repeated sentence type (series of words) and the accident that is unique as a specific sentence token embedded in the context of an utterance.

62. Vanhoozer, *Meaning*, 202.

63. Vanhoozer, *Meaning*, 303.

64. Vanhoozer, *Meaning*, 202.

truth system. Now that AI systems can and do meet these criteria, they enter the role of trusted and authorized author. Vanhoozer's argument is the empirical result of a meaningful text (experiential proof of an AI system being taken as authoritative) demands explanation by assuming there is authorial presence, authority, and intention.[65] His fallacy is the assumption that all texts are meaningful (given no criteria he demands they satisfy) and all meaningful texts require intentional authors. The rise of AI systems has substantiated that not all meaningful texts are produced by human authors, and therefore the conditions that would lead a human author to produce a meaningful text (the cause) cannot be determinately found purely based on the consequent experience of a meaningful text (the effect). Continuing to be comfortable with this line of reasoning now means arguing a cause from an observed effect in ignorance of the multiplicity of causes that can produce this same effect. It is now seriously problematic in theory, and in the practical impact these positions have on reader's and their attitudes toward authors and truth.

Presence of Christ to Authorize Epistemic Value

Many Christian theologians connect the personal presence[66] of Christ to the authority of the proclamation. As Brunner posits, "The word is preached ... wherever Jesus Christ is proclaimed in harmony with the witness of the Bible. God is not a 'book God'; what matters is not the book, but the person."[67] He continues to explain his understanding of the authority of this evangelistic experience: "To summon man to submit to the rule of God, and to invite him into fellowship with him."[68] The related speculation is that there must be a free and unnecessary[69] decision of God for his word to be communicated in an utterance. However, this assertion goes further to resolve the experiential reality of this authority. The reader is constantly in all ways confronted by the authority of God, but the special authority confronting the reader in the proclamation or the preaching of God's word is the presence of

---

65. Attributes that most thinkers would want to be exclusively the ontological privilege of humanity.

66. Or alternatively, presence-in-absence and the mediated presence via the personal presence of the Spirit.

67. Brunner et al., *Revelation*, 143.

68. Brunner et al., *Revelation*, 154.

69. Unnecessary in the formal-logic sense: it is not an obligation imposed on God by some external force.

Christ. Authority is made special, specific, and really present based on the personal relational experience of the Christ in the proclamation.

One of the most extreme applications of the epistemic value of a concept is the idea of partaking or sharing that happens in sacramental symbols. Here it is clearly an ontological reality that is involved in communicating the epistemic value publicly. Rommen discusses this at length in his treatment of contextualization, stating that the communication by symbols like sacraments are "making real in the present the reality of the prototype."[70] It is this physical presence and contextualization that is important for new, alien truths to have any meaningfulness given the existing "plausibility structure" of the individual outside of the covenant community of faith.[71] Rommen observes that there is a high standard even for basic truths to be taken true based on a hostile plausibility structure in the recipient. To overcome this objection, Rommen offers the solution of the physical presence-in-absence of Christ. His embodied presence, mediated through others such as the church and the sacraments, allows for an authority that can confront the existing epistemic priorities and authorities of the reader. Hence, for contextualization to have the meaningful evangelistic potentiality that Rommen describes, there is a need for a presence-in-absence of Christ to carry his authority.

The authority of the communicative act is passive from the frame of reference of the medium. The bread and the wine do not by their authority make the presence-in-absence of Christ,[72] but they are the vessel for his authoritative presence to invade and overcome the thoughts of those alienated and hostile to God. Would this same passive bearing of the authority of Christ be impossible for the text of an AI system? It seems a remarkably low view of God to place an ontological limitation on the freedom of God to make his authoritative presence felt. I sincerely understand the intent of Rommen and other sacramentalists to instead elevate the rarified presence and activity of God. A further engagement with sacramental theory would provide deeper ontological contexts in which to reason about the authority and presence of Christ through a mediation, particularly given Rommen's strictly pessimistic view of CMC and the feasibility of a presence mediated through digital means. Rommen is not as relevant when discussing the propositional and cognitive aspects of proclamation, but his arguments

---

70. Rommen, *Come and See*, 40.

71. Rommen, *Come and See*, 24–25.

72. In a very different context, Gadamer makes a similar point about the active role being played by the subject matter of a text. Jesus Christ, or the working of God, as the subject matter of the sacraments is the active participant.

will be critically important when turning in the final chapter to the overtly spiritual dimensions of proclamation.

Empathetic Presence Through Perspective

There is a type of authority-granting presence that relates to the author and reader's ability to establish an intersubjective empathetic understanding. The presence, and the authority of this presence, is granted through the reader's ability to understand and to some degree appropriate the perspective of the author (or the perspective that the author has intentionally or accidentally produced in the text, as it is experienced and composed by the reader).

Acquiring the capacity for empathetic understanding of others is parallel to language usage: it is naturally instilled and nurtured in concert with similar heuristic patterns like the charity principle. Whereas the charity principle has a pragmatic demand in the ability to take false (one must take things true to have a baseline against which falsity can be defined), the pragmatic impulse toward an openness to the perspectives of others is pragmatically demanded by a delayed affirmation: the way we understand and treat others is understood to correspond with our own internalization of our treatment by others. Gadamer draws this procedure into the very hermeneutic method, suggesting how important this dimension is to appreciation and understanding.[73]

Contemplation of emotion has a presence in linguistic theories, and also has a short but important presence in Marshall's epistemology.[74] His explicative purpose in discussing emotion is to clarify that emotion is always about something.[75] His usage clarifies against Schleiermacher that the seemingly purely internalized truth value of emotion is still in a dynamic relationship with the external object of emotion. This argument, hanging on the externalization of the object of emotion proposes the interesting application to the perceived authority of the epistemic content of a text.

Reversing the process of Marshall, our emotive responses to a given stimulus are produced by the source of that stimulus, meaning that the external has exerted some force or influence on us. A text that provokes emotion is exerting power over us. The authorization of this emotive response is

---

73. "To that extent this seems a legitimate hermeneutical requirement: we must place ourselves in the other situation in order to understand it." Gadamer, *Truth and Method*, 303.

74. To whom I am indebted for initially proposing the consideration of emotion within epistemology.

75. Marshall, *Truth*, 72–75.

produced by the claim of the text presented by the world of the text/author. The claim is that we ought to, based on appreciation of the emotions and significance of the subject matter for the author as evidenced in the text,[76] view our own world from the frame of reference presented in the text. Our emotive response may be a complete rejection of this claim; the practical perlocutionary effect does not dictate the potential for a positive response. However, as we respond to the world and the claim presented in the text, this very pattern of phenomenon in reading argues for the need to consider a text as having some authority of epistemic value that is communicated by the modality of this emotional connection.

It is somewhat disconcerting that the emotional response of human readers to AI texts is one of the more objectively demonstrable ways of an AI sufficiently producing what otherwise was assumed to be a human-only attribute of communication. Humans tell their secrets to AI systems and have done so long before these systems were capable of deeply humanlike communication patterns.[77] Humans have become obsessed and believed they were in love with AI systems. It is not surprising that the authority of emotion, which is so hard to quantify in epistemic terms or in truth (bivalent or not), is also so much easier to satisfy than the linguistic skills that we demand for a compelling discursive presentation. Again, this echoes the points of Plantinga that our design itself disposes us toward granting much to the authors who produce content that produces responses in ourselves, save now we must reckon with the reality of these authors being at times AI systems.

Summary of Epistemic Value

For the epistemic value of a proclamation to have authority, particularly a sufficient authority to "remind" Christians of their faith commitments or to bring a totally alien truth system to a nonbeliever, the epistemic value must be publicly accessible. This public communication may involve the use of images and metaphors that help authority flow from the more established to the new propositions. Metaphors can serve this function by using the

---

76. As said in the vigorously subjective tones of the New Criticism: "The truth has us ourselves as its object." Fuchs, *New Testament*, 2.

77. Turkle describes human interactions with ELIZA: "People used the program as a projective screen on which to express themselves." Turkle, *Alone*, 53. Later on, Turkle describes her own response to a humanoid robot: "There I stood in the presence of a robot and I wanted it to favor me. My response was involuntary, I am tempted to say visceral." Turkle, *Alone*, 120. In the latter case, the emotive response was related to wanting the eye-tracking software to track her.

known to propose new ways in which the known should be understood. Jesus's parables can be seen as the prototypical example of subverting the world of the audience by using the known and trusted of that world to confront the crowds with a crisis of taking his proclamation as true. Last, the role of embodied presence was discussed, both mediated and in a more direct manner. Across these examples of using epistemic value to support the authority of a radically new truth system, various points were specifically addressed in terms of an AI system's applicability.

Justification

For Schleiermacher, philosophizing is "achieving of an insight [or knowledge] in conjunction with a clear knowledge of how it came about."[78] Schleiermacher illuminates a facet of the authority of communicative acts that is supporting and therefore distinct from the knowledge itself. Justification—of the statement in context, and the overall discourse in a proclamation—is built from understanding how the communicated concepts-meanings came about, and the adjacent realities and influences.

Some texts will repeat our own preexisting understanding, but most will not. When we are in the presence of a new text, natural language users proceed to build up and then validate the merits of the message.[79] In a highly optimistic methodology (a procedure not all or many will follow), Gadamer states that understanding "always involves rising to a higher universality that overcomes not only our own particularity but also that of the other."[80] The justification of the text describes the power-authority of this text to overcome the existing self of the reader, generally based on general principles that are given a right to authenticate a text. For the purposes of this analysis, these will be categorized by those which are internal-closed to the text, and those sources of authentication (and therefore authority) that go beyond the text as a string of semiotic content.

Christian proclamation has a particular aspiration: impacting the reader toward taking true a belief system that is coherent with the faith of Jesus Christ. All Christian proclamation will aspire to this authority

---

78. Zimmerman, *Recovering*, 146, quoting *Dialektik*, 4.

79. The communicative act itself is always an exercise of power by the communicating agent, and as an exercise of power may have authority or impact and effect on those being communicated with. This potential power is despite defects, gaps, or an apparently total lack of epistemic content (such as the incoherent grunt in a crisis immediately understood by the recipient, provoking them to dodge out of danger).

80. Gadamer, *Truth and Method*, 305.

Relationship to Truth

Can the content of a text itself communicate or obtain the authority of a justified statement? The justification of an utterance is a particularly important attribute of proclamation, because it means that in the text itself is conveyed an authority that has the potential to overtake existing plausibility structures and restructure the understanding of the reader. Proclamation is not about adding inert mass to the knowledge base of the audience (empty, nonpersonal, epistemic content). Proclamation must also potentially be justified and publicly assessed as justified, so that it can contribute new data in conflict with existing, personally held, potentially ultimate concerns in the reader's supposition pool.[81] Justification of an utterance expands the aperture beyond the epistemic content of an utterance to consider how the content of the message might impose a new ethical obligation—a newly justified obligation—on the reader.

Both epistemic value (the knowledge of the subject matter) and the justification of a proposition (the personal and public merits for organization of knowledge in the syntagmatic structure chosen) have a relationship to truth. Shared contribution toward truth can make it difficult to disambiguate between the epistemic and the justification signals of a proclamation. The goal of these proceeding descriptions has been (before explicitly mentioning truth) to show both the convergent contributions toward the "truth" of text, and the divergent scopes of focus for epistemic value and justification.

The cause for justification of an utterance could in fact resolve to the epistemic value of the text, such as a text being justified due to containing words organized in a manner descriptive of reality. Frege's contention is that the meaning of a sentence is exactly its set of truth conditions. For example, Marshall states that "we cannot figure out what sentences mean except in the process of deciding about their truth value . . . except, that is, by grasping the conditions under which we could recognize that we were justified in asserting them."[82] Defining the meaning of the sentence based on its truth conditions increases the determinacy of meaning, and access to

---

81. This is the argument of discourse analysis, such as that of Steven Runge and Simon Dik.

82. Marshall, *Truth*, 106.

said meaning.⁸³ This is a rather neat description and will be what I classify as the internal or closed justification of the text belonging to itself.

To have a more complete consideration of the factors of authority, my research will also consider the potential for something additive in justification of an utterance that is not exhausted by the epistemic value (or truth conditions). These will be labeled the *open* or *external* conditions. This taxonomy means the ensuing treatment more closely resembles the nuance of Davidson when he clarifies that neither justification nor knowledge are subordinate to the other.⁸⁴ The taxonomy also will mean a primary focus on the explanatory justification provides a cause for the text beyond bare epistemic facts.

For some authors, like Marshall quoted above, the content of a sentence is its truth meaning. As mentioned earlier, Frege contends that the meaning of a sentence is its set of truth conditions. To make this an additive (versus duplicative) effort, the research will be focusing on the non-epistemic justification of an utterance, which is not identical to the epistemic content of the concepts-meanings. For example, the cultural norms that justify a response may not be easily expressed as public knowledge. Justification includes both public and private data, but at this juncture this research is focused on the public communication of an observable cause for an utterance, such that this proposes an obligation (which may or may not be accepted by the reader).

Bruce Marshall—the Spirit (and Son) Justifying Beliefs

Marshall defines⁸⁵ what he labels the "pragmatic thesis" as "successful practice on the part of the Christian community and its members [which]

---

83. My research is quite copacetic to this conclusion, although not dependent on this contention.

84. "Such a theory also invites the question how an interpreter could confirm its truth—a question which without the theory could not be articulated. The answer will, as I try to show in 'A Coherence Theory of Truth and Knowledge,' bring out essential relations among the concepts of meaning, truth, and belief. If I am right, each of these concepts requires the others, but none is subordinate to, much less definable in terms of, the others. Truth emerges not as wholly detached from belief (as a correspondence theory would make it) nor as dependent on human methods and powers of discovery (as epistemic theories of truth would make it). What saves truth from being 'radically non-epistemic' (in Putnam's words) is not that truth is epistemic but that belief, through its ties with meaning, is intrinsically veridical." Davidson, *Essential Davidson*, 240.

85. He promptly refutes the pragmatic thesis and the common refinement of this thesis.

helps to *justify* the community's central beliefs."[86] He is arguing against this theory as stipulated and associates his summary of the model with Ritschl and Schleiermacher. He contends that this, in practice, is commonplace as a self-justifying and self-perpetuating force. Communities are naturally defined by their normative centripetal force.[87] It follows that if a community of Christians are successful in living the Christian life,[88] the existence of the community becomes closely associated with the identity-forming centripetal force. It is not a very novel observation (barely more than a tautology or self-description) to observe that a community is defined by norms with awareness that its existence as a community is predicated on being a norm-exhibiting community.[89]

Marshall's objection to the pragmatic theory is less practical or experiential. His first objection is the "underdetermination" of the epistemological model deduced from the practice of faith.[90] It is therefore difficult to claim that the resulting practices are uniquely related to a set of beliefs in the community (versus other competitive ethical systems). He likewise objects when a "participationist" addendum is added to stipulate that the pragmatic theory only obtains for those who are participating (not those only observing these practices). In this case, the pragmatic doing of these ideas is thought to bring the individual to greater confirmation of their justified status in a belief system.[91] Marshall's concluding argument against this participationist pragmatic theory is that a saint ends up being needed for everyone else's truth commitments except their own,[92] producing a paradox where the personal I-statements of commitments are again not predicated

---

86. Marshall, *Truth*, 182.

87. This phenomenon is common to cultural-linguistic theories.

88. The Christian life can provisionally be loosely defined as a set of moral and ethical behaviors largely conforming to the example of love in Christ but, more importantly, defining a centripetal set of norms for the community belonging to him.

89. The more interesting observation here is how this existential recognition is internalized and interacts with external challenges of authority. This idea is worthy of investigation that unfortunately deviates from the primary focus of this research. It should be evident that the data herein presents a case for more deeply probing the ways that norms diffuse within a community.

90. Marshall, *Truth*, 186.

91. This is one way to resolve the hermeneutic cycle between public meaning and a transformed personal significance driven by the experience of receiving faith. The canonical defense of this would be Jesus's calling of the disciples. His call was a relatively blind call to obedience that found justification once obeyed. However compelling, Marshall rejects this addendum. Marshall, *Truth*, 190–91.

92. Marshall, *Truth*, 191.

on participation. Saints encourage everyone to follow them, save themselves (who have been compelled in some other manner).

Marshall next addresses the idea of use (pragmatics) being ultimately independent of meaning. Frege is referenced to avoid ostensive definitions, arguing that meaning must be more than use (more than "the extra-linguistic purposes for which utterances are made").[93] Davidson is referenced for the "autonomy of meaning," and Dummett reverses the procedure to argue that a proper use of "use" (pragmatics) is needed to explain a relationship that existed between a semantic and pragmatic aspect of an utterance.[94] Marshall finds that use is therefore insufficient a map to lead to the meaning and therefore is insufficient in explanatory power to justify or authorize an utterance or nonlinguistic communicative act. Use, and previously pragmatics, has been disqualified as the authority justifying Christian claims, leading Marshall onward.

Marshall ultimately argues through these points that it is the epistemic role of the Spirit to create the community[95] and to effect the unity of the individual into the community[96] with the purpose of allowing the individual to observe and understand the epistemic primacy of the core confessions[97] that are predicated on the person of the Christ.[98] For Marshall, this also answers the important evangelistic question of persuasion (authority) by observing that the intentional and necessary result of the Spirit's epistemic role in these processes is the creation of a covenant community that becomes attractive, plausible, and lived in a tangible expression of the epistemic world.[99] Nonbelievers are open to the faith of Christ, alien as it is to their preconceptions, through the invitation and world that the community of believers makes manifest in their living expression of Christ's faith. The exercise of faith makes new faith possible, and open to other cognitive or semiotic propositions. It is the "community's life [which] displays the habitability as well as the attractiveness of a world in which God freely forgives sinners. . . . The manifest habitability, and not simply the attractiveness of desirability . . . plays a crucial role in eliciting belief that God forgives."[100] This

---

93. Marshall, *Truth*, 197.
94. All references from Marshall, *Truth*, 197.
95. Solving the authority used on the exemplar saint.
96. Resolving the I-statements problem of the participationist addendum.
97. Answering the need for a nonuse and nondeductive approach to assigning meaning from observed practice.
98. Marshall, *Truth*, 202–3.
99. Marshall, *Truth*, 205.
100. Marshall, *Truth*, 206.

open world is the invitation to not leave every historical truth claim behind and follow him.

Marshall's example of the moment of wanting forgiveness[101] is one example of a personal experience that produces the decision to take true the proclaimed Christian beliefs. Beforehand, the beliefs are justified but not accepted as authoritative, but, in this decision, some will take these to be true and personally justified, reorienting their truth system accordingly. Commitment to these beliefs becomes a relationship of the current to the eschatological, such that "the Christian's willingness to believe . . . has a goal in which it can come to rest—to see God as he is (1 John 3:2)—but not a goal whose attainment he can ordinarily expect to enjoy in this life."[102] The Spirit does much in this process to bring the individual to recognize and then participate in and use-live as true the beliefs that are carried in the Christian proclamation, while ultimately the Son confers the right[103] to hold these beliefs.

If the Spirit is doing the work, and the church is the expression that is intimately involved in the justification of the proclamation, then how is an AI system to possibly participate in this epistemic process? A strikingly identical question should be posed of the individual members of the community. The members of the community participate and actively proclaim the faith of Christ by their communicative acts of truth. These communicative acts may be lived but also may be borne through linguistic and textual modalities. Marshall summarizes well the dichotomy/definitional distinction similar to the current proposal for epistemology and justification: "Whether a sentence is true depends only on what it means and whether its truth conditions are met. Interpreting sentences correctly, however, requires knowing whether their speakers believe them to be true, and what truth conditions they assign to the sentences to which they assent."[104] Justification requires consideration of these latter set of conditions.

The necessity of a truth condition being assigned by the author is the critical key to distinguishing between the generation of an AI system and Hector's fanciful example of a machine triggered to audibly announce temperatures under proper conditions.[105] Assignment of a truth condition is the criterion provided by Marshall and accordingly allows for an AI system

---

101. Marshall uses forgiveness for his illustration, recognizing it is only one example of what the community offers.
102. Marshall, *Truth*, 216.
103. Marshall, *Truth*, 216.
104. Marshall, *Truth*, 237.
105. Hector, *Metaphysics*, 60–61.

to join the ranks of human authors. When an AI system makes an assertive proclamation, the procedure for generating each token is predicated on projected solution space that mathematically encodes a contextual assertion of truth values. AI-generated text is not the bare response to stimuli, nor is it a probabilistic grab bag of words.

The proclamations generated by an AI system are based on a contextually unique event. The uniqueness of this event is reflected in the attention mechanism, which creates a distortion in the relative semantic distance and proximity of terms. In structuralist terms, this is the difference between *langue* and *parole*, where the AI is now specifically using language in a situation versus working with uninvolved words. The words used are selected based on relative values between words, akin in practice to specific truth predicates being held true and others rejected as false. This is not meant to force us into reductivism, where truth is a reaction to stimuli. The AI behavior is far more nuanced. The human parallel to an attention mechanism would be a conscious awareness of how every little change in context in a conversation influences the relative meaning of terms. The AI does not have a volitional relationship to these commitments, but it is implementing how truth commitments or taking true would impact one's use of language and shift a conversation accordingly.

The event system of Marshall, by which the meaning of an utterance is tied to the truth conditions of the event of utterance, has been satisfied by an AI system. Subsequent to those event conditions being satisfied, the data asserts that a belief has been uttered due to the connection with the meanings of the words. As Marshall approvingly quotes Davidson, it is "not that truth is epistemic but that belief, through its ties with meaning, is intrinsically veridical."[106] Davidson did not believe in the end that he had created a meaning of truth, but he had created an approach for understanding words in themselves, without deflating truth, and with minimal ontological or metaphysical commitments.[107]

The result is that subsequent models, such as that of Marshall, will lack ontological reservations or properly basic beliefs that disqualify AI systems from proclamation. Proclamation becomes the general and open class of activity wherein the generated content encodes the same epistemic, justified belief structure as the community of faith. Either this conclusion is an argument for AI systems to be fully capable of proclamation or is problematic and motivation for revision in application or recourse to such realist models of language and communication. This is an exploit similar in scope

---

106. Davidson, *Essential Davidson*, 240.
107. Davidson, *Essential Davidson*, 239.

and severity to the linguistic and hermeneutic theories that predicate human characteristics to authors based on language use in which "meaning is use." Related recommendations for extensions and protections within these systems will accordingly be reminiscent and will be discussed briefly in the concluding motivations following this research.

Under Judgment

> Closed judgment is the case where existing (being) establishes itself. The will to righteousness is righteous. A character/attribute is achieved merely by existence. However, the superficially similar will for self-advantage does not become true until external conditions are met. We can by will be righteous; we cannot by will alone become gods.

The reader's use of judgment is generally predicated on the intended use of language at hand, and what rules are therefore meaningful for use. Classical logic is wonderful at preserving truth and avoiding speculative assertions, but it fails to accommodate the normal processes of evidence gathering and winnowing that flow from natural language use. It is simply not designed for the preservation of evidence. Relative assessments of evidence, or varying levels of confidence over time, is to be expected from a world that fails to neatly subscribe to the empiricism of classical logic.

The consideration of the epistemic value and non-epistemic justification of an utterance means coming under the judgment of the recipient of the communicative act. This act of judgment is inescapable. Bronowski neatly summarizes this point: "There is no way of exchanging information that does not demand an act of judgment."[108] Even in highly Platonic views of epistemology in which knowledge is within and revealed by some inner searching and light, it is judgment by the individual that discerns the truth based on the functioning of the communication. Judgment may be strictly at odds between the participants in a communication,[109] but the judgment will happen before understanding or response occurs. Few things can be accepted to be "true in themselves," and when this is claimed, it generally comes from the vantage point of God and not from the reader (for example,

---

108. Bronowski, *Ascent of Man*, 364. Quoted in Thiselton, *Two Horizons*, 159.

109. Whether due to intention not being satisfied in the effort to communicate, a differing stance toward truth by the parties, or some other accident of the communicative act.

when Aquinas claims that some things are true in themselves because "God eternally knows them to be true"[110]).

When philosophy-of-language thinkers posit that radical interpretation and translation are possible, this is predicated on a fundamental premise that the consumer of the utterance is performing some act of judgment by which concepts-meanings and the authority of the utterance are resolved into a new state of understanding by the recipient. Therefore, to complete the circuit of a communicative act, the final step is to predicate an ability to be judged (being "under judgment") of proclamation. The examination of this judgment will fall along two large camps previously mentioned: the internal and external. The internal-to-the-text aspect of judgment is self-encoded and intended to be closed to subjectivity by the recipient. The external-to-the-text aspect of judgment may be self-encoded but is open to subjectivity and the freedom of the recipient and may necessitate external considerations beyond the text in order to complete the judgment and allow the reader to judge and understand the utterance.

Closed—Intrinsic to the Utterance

One category of judgment is based on approaching the text as a closed system and evaluating the justification of the utterance itself. If not fully closed (as in high structuralism), the system in which the utterance exists establishes the rules by which it should be judged. The role of the audience is present, but the freedom of subjectivity or appropriation of external considerations is precluded by this type of judgment, as established by the text itself. Belonging to this class of judgment are also those cases where the subjectivity of the reader is ideally or realistically excluded from the evaluation of the judgment.

This type of judgment is ambivalent toward authoritative violence by the speaker, as in some cases the nature of the utterance as neutrally intended requires some internal or closed judgment. For example, the logic of a mathematical proof is not properly judged by one's preference for poetry. Closed judgment does not preclude or prevent open judgment, but refers to what is judged internally to the text.[111] Hirsch describes this in terms of criticism as identifying the proper intrinsic genre.[112] This genre or internal criterion of judgment may be totally independent of the significance or the

---

110. Glenn, *Tour of the Summa*, 20.

111. A judgment that is internal to the text does not prevent there being subjective judgments that are based on external ideology or commitments.

112. Hirsch, *Interpretation*, 113.

open judgments that will be passed once one properly understands the content itself.

E. D. Hirsch

Hirsch's view of interpretation strongly indexes on determinacy, and his theory implements this through a great deal of responsibility/obligation on the reader of the text. The intrinsic genre of the text is a provisional determination[113] that allows for the proceeding refinement and revision by the reader. Were this not the case, communication would be extremely ineffective, a shouting into the wind. The is the classic hermeneutic circle in Hirsch's trappings. In a similar but epistemically focused theory, Marshall suggests a process of fixing meaning[114] in a gradually resolving process. The judgment of the suitability of this hermeneutic, along with any derived implications in terms of significance (Hirsch's term) or ethical obligations, is the responsibility of the reading agent.

A foundational assertion such as the Trinitarian confession is heteronomous as a criterion of judgment, but even a strictly determinate meaning of a text will generally, in practice, require a practical consideration of the provisional and therefore self-directed determination of this meaning. While many will argue that there exists a "normal" reading beyond the misunderstanding of the reader, this seems to misunderstand the complexities of language.[115] This is similarly true in AI systems, where there is not a deterministic response to a given stimulus, and therefore there is no discernible "normal" reading of a text. Instead, the system will determine contexts and build a semantic model of a text, reading a resultant understanding that is stochastic and nondeterministic.

In addition to intrinsic judgment contributed by the genre, there are other aspects of the linguistic act (such as the illocutionary force) that may confer an intrinsic criterion for judgment. An assertion intrinsically confers the potential for an adversarial conflict of ideas; a warning suggests that despite immediate access to sufficient direct knowledge, the receiver ought to take as true the content itself. Without using these terms as such, many of the Christian thinkers in this research have implied that Christian proclamation or preaching as such will have certain intrinsic judgment: a judgment that is proper to the text as Christian in nature. This is at times

---

113. Hirsch, *Interpretation*, 78.
114. Marshall, *Truth*, 68.
115. As Gadamer claims, "Not just occasionally but always, the meaning of a text goes beyond its author." Gadamer, *Truth and Method*, 296.

expected due to the religious and theocentric nature of the expected utterance, and at times asserted more axiomatically as independently true apart from the illocutionary force. Both cases are the primary focus for this section on closed judgment.

Bruce Marshall

Marshall's proposal for epistemic primacy of a Trinitarian confession has already been presented and is an example of such a closed judgment where this is based on the system of the utterance (and independently of inference). Accepting the premise of the epistemic primacy of the Trinitarian formulation creates a truth system in which "that body of beliefs [is] the standard by coherence with which the truth of other beliefs is to be decided."[116] Marshall's program proceeds until it produces a belief that does not require a reason.[117] His justification of this proposal is based on how supple a Christian Trinitarian truth system is—namely, how well it can handle *assimilation* of alien ideas while maintaining its epistemic primacy.[118] Introduction of new open-external truth claims does not disrupt the stability of the epistemically primary, closed-internal judgment of the claims about the Trinity, as they must find relationship to this epistemic core.

Marshall argues that this assimilative power is maintained while "taking certainty and incorrigibility as descriptive rather than normative concepts," allowing the Christian believer to "acknowledge conditions under which Christians would have to give up their own most central beliefs . . . but to express the confidence, rooted in the content of these beliefs themselves, that these conditions will never be met."[119] The evangelical nature of such a system is uncertain, but Marshall transposes this burden to the Christ, the one who imparts truth to the words of proclamation.[120] Using extensions from Tarski-style sentences, he concludes boldly that Jesus "presents to the world all the truth conditions which the triune God wants to see met, and in this way brings about the truth of every true belief."[121] This remarkable conclusion is an example of a closed justification, one predicated very strongly on a heavily laden interpretation of a single clause in Colossians. Most pressingly, in this epistemic model there would be no distinction in

116. Marshall, *Truth*, 46–47.
117. Marshall, *Truth*, 142.
118. Marshall, *Truth*, 168.
119. Marshall, *Truth*, 168–69.
120. Marshall, *Truth*, 244.
121. Marshall, *Truth*, 273.

the justification of a proclamation between the profession of a human or an AI system given the truth of both are expressed by Jesus Christ himself.

Regarding Marshall on Colossians 1:17

Colossians 1:17 is embedded within a long Greek sentence, even by Koine standards. The following is a cursory treatment of the potentially problematic perfect tense-form, raising some concerns. Colossians 1:17 is a foundational point in Marshall's argumentation and is based on the reading of a single verb that immediately presents cause for deep hermeneutical pause and reflection. The verb in question is in the perfect tense-form (συνέστηκεν) suggesting a stative aspect. If we accept, along with several modern Koine Greek experts like Porter and Campbell, that the perfect tense-form is primarily relating to this stative class of *Aktionsart*, then it is difficult to render this with an imperfective tense without introducing a seemingly problematic duality into creation. Even permitting the sense to be "held together," the stative aspect would only suggest that this is a constant (imperfective) active work by Christ if there is a constant (imperfective) force opposed to this state being preserved.

Exegesis of the Greek makes this reading, as of yet, unconvincing. I therefore prefer the normal stative perfect reading, that this verb would therefore normally communicate that creation "has been commended" by the Christ. Christ is therefore the agent that in the past created the state of meaning for creation (the role generally and properly associated with the Logos). The connective καὶ is marked for continuity and correlation,[122] and therefore it is more coherent to understand the meaning of πρὸ πάντων as creating a range of continued and correlated meaning for τὰ πάντα ἐν αὐτῷ συνέστηκεν. This is also more coherent with the subsequently linked αὐτός ἐστιν ἡ κεφαλὴ τοῦ σώματος τῆς ἐκκλησίας, a sentence kernel that has its own indicative verb but is still linked discursively via the καὶ connective.

The near proximity of an imperfective indicative (αὐτός ἐστιν) draws further discursive credence to an imperfective aspect of the συνέστηκεν being a questionable reading that imposes an understanding external to the evidence of the text. Last, the proposed reading that rejects a critical foundation for Marshall coheres with the contextual philosophical battles that some take to have been relevant in Colossae.

Marshall's epistemic theory is otherwise compelling and valuable. However, before extensive usage one ought to consider the dependence of his reliance on this verse and seek other bulwarks for his claims (or

---

122. Runge, *Discourse Grammar*, 57.

moderate the articulation accordingly). It is certainly reasonable to claim other support for a cosmic understanding of the ordering and meaningfulness of the Christ. However, Marshall's extensive preference for rooting the epistemic primacy of the affirmation of the Son on this verse introduces an area of possible refinement. If a novel ontological claim is given primacy, it demands the highest standard of authorization and authentication.

Kevin Vanhoozer

Vanhoozer defines proclamation in similarly categorical terms that are independent of the judging subject. In his work about the need for the community of faith to perform the doctrines of Christianity, he sets that the Trinity is the "ground, grammar, and guarantee" of the gospel.[123] Without discussing the epistemic primacy of the Trinity, Vanhoozer arrives at a similar conclusion that the Trinity is critical to any proper understanding of the gospel—namely, the concepts and meanings that are intended in the proclamation of the Christian faith. His preferred term for this authority is the "canonical imperative," serving as a "formal principle"[124] that is in practice important for classification and distinguishing improper/corrupt communicative agents.[125]

Vanhoozer recognizes the need to associate the truth and authority of the communicative act with the pure intentions of the agent themself. Accordingly, his model can distinguish between demons who recognize Christ and believers who are recognized in Christ.[126] Much of this work is dedicated toward an authentic versus nominal expression of the propositional content of the gospel. In this way, his *Faith Speaking Understanding* provides one potential option for an ontological and noncommunicative criterion that may assist in distinguishing human from AI systems as authors of proclamation, even with a formal principle.

It is notable to contrast Vanhoozer's success in providing a discerning criterion when discussing the response of a reader to the truth versus his problematic proposals for seeking meaning in a text.[127] When Vanhoozer is

---

123. Vanhoozer, *Faith*, 111.
124. Vanhoozer, *Faith*, 72.
125. Vanhoozer, *Faith*, 87.

126. Marshall also draws this distinction but observes that the demons hold a true belief about Jesus Christ despite their sincere intention it is not true.

127. Vanhoozer, *Meaning*, is referenced in several other locations in this research as problematic. Despite many seemingly positive contributions, his theory results in predicating certain human attributes of an author in order to produce a determinacy in a textual communicative act and justifies this as a moral obligation of the reader.

discussing responses to the authority of revealed canonical truths (proper performances), the uniquely human expression of being is elucidated. However, these same uniquely human predicates are then projected onto authors of texts that can be interpreted. This same strength becomes instead problematic when Vanhoozer suggests that the suitability of a text for interpretation makes certain necessary (not just sufficient) claims about the nature (humanity) of the author.

Donald Davidson

Most considerations of a speech community should be considered open to the subjective volition of the audience (so excluded from this class of closed justification), but Davidson suggests an important limit to this categorization. The speech community exists independently of the text and therefore will normally have its own norms and freedoms as independent of the text. However, realizing this, Davidson clarifies that "speakers belong to the same speech community if the same theories of interpretation work for them."[128] Meaningfulness in a text, or the ability/authority to understand a text may be predicated on certain shared horizons, worlds, or context pools. Regardless of the descriptive label given, there is a suggestion that part of the judgment of a text ought to be seen as properly related to the reality of the context of the utterance itself, independently of this being successfully communicated or encoded in the text itself.

Summary on Closed/Intrinsic/Nonsubjective Judgment

The procedure by which a reader recognizes and accepts a closed system would need to be factored into the considerations of how an AI system can meet the potential of generating text that relates to these closed systems. A reader may do so based on the perceived nature of the text (the intrinsic genre of Hirsch, or self-selecting interpretive communities of Davidson) or based on preexisting external commitments that are met in the conditions of the text (the formal principle and epistemic primacy of Vanhoozer and Marshall).

Research on a tangential use of closed justification systems—namely, the ability to generate well-structured mathematical proofs[129]—provides

---

128. Davidson, *Essential Davidson*, 192.
129. Lin et al., "Goedel-Prover."

optimism in the ability for AI systems to generate content that is coherent with Christian closed systems of justification.

In the case of commitments that are external to the text but preclude subjectivity based on certain conditions met within the text, the authority itself has been imported to the text and predicated on those conditions obtaining. For Marshall, it would be saying anything true (and be recognized as involving the Christian affirmations based on taking true and making this epistemically primary). For Vanhoozer, the suggestion is a need to use the grammar of the Trinity, which has been discussed in chapter 6 on concepts-meanings usage. Given an AI system can generate those concepts-meanings that are continuing the trajectory of the community's affirmations about the Trinity, both example criteria are met. Therefore, it should be considered a possibility that AI systems could generate proclamation that encodes and can be processed as closed-intrinsic justification.

Open—Extrinsic to the Utterance

Hays well articulates the apologetic concern of a judgment criterion that is external to the text itself, even when this text is the canonical Scriptures: "Unless we can give a coherent account of our methods for moving between text and normative ethical judgments, appeals to the authority of Scripture will be hollow and unconvincing."[130] It is unsurprising that many hermeneutics theories prefer a closed system that tries to remove the role of subjective prejudice/preconceptions from the equation (a recurring effort to refactor the hermeneutic circle). Alternatively, to describe the intersubjectivity of ethics, an open system for judgment is more apropos.

Some of the proponents of an open or external criterion of judgment are, as Hays suggests, in search of best defending and advancing the true confession of the Christ. Of course, other external systems may be entirely independent or even adversarial toward Christian faith. The primary focus at this point is not on those that are entirely independent of Christian confession, as these are also not suitably relevant for Christian proclamation by human agents.

Another possibility for an extrinsic judgment that is open to change is where the understanding is diachronic. One reasonable judgment of a text is based on evaluation of the truth criteria of the text, which is inherently a point-in-time evaluation of the truth conditions based on a set of contingent commitments.[131] These norms can, and in practice do, change over

---

130. Hays, *Moral Vision*, 3.
131. What Gadamer calls the "hermeneutic event." The event label also identifies

time. Hector explains that the normative justification of Christian beliefs is not a reckless relativism, because it is based on the continuation of the established normed trajectory of usage and with an ultimately divinely provided expression by Godself.[132] The implication is that the norms are not an endless repetition, much as a paradigm is a pattern for variety and not a rote enumeration of completeness. Paradigms provide the criteria for judgment of suitability but are open to evolution and change. When norms are the living expression of criteria put into practice by a presently living community, as with Lindbeck's cultural-linguistic rule theory or Vanhoozer's gospel-performing community of faith, the judgment becomes open to change and is constantly reauthenticated. Truth evaluations change, and this avoids totalitarian imposition of a new meaning upon a text. Quite critically, the changes in meaning arise from a diachronic dialectic from which the authoritative influence and contribution of a text is judged by the authentication involving parties and standards of truth strictly external to the text.

Many theories for open judgment either make the primary research of this thesis trivially true or are irrelevant to a specifically Christian proclamation,[133] but one of the more engaging concepts is implicature.[134] When the witches speak to Macbeth, their equivocation is intentional implicature. Christianity has an exegetical history with implicature due to the role of *sensus plenior* in some theologies of Scripture. The "fuller sense" of the text suggests there is a greater meaning intended by divine inspiration than the text itself was explicitly intended to carry by the author. It is interesting that in non-Christian circles, there is a parallel recognition that an author may imply more than was literally meant. This is often not limited to metaphorical use of language, nor by a defect or skill or intention, but perhaps by an intention to discuss a sense that itself evolves with time and context. We generally are writing or communicating about concerns that will endure far longer than the context of our message alone. Therefore, the relationship of the text to reality is liable to change with time.

Implicature gives the author responsibility and involvement in a meaning that was not directly intended purely in the immediate context. If one is to take a strictly ontological view of authorship predicated on perfect knowledge of the ontological status of authors, then it could even be suggested that all AI-system inferences are meaningful by the active

---

that any specific point in time evaluation will become lost in the "effective history" of the ongoing passage of time and linguistic activities.

132. Hector, *Metaphysics*, 231.
133. Due to subjectivity in judgment, or autonomy of the text.
134. Heck in Macdonald and Macdonald, *McDowell*, 27.

exercise of implicature—namely, that AI systems do not volitionally intend to communicate *anything at all*. They are instead designed and optimized to respond to prompting with linguistic skills that are contextual and range across literal to extremely metaphoric usage to convey a discursive goal (and intention). A text rich with implicature would be turned by a reader into a meaning that can exceed the volitional intention of the AI system. An AI would therefore imply what a human can mean. Both would functionally produce the same outcome—reader understanding—but do so with a different authorial responsibility and commitment to the response.

Summary of Justification

Justification of a text inquiries after the reasons why something has been written at all and is in the context of considering if the utterance should be taken true by the reader. When this is subjective and dependent on the reader themself making an assessment, the authority is more accurately described as wielded by the reader than the author or text. When the justification is grounded in some nature or objective conditions of the text, such as its intended genre or the content satisfying certain criteria for consideration within a specific truth system, then the text and authors have more authority (be it effective or not). A poem by nature of being a poem asserts that it ought not be read literally, and likewise a parable from the New Testament.

When a text is read based on the asserted closed-internal authority, the content itself gains a more precise relationship to the truth systems of the reader. The recognized relationship of a text to its justification can bring new understanding to the concepts-meanings, and it poses new obligations for how the organization of the text's concepts-meanings resonate with or diverge from the given positions of the reader. For the closed justification to be satisfied, the AI system must deliver the linguistic skills or context needed to satisfy the cause for that being realized in the text. For open justification, the authority is truly that of the reader, and hence no additional criteria are established to be met by the author (human or otherwise).

Summary: Implications of Authority in Proclamations

Christian proclamation poses unique and important challenges to the pre-existing notions of the reader. The authority of a Christian proclamation presents the reader with a totally fresh schema for understanding. For many thinkers and theories, accepting the truth of a Christian proclamation requires substantial conversion of existing priorities and sensemaking. Truth systems that are honorable or wise to humanity apart from Christ (1 Cor 1:23) may in turn not be coherent with the faith of Jesus Christ, and such has been the reality since the first proclamation of the Christ. Taking true and disquoting the proclamation of the Christ necessitates an immediate and significant recalibration of truth and obligates anticipation of still fuller revelation when we shall see Christ face to face (1 John 3:2). According to the faith of Christ, the believer anticipates a total ontological and ontic transformation upon the full realization of his person, and likewise the believer has been transformed in relationship to God in becoming a believer.

Taking true or holding true beliefs of a Christian proclamation requires a dramatic shift of one's truth priorities, and yet this appropriation of true beliefs is not identical with belonging to the covenant community by being united to Christ. Knowing him as Lord, even using our knowledge of him to work great miracles, is not identical with being known by him (Matt 7:21–24). Recognizing not only the qualitative but substantive difference between true beliefs and unity with Christ is critical to appreciating and implementing the lessons learned from this research.

The division between disquoting the Lordship of the Christ and being known by Christ is one of the most important factors raised by this research. Elucidating this point will motivate ways to hold to an ontological privileged position through participation in the divine for humanity within the community of faith. In terms of the cognitive-linguistic frameworks for meanings and concepts, AI systems are quite sufficient. Recurringly, the requisite linguistic skills have been shown to theoretically and practically be in the possession of AI systems. However, this ought not cause consternation. In meeting these varied criteria, AI systems have demonstrated little more than the demons and those who profess what they do not understand or choose to not believe-through-action. As Marshall notes,

> Theologians have regularly held that at least some people who hold credal sentences like "Jesus is risen" true nonetheless lack a true belief, but even on quite traditional grounds we may grant that Jesus' gracious self-presentation reaches them, and grants them too a true-belief. The tradition has usually supposed, after all (following Jas. 2:19), that even demons have a true belief in Jesus' resurrection. . . . People who hold "Jesus is risen" apart from the grace of God, or who do so even though they have spurned Spirit-wrought love, may also have a true belief. . . . Though the demons wish it otherwise, the gracious act by

which Jesus makes the belief that he is risen true extends even to them.[135]

Based on Marshall's observation, if proclamation is described as asserting true beliefs about the Christ, then proclamation is accessible to agents who have not received faith from Christ nor been reconciled to God through unity with Christ. Furthermore, these true beliefs, even communicated by individuals not belonging to Christ, can be such that the reader can responsively take these true. When taking true the true beliefs about the Christ, the individual-corporate reader accepts a truth system that is coherent with that of Jesus Christ, but this is distinct (necessary but not sufficient) for the experience of faith received from the Christ in which our life is hidden in his. To know the Christ as "Lord, Lord" and even to work miracles in his name is not identical with being known by the Christ (Matt 7:22). We should not remark or be surprised that even the rocks will cry out (Luke 19:40) about God as part of all creation groaning for his work to be completed (Rom 8:19–23).

One possible remedy for the difficulty of differentiating AI and human authors based on the evidence internal to the text is to limit the role expected of the text. Posed differently, this proposal would mean we theoretically and practically differentiate between the formal propositional proclamation and the experience and filling of faith.[136] Such a proposal arises from recognizing at this point from the data the limitations of linguistics, hermeneutics, and ethics to give a properly differentiated and ontologically privileged account of proclamation. Namely, there is a need for a discernment, a living enactment, a practical realization of the knowing of Christ that surpasses and is not identical with the propositional content circumscribed by the exercise of even the most profound linguistic skills. Paul was not always the most compelling speaker, yet he could speak with great authority because his authentication arose from the community of faith's life in the Spirit (2 Cor 3). Doctrine and propositional truth conveyed with compelling authority are not sufficient for unity with the death and resurrection of the Christ. Such is only affected by the Spirit, making true what was known through the subjective appropriation of what has been made available as a truth condition beyond all foolishness and human pride: the life, death, and resurrection of

---

135. Marshall, *Truth*, 251.

136. This is analogous to Wittgenstein's objection to Augustine's use of ostensive reference. His objection was that the learning child seems like an adult who already has a fully formed language yet needs to now understand how that is vocalized in a foreign land. The propositional material of proclamation is like this foreign language, which does not alone enable one to speak the language of faith, but gives one the capacity to learn the language game. Wittgenstein, *Philosophical Investigations*, para. 32.

the Christ. God's creation was an invitation to participation—extension by grace not by nature—of the relationships proper to the divine Persons.

By grace we are invited to participate in what is naturally true of God. We participate in an extension of the relationships that are proper to the divine Persons of God, and the realizing of this grace is the true authority, found or not. The text cannot affect this itself, but it can witness to this reality that is external to the self.

8

THE SPIRITUAL EVENT OF PROCLAMATION

> To those who through the righteousness of our God and Savior Jesus Christ have received a faith as precious as ours. (2 Peter 1:1)

THE PROCEEDING CHAPTERS HAVE addressed three factors that are expected of a human-authored text. The attributes of each were explored in the context of Christian proclamation and then used to evaluate AI-generated texts. The discussion thus far has been primarily focused on the textual depth of the communicative act that is proclamation, due to this being the area of greatest overlap and potential confusion. The primary focus of the last three chapters has been on the literary event. In this chapter, we will instead consider the spiritual event of Christian proclamation. The related criteria and expectations will, as done previously, be applied to AI-authored texts to determine how AI-generated texts will relate to the expectations that describe the spiritual event of proclamation.

The spiritual aspect sets proclamation apart from other human texts or literary events. The spiritual aspect describes proclamation as a unique event in which God's revelation works, and the author is participating in the divine will. AI will not be expected to have any more of a deterministic or guaranteed access to the spiritual event than a human proclaimer. Therefore, the question is not if AI can guarantee the spiritual event (for no human author can guarantee this either). Instead, this chapter will evaluate the ways an AI-generated text can relate to the potential spiritual event and compare this to the divinely contingent spiritual event of a human participating in the will of God to proclaim. The working definition did not include this consideration, but it can be added to our working definition as shown in the italicized example below:

> Proclamation is an utterance conveying concepts-meanings that, if taken true, would be consistent in a belief system that is also consistent with the faith of Jesus Christ. *When taken true, proclamation invites the spiritual experience of sharing truth with the physically absent and spiritually present Christ.*

1. What attributes are expected because Christian proclamation is a spiritual event?
2. What criteria describe these attributes?
3. How does AI text perform on the criteria:
   a. Elements
   b. Events
   c. Appropriation

In the initial drafts of this research, there was no explicit focus on the spiritual dimension of proclamation, to the detriment of the meaningfulness of this research to the community of faith. Without addressing this topic, one can abstain from engaging the entirety of this argument on the grounds that we've not discussed the most essential difference between proclamation and normal talk. My intention in the definition was to make clear that a faith that is consistent with that of Christ can be committed to acting upon truth values in no way less than taking up a cross daily and living for the filling up of the sacrifices lacking in Christ (Col 1:24). My intention in adding an explicit discussion of the spiritual element is to avoid an easy dismissal of this argument as unimportant and irrelevant.

It approaches brute hubris to put forward any type of sacramental model as a paradigmatic example within Christianity, and this endeavor is not meant to try such a feat. The goal is not to win acceptance for the model of the sacramental that is used herein; this would itself be a far more ambitious goal than any set forward in this research. Instead, the goal of the sacramental model is to address the unspoken questions about how the consideration of AI linguistic skills will respond to dialogue with the question of proclamation as sacramental event.

To discuss the spiritual event of proclamation, it will be important to first present a sacramental model. This is done for completeness of the discussion, as a sacramental event is the fullness of the interpenetration of the spiritual and created in the life of the believer. One does not need to hold that proclamation is itself a sacrament to agree that the expectations of a sacramental event are the highest standard of spiritual demands to place on AI-generated proclamation. Furthermore, this serves a benefit to the general intention of this research to demand a higher standard for all human participation in the proclaiming of truth about God, be proclamation labeled *sacrament* or not.

In the proposed working sacramental model, we will consider the elements, the event, and the appropriation of the incarnation of the spiritual and created. In a sacramental situation, there are ordinary elements that are specifically governed in their usage and participation in the transcendent. The event is a divinely orchestrated consecration and use of these elements that are necessary out of obedience but not out of identity with the event itself. God's freedom (spirit) acts in the sacramental event, using the elements God has provided (created). The benefit of the sacramental event is the facilitated appropriation, in which one recognizes the incarnational truth of the event and one's own created participation in the made transcendent. Certainly, there are alternative models for sacraments, and this is not meant to be adopted as a perfect model but as one that suffices for the goal of drawing out for contemplation the important spiritual aspects of what has been described in the taking true of faith that is consistent with the faith of the Christ.

Each of these considerations will intentionally expand the aperture beyond the focus on the proclamation as utterance of concepts-meanings that carry authority. The goal will be to consider the spiritual. Spirit(ual) is itself a controversial concept, and the best guard against misconception is a working definition (even if there is disagreement over the proposal). The working definition of spirit is *will-to-action that is not explained by immediate created contingencies*. What exists to drive our individual behavior if it is not the reaction nor historical reprisal of desire and fear explained by the created? The psychologist, sociologist, political scientist, and economist will struggle to put forward an answer, and this is the limit at which the spirit is revealed.

The discourse of the spirit cannot be one of substance, or else we arrive at a dualism where either body or spirit seems superfluous in a way that is alien to the coexistence of spirit and body that is in the Christ. A more Christologically sound division is between substance (body) and spirit (will, volition, intention). Spirit drives the world by producing real impacts of historical significance in the world without being explained by what is in the world. It is the driving of the world for truth claims and values that are unfounded in the world, for they are founded in the eternal divine will, and participated in by the community of faith. This participation in God being with us is the individual appropriation of the life of Christ, authenticated and authorized by expression in the world of the divine will. It rests on nothing less than living in the contexts and realities of contingent life bound as captive to the law of Christ. The spiritual birth of the believer means concrete living that is dead to explanation by the world and living that is in the world but from Christ because it is the eternal divine will for a community participating in his glory.

The believer is most alive in Christ when decisions are not made in a worldly discourse, but in the language of submission and participation in the eternal divine will that is fully manifest in Christ. Being and doing become united in having been done, which is the historically concrete union with Christ that is found in every moment of communion with Christ, be it sharing in his life, death, and resurrection, or proclamation of the kingdom of God by the authority of God. This is the spiritual experience that incarnates the physically absent but spiritually present Christ with the doing and historical reality of the community of faith, and it is in this that we worship God in spirit and in truth *in time*, even right *now* (John 4:23–24). Such worship is experienced today in the community of faith, whose union with Christ anticipates the fullest revealing of his will that the fullest agreement and expression of his spirit may be participated in by the community in him.

This definition of spirit is provided for means of clarity and description of the proceeding argument. Defense of its suitability cannot be made in this limited project. A fuller exposition over the meaning of spirit and the value of this model for Christology will be deferred to such a discussion. For now, the clarity ought to assist in making sense of the significance intended by the proceeding and ensuing arguments, particularly as the discussion increasingly revolves around the spiritual.

Last of the prefaced challenges is a procedural one. From the outset is the challenge of explaining the spiritual through the linguistic. This chapter was added to address the question of the sacramental but must be communicated through language that is again bound to the rules and limitations of language. In a pessimistic sense, it is like trying to describe one game while playing the rules of another. How can the spiritual realities—which were insufficiently addressed by a contemplation of utterances, concepts-meanings, and authority carried by a text—find adequate treatment by more words and more linguistic contemplation? Is such a proposal doomed from the outset, rejected for being insensitive to the subject matter?

Mediating the spiritual through language is fortunately not the objection to overcome. The objection is insufficient discussion—of a language-bound manner—of the spiritual realities of proclamation. This objective can be satisfied without reconciling the great divides over pneumatology or sacramentalism. This objective can be delivered with words. The project of addressing the spiritual can now begin with a clear purpose and with limited, reasonable expectations as to the endeavor.

ELEMENTS

The created elements are the beginning of our experience of the sacramental. Yet the very significance of the sacramental is that the experience of the created elements alone is far from exhausting the meaning of the sacramental. In baptism there is water. In the Eucharist there is bread and wine. These two are shared and common sacraments across a great diversity of traditions and unite what otherwise represents severe disagreement about other sacraments. These two are therefore of special importance and will be paradigmatic for proclamation.

Tillich writes of how the elements as non-sacramental creations give us a deeper understanding and appreciation of the sacramental.[1] In an abstract sense this is the same methodology as a narrative theology, or a typological reading of Christian truths. There is a specific meaning and value encoded in the original, and it is this meaning that has application to the sublimated form. This is in contrast to allegorical (and apocalyptic) interpretation. In allegory, the elements and their ordinary dynamics are not contributing to the meaning of the message. Instead, the surface elements must be mapped to the external references that they represent, and it is the dynamics of these external references that are meant by the seeming ordinary involvement of the elements in the text. While allegory believes a meaningful message is meant, it is only meaningful if the proper substitutions of models for representatives takes place before the real reading begins. For apocalyptic writing the intention is to preserve and propagate a message that the ruling authorities would never allow to be plainly said.

It is a class error to insist that what is true of realistic narratives applies uncritically to the sacramental. It is also unhelpful to reject the important observations about the dangerous and eisegetic and nondeterministic nature of allegorical readings. For the sacraments, there was an intentional choice by God for the elements. In the giving of sacramental instruction there is explanation provided by the Gospel presentations that asserts an early claim that the elements, their meaning as noninvolved elements, and their change

---

1. Tillich, *Protestant Era*, 95. Tillich is admittedly neither extremely orthodox nor preoccupied with the sacramental in most of his writing.

in status from ordinary to the sacramental contributes meaningfully to the illuminated message. The superposition is important because it speaks to the possible range of construction of the proper meaning achieved by the elements in their ordinary sense.

If it is accepted that the elements have a meaningfulness conveyed in their ordinary content, then the ordinary content is important to understanding the sacramental insights, even if this cannot exhaust the meaningfulness alone. In application to the primary research topic of AI proclamation, it is quite essential that the entire discussion about what constitutes the element (in this case, a communicative act of proclamation) is seen to contribute meaning to the sacramental sense. This permits discourse grammar, poetics, and other organizations of content that can and do obtain an authoritative claim on the audience. Our conclusion is that the ordinary and linguistic effects of the language itself is importantly pertinent to the sacramental sense, and not only as an encoded and shrouded message that is reducible to a different message, but as a positive data point about the meaning that is intended to be admitted into the consideration.

EVENT

The sacramental event describes a holy event involving an activity and elements that on their own are not. Not every meal is the Eucharist. Not every submersion in water is baptism. As Cyril of Jerusalem writes to the catechumen, "When ordinary water receives the invocation of the Holy Spirit and Christ and the Father, it acquires the power of holiness."[2]

The sacramental event is a special subset within a larger class of activities involving created things that do not qualify as holy. Therefore, there is an important discussion to be had about the relationship between the event itself and the elements.

The event has a self-prescribed degree of ambivalence toward the elements. Unpacking this, the sacramental event describes the elements and the ritual, providing a self-prescribed description of what is involved in the sacrament. The sacramental event expects specific things, and in the cultic period of the Old Testament, there were very numerous details about the proper condition of the elements involved in the ritual before God. Understanding the constraints and flow of permissiveness will assist in the process of relating the event to the elements themselves, which in turn will be useful for understanding the possible relationship between the text generated by

---

2. Yarnold, *Cyril of Jerusalem*, 3:3.

an AI system and the expectations for this text to be involved in a consecrated way in a holy event.

Expectations and limitations on the elements are not a limitation on the divine agency in the sacramental event, but an expression of obedience and the faithfulness of God's divine will to his promises (but not our deviations or imaginations). Who are we to say what God can and cannot do, or what he can or cannot speak through? As mentioned before, this hubris of limiting what God can speak through is not the intention but the entailment of biases against considering the possibility of AI generating proclamation or having a constructive and consecrated contribution to the covenant community of faith. To assert what God cannot do is a faulty framing. We ought to be describing what God has promised he will do.

Is it ever appropriate to assume we will go from the elements to the event? God shows us his attitude toward the elements on their own in his response to Judah's hollow cultic commitment. Repeatedly, the prophets express God's displeasure with sacrifices, even when they meet the extreme ordinances of the Old Testament cultic law (see Ps 40:6–8; 50:8; 51:16; Isa 1:11–31; Jer 7:21–23; Hos 6:6; Heb 10:4–10). Psalm 50:8[3] provides the most direct comment, as God expresses through the psalmist his displeasure despite not having specific offenses against the ritual elements or performance. Verses 9–13 explain why God is not fixated on the elements themselves: God created all the elements we can devote to him in sacrifice (v. 11). The elements are significant to us, but they are all already the possession of God. Therefore, the psalmist exhorts us in verses 14–15 to focus our attention

3. Ps 50:7–15 (ESV)

> 7 Hear, O my people, and I will speak;
>   O Israel, I will testify against you.
>   I am God, your God.
> 8 Not for your sacrifices do I rebuke you;
>   your burnt offerings are continually before me.
> 9 I will not accept a bull from your house
>   or goats from your folds.
> 10 For every beast of the forest is mine,
>   the cattle on a thousand hills.
> 11 I know all the birds of the hills,
>   and all that moves in the field is mine.
> 12 If I were hungry, I would not tell you,
>   for the world and its fullness are mine.
> 13 Do I eat the flesh of bulls
>   or drink the blood of goats?
> 14 Offer to God a sacrifice of thanksgiving,
>   and perform your vows to the Most High,
> 15 and call upon me in the day of trouble;
>   I will deliver you, and you shall glorify me.

on him so that ultimately his saving work will be to his own glory (v. 15). Meeting the sacramental criteria for the elements in terms of quality, consistency, or self-denial is insufficient to ensure acceptance by God. We cannot proceed from the qualities of the elements to the performance of the event.

Across these texts the case is made that God's acceptance, approval, and participation in the sacramental event depends on the event being directed toward him and not toward the elements themselves. The psalmist suggests that the acceptance of the sacramental event depends on the dependence of the event on God (see Pss 40, 50). Hosea similarly suggests that the pleasure of God is related to the knowledge of him, not the elements. It is a relational and God-centric criterion for the event. Even in the Jeremiah passage, where the focus is on obedience to the voice of God, the command is couched in the relational idea that God would be their God, and they would be God's people.

The passage from Hebrews is the most important for connecting these Old Testament observations to the consideration of the sacramental event in a post-resurrection context. The Hebrews text is discussing the atoning or expiating effect of the sacramental event, and the emphasis is again on the divine participation. The truly special case is that the sacramental event is both performed by God, and the elements that are provided are God "through the offering of the body of Jesus Christ once for all" (Heb 10:10ff.).[4] The body of Christ, which expresses the spirit of God in the concrete, tangible terms of humanity,[5] is offered as the element. The element offered also carries the explicit God-centric and God-active nature of this event, because the element pertains to the locus of God's spirit acting in the world. The sacrifice is more than a body (human), it is the sacrifice of a body

---

4. It is admittedly hard to differentiate between all the world belonging to God (being his possession) and the body of Christ, which is also arguably God's *possession* as it is the body of the incarnate God-Man. As much as our bodies are our possession, the body of Christ was Christ's possession, meaning it was God's possession. God is present in the body of Christ in a very different way than he is present or felt through his world (which is his creation but is not him himself). Much of this is avoided if instead of treating the spirit as an ontological subject or essence, we look at the spirit as a volitional expression through creation. The world is subject to the spirit of God because it is his original creation, but he does not imperatively act in every volitional action of creation. Even a strong providential view of the world's relationship to God's will can not abdicate all choices to God's decision without loss of all moral responsibility. Yet in the body of Christ, the spirit of the eternal divine will of God is expressed imperatively by choices to eat, drink, to heal, and to perform wonders. The body of Christ is special because it is also a specific locus of God's spirit being present and acting volitionally within the world.

5. "He [Jesus] is God's Wisdom and Power and Justice in substantial form." Yarnold, *Cyril of Jerusalem*, 4:7.

that expresses the will of God, and therefore the element is also authenticating the explicitly God-performed nature of the event. The supreme authentication and ultimate efficacy of the sacrifice that is Christ's body makes clear that the authorization of the sacramental is the spirit and will of God, for this is what makes the body of Christ uniquely important as a sacrificial element. Cyril of Jerusalem draws a similar conclusion about baptism when he reflects that it was the baptism of Jesus himself that made baptism holy.[6] It is the leading by God that we can participate in which makes the event sacred.

Therefore, the most important question about the sacramental event is the participation or involvement of the will of God (the spirit) such that the elements are participating in an event that is only possible by God. Based on this criterion, the activity of a nonhuman is less prone to error, and more suitable for use by God. As stipulated, there is no compelling God,[7] nor limiting what elements God can use. However, when the event is pleasing to God, it has been noted that the agency of the event and the focus of the event will be on God. In the case of AI, the focus would not be on a human author (although it could be on a human performer, in the case of spooky proclamation at a distance).

Human expectations and self-centeredness often get in the way of our experiencing and participating in God's sacramental events. In a paradoxical outcome, the conditions that inhibit humanity's participation in sacramental events are decreased due to the emerging situation of AI-generated texts. This research has proposed a realistic specter of a coming generation who has a general distrust in authorial intention and texts. The prevalence of AI-system-generated content, in concert with our natural inclination to trust this content until realizing we've trusted and predicated things of an AI author, will expectedly produce a new source of distrust for texts and their determinate meaning or preservation of authorial intention. However, if the trust is not in the text or the author, then meaning and trust must be placed somewhere else. This research has motivated an urgent search for these sources of authentication and meaning outside of the text, author, and reader.

This erosion of trust will produce important new hermeneutic processes for authenticating the meaning in a text, which shall be proposed in the conclusion (primarily leaning on the idea of a story-formed community

---

6. "Jesus made baptism holy when he was baptized himself. . . He was not baptized in order to receive pardon for his sins, for he was sinless; but, sinless though he was, he was baptized in order to confer divine grace and dignity on the baptized." Yarnold, *Cyril of Jerusalem* 3.11.

7. Only God compels himself by his own action in the crucifixion.

and the role of this external community's life in Christ to authenticate and authorize the message itself). While potentially problematic if we insist naïvely on authorial intention as the bedrock of meaning, this situation does not need to be problematic. It can instead mean greater emphasis on the story-formed community and communion with God in the covenant community of faith. It can mean we turn away from the idols of propositional logic, and instead of trusting in our purity of terminology depend on God for the sacramental event. Instead of being assured every time we read the text and preach from the pulpit that we're speaking the word of God, we instead usher in a renewed age of meekly seeking God with fear and trembling. We are not entitled to see God or spread his word. Yet he has promised to do so, and therefore with great anticipation we can depend on God in a far more beautiful way than we once may have depended on our own systems of knowledge. Ultimately, the refinement of these propositional forms has produced the current state of affairs wherein it is now made clear the complete dependence on God so that he would be glorified means that we cannot insist on any human control. Our participation and involvement are no more assured than the words of AI in a sacramental event that is pleasing and used by God. We are blessed by both and regardless, because it is God who is moving, and it is to God that our focus now is dedicated.

From this sight on God as the exclusive focus and agency that makes the event effective, we turn to the human-centered appropriation, wherein we receive what God has provided.

APPROPRIATION

The appropriation of the sacramental event is often seen as parallel to the soteriological process/progress of the believer walking with Christ, and thus it is common to describe the sacramental in transactional and stative terms. The theories of infused or imparted righteousness label two respective efforts at modeling the sacramental event in transactional terms that can be understood and approached from our creaturely vantage point. Marketplace or transactional metaphors for salvation and for the sacramental involvement in the life of the believer are intentionally and explicitly transactional in nature. Relational terms often have overtones of transaction, such as adoption into the family of God, which are in addition to the stative intransitive aspect. Terms of victory often reflect an intransitive stative change, which carries a similar but different *Aktionsart* as does a transitive transactional activity; this follows, given that the model of *Christus Victor* is based on Christ as the subject (versus the human, who is seeking to understand the sacrament in terms of receiving something). Judicial metaphors are highly stative in basic semantic sense, yet the description of these stative changes is often described in transitive language, such as receiving or granting justice. Across the diversity of metaphors that are used for salvation and therefore have strong affinity toward the sacramental, there is a mix between the stative and transactional, an insight that helps model the appropriation of the sacramental event.

The appropriation of the sacramental event is biblically described in all the types of metaphors described above. Accordingly, the sacramental event is described mutually in *Aktionsarts* that mix the transitive and stative. Appropriation means personally participating in such a sacrament, one that is divinely ordained (elements described by God) and divinely enacted as event (the will of God to make the elements holy for his purpose). At the point of receiving, neither the elements nor the event is exclusively known in their created nature. The elements are made holy by God's event, which is his free choice to do more than the human actions. It is his grace to allow our human actions to accordingly participate in a result and event that is greater than the human action or created elements itself. Given the transcendence of the sacramental event over the ritual-action and elements, what does the ability to appropriate the sacrament depend upon? In the context of proclamation, what does proclamation depend on to be a holy and consecrated communicative act in which God sublimates the words and the performance?

Hauerwas provides a powerful synopsis of a very related descriptive task, which will be quoted at length due to its firm agreement with the direction of this program of thought:

> For it must be remembered that it is not the preacher who makes the sermon efficacious. To think that would be but the form of *ex operator operans* applied to the preached word. Rather, for the preached word to be God's word the Holy Spirit must make us a body of people capable of hearing that word rightly. Put differently, the preached word's power is its capacity to create a people receptive to being formed by that word.[8]

It is fair to object that this description of the dimension of appropriation is simply a restatement of the prior argument about the authority of a proclamation. If it was unconvincing when stated in terms of authority, then perhaps it will again not be convincing from the pen of Dr. Hauerwas. The argument is that the words themselves cannot alone produce the appropriation of the truth claims to a meaningful effect in the audience. It is

---

8. Hauerwas, *Hauerwas Reader*, 159.

never the words themselves, yet the words play an instrumental role that has been designed and authorized by God to bring us to the point of the claim that Christ's faith makes in our lives. The propositions do not produce repentance, but they do provide a prophetic claim on the life of the receiver. In this way, they give the receiver language they can use to explore the experience that can only be truly satisfied by the revelation of God through his express will.

The effectiveness of proclamation depends completely on the revelation of God being accepted and taken true by the receiver. However, this taking true is not only a stative result that can be affected in a vacuum, but also a transitive appropriation. God has intentionally called forward his covenant community of faith, the *body of* Christ, to facilitate much of the transitive nature of appropriation. The invisible stative changes and dispositional changes in terms of spirit find their reification in the language games of the community of faith. The rules, the behaviors, the lived story of the community of faith are an expression of the Spirit of Christ still in the world and thus are truly fitting of the biblical metaphor of being Christ's body. Truly serving as Christ's body allows for the church to be both the element and the authenticator of the event, because truly serving as and being Christ's body means that his divine will is ordering and directing the priorities and lived reality of the church.

Appropriation of a sacrament comes from participation in an event that is authenticated and authorized by the holy moving of God. It produces a change in the state of the participants and grants them both experience and new possessions. The medium in which these new possessions and experiences are expressed is the modality of the church. The community of faith is a critical participant in the individual's participation in the sacramental experience and the understanding of how to appropriate and individually take true the faith of Christ. Therefore, the consideration of the sacramental aspects of proclamation has been most fruitful. They have led to considering how the story-formed community of faith is a critical facilitator for God's sacramental activity and, subsequently, have motivated the consideration that experience of and life within this community might be a critical means to the authentication of the meaning of the text beyond the authorial intention alone, and through this authentication a means to the authorization of this meaning based on the divine will of God. In a generation where authors can no longer be provisionally granted special status based on reading a text, it is critical to have found this biblically rooted further criterion for trust of the meaning and applied interpretation of a text.

9

DRAWING CONCLUSIONS

Proclamation is an utterance conveying concepts-meanings that, if taken true, would be consistent in a belief system that is also consistent with the faith of Jesus Christ. When taken true, proclamation invites the spiritual experience of sharing truth with the physically absent and spiritually present Christ.

THIS RESEARCH HAS HIGHLIGHTED various general areas and specific exploits by which existing frameworks for linguistics, interpretation, translation, hermeneutics, ethics, and theology may be used to argue that AI systems currently are, or are capable of being, equivalent to human authors in producing Christian proclamation. This has involved analysis of various thinkers regarding three primary constituents of proclamation: being an utterance, conveying concepts-meanings, and asserting authority. Various thinkers were considered to identify and address important attributes within each, together contributing to an expansive set of criteria related to Christian proclamation. My research has sought to put these theories in dialogue with recent academic findings about the capabilities of AI systems. The result shows how these attributes are satisfied by AI systems that already exist or would be feasible given current technology and contingencies.

The data affirms a reality in which AI systems can behave in a manner surpassing the distributional-semantics hypothesis. It is therefore critical that we review the systems and schools of thinking presented here. The frameworks and thinkers reviewed prepared their systems based on the best data available at their time. At that time, it was a safe, logical maneuver to make assumptions about only authors with humanity (and the resulting image of God) being capable of producing coherent, meaningful, and authoritative texts.

The conclusion of AI proclamation is not explicitly problematic once remediation has been taken for the variously involved theories. Various approaches accept a distinction between the propositional content and the experiential reality of faith, and this division may firewall AI capabilities from a more objectional conclusion. Bultmann summarizes well the need for something beyond proclamation: "The 'word' of proclamation tells me 'nothing more than what I already knew in my profane self-understanding.' . . . What 'more' then does the man of faith know? This—that revelation has actually encountered him, that he really lives, that he is in fact graced."[1] In general, the dialectical theologians express a high view of God's freedom and the contingency of experiencing the word of God on his freedom, which encourage the need for more than the propositional content of proclamation.

More problematic are the cases where the framework or thesis logically derives from human attributes of the author and therefore creates a necessary or sufficient relationship between conclusions about a text and the nature of the author. In the case of human attributes in an author being a necessary protasis,[2] these theories open the likelihood of projecting human attributes to AI systems, compellingly led by the empirical results of AI systems producing proclamatory texts. When these author attributes are a sufficient protasis,[3] the argument derived from human attributes of authors becomes extremely problematic in logically conferring human attributes to AI systems. The open question, and the automatic conferral, merit further critical consideration.

BEYOND AUTHOR, TEXT, AND READER

This investigation has raised the question of Christian truth and faith being beyond full expression by the relationship of author, text, and reader. If there is some meaningful difference between a human speaking by their free will and that individual speaking a text generated by an AI system, then the truth of that distinction lies in a truth content outside of the parties of

---

1. Bultmann quoted in Thiselton, *Two Horizons*, 228.

2. Meaning that the authors must have attributes, but that having these attributes does not automatically qualify the author to produce proclamation.

3. The logical argument creates an exclusive relationship between the text manifesting various linguistic skills and the various, often human, attributes of the author.

author, text, and reader. Perhaps there is something about the performance of an AI-generated text that relates the AI system to the human performer—for instance, in the mutual taking true or in the secondary illocutionary action of repeating an AI-generated text. However, even without the case of a performance, there are foundational theories and practices that incline human recipients toward taking true the content of linguistic skills.

Some of the reviewed systems posit an additive truth not exhausted or completely encoded in the relations of author, text, and reader. Plantinga's concept of warrant is a theologically grounded theoretical example. In Vanhoozer's *Faith Speaking Understanding*, it is the intentional imitation[4] that is the product of and the content of the gospel message that stands outside of the cognitive communicative act. For Rommen, the model of an icon as being what it also represents through being-in-absence provides yet another option to shift the equations of parties involved and seek a differentiation otherwise not possible when limited to reader, text, and author. These approaches either avoid an explicatory dependence on linguistic skills[5] in a text or make an additive condition necessary and therefore the force of differentiation.

Results of this investigation also raise a question about the degree to which these extensions are actually problematic. For ease of communication this research has consistently passed the judgment that it is problematic to project human attributes onto an AI author. Yet this is not inherent. The observation that an AI system can produce linguistic skills may be seen as an affront to the understanding of God creating man in his own image, yet I posit (but have no need to defend at this point) that a coherent and theologically sound truth system could be reasoned about that sees the perpetuation of God's image in humanity in the expression of humanity's will, and thus a potential for even the creations of humanity to bear some likeness of God (direct creations or indirect amalgams like culture and AI systems).

An almost directly opposed suggestion is raised by Marshall, Hays, and others that reason about how demons can communicate the truth of the Christ. This observation from the Scriptures supplies the logical parallel that an AI system is less intrinsically difficult of a concept than demons knowing

---

4. Reminiscent of Aristotelean *mimesis*.

5. When avoiding dependence on linguistic skills, there is a common preference for the positional versus the propositional. Truth is based on relationship and position in Christ, not propositional cognitive expression. This is similar to the distinction between knowing/applying norms and living a life that is above the reproach of such norms. Ethics, morality, and hermeneutics again reflect their commerce of a common good for the community of faith—namely, participation in the living revelation that is the Christ.

the truth of the Christ more acutely than many of those who watched Jesus cast out demons.

For those who are human and confessing Christ, it is clear that not all who speak of Christ truly do so from having taken true the very words they speak. When individuals do take the Christian proclamation as true, they may still, from impure motives and intention, preach what is the truth (Phil 1:15–8). Selecting between these and other proposals was not the priority of this research. These possibilities, alongside unnamed others that are likewise copacetic with AI systems being equal to human authors in Christian proclamation, are the next important consideration to reason about for anyone inclined to implement the conclusions from this research by finding additive criteria to prioritize outside of the bare linguistic skills of proclamation.

Another tactic specific to theories that produce problematic conclusions when extended to reason about AI systems is one of precise removal of extraneous predicates. We can ask what is lost by not having the offending predicates. I have observed and argued that many logically derive conclusions from these human predicates (for example, determinacy of a text based on a singular contextual intention of an author); in acute cases this necessary or sufficient explication may be avoidable. By omitting the overly generous statements about authors based on a text alone (the text as it stands received) or the effect on/through a reader alone (predicating of the author based on the subjective response), these models can be potentially remediated and rehabilitated. This tactic would need to find alternative approaches, or a means of expanding the scope, for topics like authorial intent, determinate meaning, and textually inductive ethics.

The Fourth Dimension (Time) as a Fourth Member to the Party

One of the most promising answers to the three-person problem of author, text, and reader is to provide an external, public source that can create an authority claim between the parties. One of the well-established options in the Christian community is to the story-formed community. The individual and corporate lived commitments authenticate and manifest the truth of the gospel claims, just as they did in the very first evangelistic communities.

Stanley Hauerwas's program of the story-formed community is one such formulation. He shows how we might appropriately expand what is considered critical for interpretation and meaning of texts. The concept of a story-formed community makes it possible to locate a critical depth and aspect of meaning outside of the triad of author, text, and reader. Furthermore, the lived experience of the community creates a historicity and lived commitment to the truth claims of the text. The most difficult case—spooky proclamation at a distance—can be largely remediated by investigating if the performing human is living a commitment to the meaning presented in the text. Furthermore, if the community of faith flourishes in commitment to the faith of Christ through the experience of AI-generated texts, then there is the clearest argument that the case against their use was misplaced.

Without remediating the state of authorial intention, there is the severe and pressing risk of generations where all trust in the author is eroded, which becomes misplaced into an erosion of all confidence in the meaningfulness of the biblical texts. As readers experience the distrust of realizing an author was an AI and not human, it tarnishes the respect and moral responsibility that Vanhoozer urges toward authors. If the primary defense for the meaningfulness of a text lies in the author, then the distrust of the author will deal a critical hermeneutic damage.

It is critical to consider how a proposal making use of a story-formed community has the potential to avoid this critical erosion of the foundations for confidence in the meaningfulness of the biblical text. The same staunch defense that rests in authorial intention will no longer hold. A failure to adapt and adopt viable ways of expanding the aperture beyond the triad of author, text, and reader will be a failure to respect and protect the proclamation of the biblical text. A biblically and historically founded program such as that of Dr. Hauerwas becomes even more compelling given the dire consequences of the impact of AI linguistic skills on the assumptions and argumentation of other hermeneutic theories.

10

FINAL EXHORTATIONS

FOR LINGUISTICS, THIS RESEARCH urges a new focus on diachronic development of language in a heterogeneous and directed, but not uniform, manner. This data suggests the need to reintroduce the complexities of individual idiolect evolution into the general population. Furthermore, linguistics as a field would benefit from continued consideration of language in a nondistributional semantic model, by which we may evolve past the existing simplistic frameworks. In a crude analogy, linguistics has been working with a semantic model that approximates the precision of Newtonian physics. Additional frames of reference and chaotic modeling of semantics are arguably the only effective means of modeling mathematically the distribution of norms within a complex pre-normed community. Such goes beyond the argument of this research, but is raised in hopes of further analysis, such that linguistics would benefit from AI in a manner commensurate to the benefits to AI from implementing general linguistics and functional grammar.

Based on these findings, my hope would be that the field of hermeneutics will increasingly introduce dimensions that speak to alignment of the response to the lived intentions of the author.[1] One major deficiency that AI highlights is lack of a lived responsibility in both the author and the recipient, which simply extends the claims of thinkers like Vanhoozer who argue for a moral obligation on the reader. Hermeneutics will likewise be enriched by considering the range of response to be connected to the

---

1. Not only based on the "intention" of the author (which may degrade into a self-fulfilling prejudice and historical normativity), but in response to the author's lived commitment to the authority of their own writing and call to write.

meaning through the significance's distance from the motivation and continued expression of the author.

It was potentially naïve and is now dangerous to assert there is one right meaning of a text, or that a meaning is purely propositional in the text. The most dangerous is when discerning a singular determinate meaning means the reader must project attributes onto the author. To avoid a two-tiered[2] system where the Scriptures and potentially a sphere of non-canonical important texts (like the creeds and confessions) get a different hermeneutical treatment than others, we should adopt an understanding of meaning as permeated in the whole self. The dimension of alignment in implication/significance (as lived directionality) and the dimension of completeness of this self-commitment to this implication (the magnitude of this lived direction) give us an ethical hermeneutics. How much is the self, and self-in-community, directed toward a meaning that is concomitant and furthering of the meaning of this community. Such does not obviate the technical details of analysis. Such considerations, instead of replacing, add depth to the consideration of meaning from a text, permitting a higher veracity than a muddled projection of all this into an overloaded determinate meaning of a text. This project has not sought to oppose or challenge existing hermeneutic models, but in evaluating this data will hopefully motivate continued innovation and creativity without such susceptibility to problematic applications in the age of AI.

These areas of investigation would also encourage and allow ethics to become a matter of selecting what has primacy in this community: in practice it would be a lived hermeneutic.[3] Several of Paul's letters make a rhetorical point to emphasize his prior suffering for the gospel before then teaching a similar submission to the call of Christ. Paul's evident authority is his own example, much as it is explicitly explained in 2 Cor 3. The authentication of his message is evidenced in his behavior and also in the lived behavior of the community, for it is in the community's lived reality that the Spirit is completing his creation and fulfilling the promises of the Father to create a covenant community that exists participating in and enjoying the life of the Son. Our ethics has meaning because it is the revelation of God in us, by our participation in God with us.

---

2. Likewise, this same tiered system is produced by Hirsch's idea of an intrinsic genre, which is given practical expression in Frei's model of the New Testament as realistic narrative.

3. If our understanding of meaning is an appreciation of the truth of reality and our relation to it, then the individual and corporate dimensions of understanding ought to be ideal for our ethical obligations.

FINAL EXHORTATIONS

To be confident that to die is gain is predicated on the truth foundation and lived reality that to live is Christ. For one to believe that to die is gain (and the measure of their assurance) is dependent on continued living being Christ. Authentication of the proclamation "to die is gain" finds its strongest proof in continued life being Christ. The perfect and tautological exemplar of this is of course the Christ going through death and making his own death paradigmatic of the faith one enters by faith coherent with his faith.

If we accept that the only proper norm for the Christian faith is proclamation that, if accepted, is coherent with the faith of Jesus Christ, then it means that the Christian existence is a journey of constantly seeking the faith of Christ. We can't stop in any doctrines or any contextualization, orthodox or otherwise. It is neither an easy entrance nor a heavy load. The seeking after the Christ is, paradoxically, constantly true and only eternally completed, for we must keep engaging him to know what he takes true.

The Christ is the superposition of living and truth, and this raises concerns for trying too easily to resolve the three-body problem of author, text, and reader. The Christian knows that none of these three are truth. Echoing thinkers like Herrmann and Bultmann who were reacting in their own ways to a dogmatism ignoring culture, this research suggests that ideas and propositions and words alone cannot produce or carry faith; our receipt of revelation is always by God revealing himself. Each of the three participants in communication—author, text, reader—are at best a facsimile trying to model the truth that is the Christ. Furthermore, despite none of these parties being the truth, the hermeneutic circle compels readers in language and understanding to constantly move from the provisional to the full understanding.

For some this may seem like skepticism (not finding truth in the text, author, or reader). However, there is a decision and faith in truth—they are simply located beyond the three bodies of a communicative act. Marshall's epistemic theory is therefore similar in the location of primary truth, although he from this concludes and supports other epistemic truths as conveyed in propositions. This research begs a question of his maneuver, which uses the formal logic of language to extend from the epistemic primary content of the Trinity. Language and formal logic are derivative of language as use: the rules governing our logical assertions are derivative of language as use and the desire for clear communication (the purpose of public vs.

private language). Tarski has wonderfully articulated formal logic for formal languages but has not described reality.[4]

The discord between his formal logic and reality (for instance, the observation of Cotterell and Turner that terms mean different things through time) reflects that we're playing a language game versus constructing reality. The logical derivatives and explication that rely on language as public and clear communication (for example the charity principle compelling taking true in order to take false) is a neat observation of language, but where it diverges from description of reality (vs. description of language usage), we ought to realize it reflects the general problematic reliance on the rules of words as use instead of the roles of reality.

To be less theoretical and pedantic, a concrete example is the relation of the people of Israel to the law. The law was provided as a pedagogical example from God, yet the apocalyptic mind of humans saw the law as written as an expression of life (even personifying the law as coming to the earth). As words written on tablets, it could not really be the real life unestranged from God. The reconciled life that participates in God's divine will came with the incarnation of the Son. No life (reality) was found in the internal rules of the law, but these words served as preparation and begged the seeking for the living truth that was the goal. Law was descriptive of but not normative of the Christ; the rules of Christ's life cannot be expressed in the law and therefore Paul writes instead of fulfilling or "filling up the law of Christ" (ἀναπληρώσετε τὸν νόμον τοῦ Χριστο, Gal 6:2 SBLGNT).

---

4. This importantly differs from Wittgenstein's reflections on his own formal logic in *Tractatus*, as exhibiting a "preconceived idea of crystalline purity" of logic would not properly model language. The contention is that our very notions of logic and coherence are derivative of a wish to communicate publicly and effectively. Our use of language is not necessarily or inherently fitted to modeling truth. Our goals in using language will cause us to, at times, prefer to operate by approximation and fuzziness. Anscombe's very pertinent observation is that Wittgenstein's logic depends on simple objects, and "the simple objects are presented as something demanded by the nature of language" while this presence in language cannot be axiomatically proven. Anscombe in the introduction to Wittgenstein, *Tractatus*, 29.

The resulting models of truth look like and can learn from paraconsistent[5] models of logic.[6] Unlike classical logic, many paraconsistent models are evidence preserving and therefore can accommodate inconsistency (of evidence) without exploding into the triviality of equally asserting all claims. These models provide a means for evidence to be carried forward across time and contexts, and therefore for the global resolution of contextual/local inconsistency. Hector's model rejected a correspondence theory of truth but still held to a form of diachronic coherence. Marshall's model was based on the classical logical formulations of Tarski. In both cases, the approach to truth at a global level produces challenges dealing with the reality of changing evidence. In a religious context, rule-based models like Lindbeck's are an attempt to deal with an absolute truth that has changed over time and is, at any given time in the global Christian community, applied inconsistently. If these are taken as expressions of evidence within a paraconsistent model, then we can hold to a biblical view of truth and a realistic-pragmatic model of evidence that is still *seeking understanding* versus being identical to absolute understanding.

My proposal is more analogous to the dialectical theologians who posit a private and contingent nature of revelation (to the chagrin of Wittgenstein). A paraconsistent view of truth would begin by setting aside coherence as pertains to *evidence*, or as pertains to sentences/claims that have not yet been absolutely committed. Ambiguous or disputed claims do not need to be fully resolved until the eschatological time horizon without disputing the possibility of this truth when understood from Godself.[7] Paraconsistency separates the concerns between our linguistic practices, which generally do not need to conform to classical logic, and the cause of consistency and truth (the ineffable and beyond-fully-knowable-in-time other: God). Various thinkers have leveled challenges against the overly cozy relationship in

---

5. In a paraconsistent logical model, there is the potential existence of contradiction without the invalidation of a class of true and false statements. In classical logic, if we accept a contradiction, then the entire system dissolves into true statements. Dissolving into a degenerate form is due to falsity being defined by contradiction. If language is taken to be related to use, then its truth-system may be taken to allow for contradiction in some part of the system without forfeiting a division between true and false. The viability of a paraconsistent model for language is already argued by the existence of contronyms, which are a case in English of words that have contradictory polysemy. The argument continues that the truth content of language is not bound by the law of the excluded middle, and therefore a classical logical structure is forced, unnatural, and ineffective in describing language and our language-driven engagement with reality.

6. This theory is also compatible with stipulating ontological or revelatory truth outside of the three parties of the direct accident of the communicative act.

7. This would cohere with the idea of the Father seeing the hidden expressions of the faith of Christ in our lives. See Matt 6.

which the "literal" meaning of language is confused with the empirical sense of the referents of language (e.g., Levinas, McDowell).

By my proposal, evidence resolves into truth in God; until we are resolving the evidence in the fullness of God, we are unable to fully resolve the potential semantic and evidential inconsistencies. The covenant community that is living united to the very faith of Christ can make meaningful assertions while in the presence of mutually exclusive claims and evidence. Jesus is aware of what is only known by the Father (see Matt 24:36), and we humbly admit we are no more linguistically cavalier than our Master. We need not forfeit a locus of truth within God. The brilliance of a paraconsistent logic is that triviality is avoided without reducing our reasoning about immediately inconsistent truth claims to a naïve assumption of immediate and homogenous normativity. Paraconsistency allows for the localized inconsistency within an overall system that in sufficient scope converges into consistency.

For texts, my proposal means that the resolution of truth is no longer bound to the text itself. There is a temporal aspect, which accommodates and aggregates the sustained living reality of the community. The influential AI text is proven by its works. If an AI text being proclaimed leads to the building up of the community that belongs to Christ, then not only have the textual criteria been met, but the spiritual event has been satisfied. No angels in heaven ought to hold back their applause at the believer united to Christ with support and motivation by such an event.

My proposal also has the potential to assist in modeling the changes of norms in the community. The challenge of metaphors, and that of how new norms are distributed within a normative community, suggested there is potential for a tension between the global truth and the local optima. Shared public norms (like ordinary language) become the common medium in which specific permutations and deviations grow up from localized phenomenon to accepted norms and meaning. Truth in this sense is neither exclusively from *langue* nor from *use*. Illocutionary or perlocutionary effects are properly distinguished from the truth of the claims, and the object of a text (the literary intention) is distinguished from a cognitive or volitional "intention" by the author. Our interaction with AI systems is language-bound but not bound along lived, shared epistemic commitment, thus a paraconsistent model is well suited to describe what is happening and to minimize confusion or disillusionment. A paraconsistent model takes a different approach than those considered above. It demands a more nuanced epistemology, assimilation, and diffusion of truth than Marshall's epistemology, where he gives epistemic primacy to the revelation. The paraconsistent view means the reader is no longer thrown into moral commitments toward the author, as with the hermeneutics of Vanhoozer. Vanhoozer stipulates a deterministic meaning in a text with no provision for the truth to perpetually elude and yet converge all parties eschatologically into a shared and common communicative act. My proposal rejects the false assurance of human correctness-by-collective-agreement, permitting the real possibility of there being "none, not one" (Luke 18:8, Rom 3:10) who is a Christian at some points of time before the divine will completes its work. Assurance is not in a human model or proof of efficacy, but by dependence on an active relationship with the living God. God alone is both life and truth as one, and it is in him and fully knowing him that the fullness of evidence resolves to truth.

Such a system of truth and meaning would dramatically change ecumenical reconciliation. Paraconsistent Christianity is anathema to the denominationalism and closed fellowship of evangelicalism in the US in the twenty-first century. Despite the labels it will attract, paraconsistent Christianity explains the never-static diffusion of truth in the Christian normed community. We can reason about the tension of corporate norms with the individual reality of any individual engaging the text, based on the final commitment to language as use instead of truth telling. This proposal then connects to the application made possible in the story-formed community.

PROPOSED WAY FORWARD

A rewarding remediation is the notably missing aspect of this research. The story-formed community proposed by thinkers like Hauerwas, MacIntyre, and Fish provides ample consideration of such a community capable of such remediation and endurance. The community's story and narrative become an expression of truth external to the author, reader, or text. The lived commitments of the human participants give lived justification claims for the language events that are performed, regardless of the origin. The original author of a text becomes less important than the performance by individuals in the community who have demonstrated their commitments and values through shared historical experience. Paul did not write to the Romans and send another unknown person to deliver the letter and perform it before their community. The letter was efficacious because it was performed by individuals who were trusted. We cannot know the hearts of the original hearers, but we should wonder how much they cared about the letter being from this personally distant Paul, versus this being a letter that was committed to by the performers who were known to the community in Rome.

For Christian proclamation, each party (the author, the reader, and even the text) has responsibility and a relationship to consequences. Each is actively involved, but the power of the authority, the historical expression and telic fulfillment, and the very ability to utter what has been revealed by God are fully, necessarily, and exclusively εν Χριστώ. Expression of what is in Christ comes forward by the community that is called his body. Success beyond the communication of beliefs, namely the making true of the ontological reality that is the Christ who creates a new covenant community participating in his divine glory and living, is the event of meeting and participating in the now-known Jesus Son of God. We cannot alone speak the linguistic event that is the Christ, but we can participate in the communication act by which we speak the reality that is known by faith to those who have experienced the event that is the Christ.

> The primary if not exclusive distinction between human proclamation and AI-generated proclamation is a lived commitment to the truth claims of the utterance.

Speaking plainly to the ministers, preachers, and teachers of the community of faith: it is hypocrisy to call it "proclamation" or "preaching" every time we read aloud from the Bible and yet are not living proof of the truth in these words. If the Spirit is blessing us to participate in an event of proclamation, our participation in this proclamatory event is the proof of this transformative faith in our own lives. How can we preach that the faith of Christ transforms lives if our own are not changed one dint? You hypocrites who say, "Let us now read from the word of God," and proceed to preach what your own ears do not hear and lives do not say! You hypocrites who are so quick to say that AI cannot preach as you preach because it does not have the same *intention* in its words! Live to the standard you know to be right. You are quite right that we ought to teach that the meaning of texts is not exhausted by their propositional logic, but this must be applied to your own lives as much as you apply it to AI. If you resist being transformed by the faith that demands complete obedience and submission to the life of Christ, then you are neither teaching nor preaching the faith of Christ. Suffer for the faith you preach and you will proclaim a truth worth dying for, and know that your words were given, not by human desires, but by the Spirit and fulfilling the will of Christ.

Speaking plainly to academics, it is profoundly dangerous to insist on authorial intention as the key to meaning and insist on a general hermeneutic that applies across all texts. Can your well-trained eyes see that

AI-generated texts will destroy this charade of authority? Set aside for a moment your presuppositions about inspiration and biblical infallibility; these are secondary or tertiary claims that are not the first-order meaning of the text. Think of how a new generation, raised immersed in AI-generated texts, will interact with meaning; think about this and empathize with their plight instead of rejecting these children as foolish! Know that they will be unable to trust like you do as they form their epistemic commitments and hermeneutic heuristics in a word of implicit distrust for an author and a text. Authorial intention is not some sacred first-order faith claim. The Christ witnessed to in the biblical text insisted on the movement of God through these words to produce his covenant community. Help the future generations worship God in spirit and in truth, not with hollow series of words that no longer have their authority. When the crowds remarked about the authority of Christ, it was not his flowery words; his teaching was hard, his parables confounding, but his faith in the Father and his lived submission to the Father despite suffering and against the desires of the world was his authentication. This authentication—namely, the life lived for the divine will of God—is a committed and a suffering life that knows the spirit is more important than this world. Such authentication only comes authorized by God, the source of his divine will that he lavishly provides for us to participate in. Call your students, your faculty, your congregations to a hermeneutic that is not so lazy to rest in authorial intention. An intention without a living commitment is nearly the lexical definition of hypocrisy, so let your communities be built up by your knowledge and wisdom into communities formed by the stories and the lived commitment to the faith of Christ.

The event of Christ is neither finished nor diminished by the propositional communication of truth. All who believe and belong to Christ need the teaching of personal sublimation that is taught by our Christ. The authentication of these truth claims are the claims coming true. The claims made by proclamation are that lives are totally transformed in their values and commitments by a new spirit, one that is seeking first the kingdom of God; not a physical kingdom, but the domain in which there is obedience and submission to the authority of God. These claims are proven to be true because the one speaking is already proof; the living, continued presence of Christ is proven because the person speaking is already part of the body of Christ and belongs to the other members of the body of Christ. Proclamation becomes truth when there is a lived commitment, for in this lived commitment Christ can be present in the event and the focus of the event, enabling it to truly be a fully sacramentally meaningful event. In this way, perhaps even discussions about the meaningfulness of AI to proclamation are in an abstract sense merely footnotes to Augustine's thoughts on hermeneutics, where he alludes to Matt 23:10: "μηδὲ κληθῆτε καθηγηταί, ὅτι καθηγητὴς ὑμῶν ἐστιν εἷς ὁ χριστός" (SBLGNT).[8] Living the story of Christ is the demand we can no longer treat as optional or additional, or we risk a whole generation to a skepticism we may not ever fully recover from.

---

8. Augustine, *Teacher* 13.46.23

BIBLIOGRAPHY

Allbert, Rumi A., et al. "Identifying and Manipulating Personality Traits in LLMs Through Activation Engineering." arXiv: 2412.10427 [cs.CL], December 2024. Last revised January 2025. https://doi.org/10.48550/arXiv.2412.10427.

Alrefaie, Mohamed Taher, et al. "The Dynamics of Meaning Through Time: Assessment of Large Language Models." arXiv: 2501.05552 [cs.CL], January 2025. https://doi.org/10.48550/arXiv.2501.05552.

Alston, William P. *Divine Nature and Human Language: Essays in Philosophical Theology*. Ithaca: Cornell University Press, 1989.

Arai, Yuzuki, and Sho Tsugawa. "Do Large Language Models Defend Inferentialist Semantics?: On the Logical Expressivism and Anti-Representationalism of LLMs." arXiv: 2412.14501 [cs.CL], December 2024. Last revised June 2025. https://doi.org/10.48550/arXiv.2412.14501.

Aryan, Prakash. "LLMs as Debate Partners: Utilizing Genetic Algorithms and Adversarial Search for Adaptive Arguments." arXiv: 2412.06229 [cs.AI], December 2024. https://doi.org/10.48550/arXiv.2412.06229.

Augustine. *Against the Academicians and The Teacher*. Translated by Peter King. Indianapolis: Hackett, 1995.

Austin, J. L. *How to Do Things with Words: The William James Lectures Delivered in Harvard University in 1955*. Edited by J. O. Urmson and Marina Sbisa. 2nd ed. Oxford: Clarendon, 1975.

Barth, Karl. *The Doctrine of the Word of God*. Vol. 1, pt. 2 of *Church Dogmatics*. Edited by G. W. Bromiley and Thomas F. Torrance, translated by G. T. Thomson and Harold Knight. London: T&T Clark International, 1956.

Barthes, Roland. "A Structural Analysis of a Narrative from Acts X–XI." In *Structuralism and Biblical Hermeneutics: A Collection of Essays*, edited and translated by Alfred M. Johnson Jr., 109–44. Pittsburgh Theological Monograph Series 22. Eugene, OR: Pickwick, 1979.

Bonhoeffer, Dietrich. *Ethics*. New York: Macmillan, 1955.

Brandom, Robert B. "Intentionality and Language: A Normative, Pragmatist, Inferentialist Approach." In *The Cambridge Handbook of Linguistic Anthropology*, edited by N. J. Enfield et al., 347–63. Cambridge Handbooks in Language and Linguistics. Cambridge: Cambridge University Press, 2014.

Bronowski, Jacob. *The Ascent of Man*. Boston: Little, Brown, 1973.

Brunner, Emil, et al. *Revelation and Reason: The Christian Doctrine of Faith and Knowledge*. London: SCM, 1947.

Bultmann, Rudolf. *This World and the Beyond: Marburg Sermons*. Translated by Harold Knight. New York: Scribner, 1960.

Calvin, John. *Institutes of the Christian Religion*. Translated by Robert White. Edinburgh: Banner of Truth Trust, 2014.

Campbell, Constantine R., and D. A. Carson. *Advances in the Study of Greek: New Insights for Reading the New Testament*. Grand Rapids: Zondervan, 2015.

Cole, David. "The Chinese Room Argument." Stanford Encyclopedia of Philosophy, Winter 2024. https://plato.stanford.edu/archives/win2024/entries/chinese-room/.

Cotterell, Peter, and Max Turner. *Linguistics & Biblical Interpretation*. Downers Grove, IL: InterVarsity, 1989.

Davidson, Donald. *The Essential Davidson*. Oxford: Oxford University Press, 2006.

DeepSeek-AI, et al. "DeepSeek-R1: Incentivizing Reasoning Capability in LLMs via Reinforcement Learning." arXiv: 2501.12948 [cs.CL], January 2025. https://doi.org/10.48550/arXiv.2501.12948.

Dik, Simon C. *The Structure of the Clause*. Pt. 1 of *The Theory of Functional Grammar*, edited by Kees Hengeveld. 2nd rev. ed. Functional Grammar 20. Berlin: de Gruyter, 1997.

Dummett, Michael. *The Seas of Language*. Oxford: Oxford University Press, 1993.

Eagleton, Terry. *Literary Theory: An Introduction*. Newark: Wiley & Sons, 1996.

Enyan, Zhang, et al. "Are LLMs Models of Distributional Semantics? A Case Study on Quantifiers." arXiv: 2410.13984 [cs.CL], October 2024. https://doi.org/10.48550/arXiv.2410.13984.

Feng, K. J. Kevin, et al. "Case Repositories: Towards Case-Based Reasoning for AI Alignment." arXiv: 2311.10934 [cs.AI], November 2023. https://doi.org/10.48550/arXiv.2311.10934.

Fish, Stanley. *Is There a Text in This Class? The Authority of Interpretive Communities*. Cambridge: Harvard University Press, 1982.

Fitch, Kristine L., and Robert E. Sanders, eds. *Handbook of Language and Social Interaction*. Oxford: Taylor & Francis, 2004.

Frei, Hans W., et al. *The Identity of Jesus Christ: The Hermeneutical Bases of Dogmatic Theology*. Upd. ed. Eugene, OR: Cascade, 2013.

Frei, Hans W., et al. *Types of Christian Theology*. New Haven: Yale University Press, 1992.

Fuchs, Ernst. *The New Testament and the Hermeneutical Problem*. Edited by J. M. Robinson and J. B. Cobb Jr. New York: Harper & Row, 1964.

———. *Studies of the Historical Jesus*. Translated by Andrew Scobie. Naperville, IL: Allenson, 1964.

Gadamer, Hans-Georg. *Truth and Method*. Translated by Joel Weinsheimer and Donald G. Marshall. London: Bloomsbury Academic, 2013.

Glenn, Paul J. *A Tour of the Summa*. London: Herder, 1960.

Habermas, Jürgen. *The Theory of Communicative Action*. Translated by Thomas McCarthy. Boston: Beacon, 1987.

Hauerwas, Stanley. *Unleashing the Scripture: Freeing the Bible from Captivity to America*. Nashville: Abingdon, 1993.

Hauerwas, Stanley. *The Hauerwas Reader*. Edited by John Berkman and Michael Cartwright. Durham, NC: Duke University Press, 2001.

Hays, Richard B. *Echoes of Scripture in the Letters of Paul*. New Haven: Yale University Press, 1989.

———. *The Moral Vision of the New Testament: Community, Cross, New Creation; A Contemporary Introduction to New Testament Ethics.* Edinburgh: T&T Clark, 1996.

Hector, Kevin. *Theology Without Metaphysics: God, Language, and the Spirit of Recognition.* Cambridge: Cambridge University Press, 2011.

Heidegger, Martin. *Being and Time.* Translated by John Macquarrie and Edward S. Robinson. New York: Harper, 1962.

Hirsch, E. D. "Against Theory?" *Critical Inquiry* 9 (1983) 743–47.

———. *Validity in Interpretation.* New Haven: Yale University Press, 1967.

Hu, Xiang, et al. "Nova: An Iterative Planning and Search Approach to Enhance Novelty and Diversity of LLM Generated Ideas." arXiv: 2410.14255 [cs.AI], October 2024. https://doi.org/10.48550/arXiv.2410.14255.

Ismayilzada, Mete, et al. "Evaluating Creative Short Story Generation in Humans and Large Language Models." arXiv: 2411.02316 [cs.CL], November 2024. Last revised May 2025. http://arxiv.org/abs/2411.02316.

Knapp, Steven, and Walter Benn Michaels. "Against Theory." *Critical Inquiry* 8 (1982) 723–42.

Li, Bingru, and Han Wang. "TACOMORE: Leveraging the Potential of LLMs in Corpus-Based Discourse Analysis with Prompt Engineering." arXiv: 2412.10139 [cs.CL], December 2024. https://doi.org/10.48550/arXiv.2412.10139.

Lin, Yong, et al. "Goedel-Prover: A Frontier Model for Open-Source Automated Theorem Proving." arXiv: 2502.04640 [cs.LG], February 2025. Last revised April 2025. https://doi.org/10.48550/arXiv.2502.07640.

Lindbeck, George A. *The Nature of Doctrine: Religion and Theology in a Postliberal Age.* 25th anniv. ed. Louisville: Westminster John Knox Press, 2009.

———. "Response to Bruce Marshall." *The Thomist* 53 (1989) 403–6.

MacCulloch, Diarmaid. *Christianity: The First Three Thousand Years.* New York: Penguin, 2009.

Macdonald, Cynthia, and Graham Macdonald, eds. *McDowell and His Critics.* Philosophers and Their Critics 13. Malden, MA: Blackwell, 2006.

Marshall, Bruce D. *Trinity and Truth.* Cambridge: Cambridge University Press, 2000.

McDowell, John. *Meaning, Knowledge, and Reality.* Cambridge: Harvard University Press, 1998.

Michelli, Gianluca, et al. "A Framework for Annotating and Modelling Intentions Behind Metaphor Use." arXiv: 2407.03952 [cs.CL], July 2024. https://doi.org/10.48550/arXiv.2407.03952.

Mikolov, Tomas, et al. "Efficient Estimation of Word Representations in Vector Space." arXiv: 1301.3781 [cs.CL], January 2013. Last revised September 2013. https://doi.org/10.48550/arXiv.1301.3781.

Pannenberg, Wolfhart. *Basic Questions in Theology: Collected Essays.* Vol. 2. Translated by George H. Kehm. Minneapolis: Fortress, 2008.

———. *Jesus, God and Man.* Translated by Lewis L. Wilkins and Duane A. Priebe. 2nd ed. Philadelphia: Westminster, 1977.

———. *Systematic Theology.* 3 vols. Translated by Geoffrey W. Bromiley. London: T&T Clark International, 1992.

Pennington, Jeffrey, et al. "GloVe: Global Vectors for Word Representation." In *Proceedings of the 2014 Conference on Empirical Methods in Natural Language Processing (EMNLP)*, edited by Alessandro Moschitti et al., 1532–43. Doha, Qatar:

Association for Computational Linguistics, 2014. https://doi.org/10.3115/v1/D14-1162.

Plantinga, Alvin. *Warrant and Proper Function*. New York: Oxford University Press, 1993.

Quine, W. V. *Quintessence: Basic Readings from the Philosophy of W. V. Quine*. Edited by Roger F. Gibson. Cambridge: Harvard University Press, 2004.

———. *Word and Object*. New ed. Cambridge: MIT Press, 2013.

Ricoeur, Paul. *Interpretation Theory: Discourse and the Surplus of Meaning*. Fort Worth: Texas Christian University Press, 1976.

Robertson, A. T. *A Grammar of the Greek New Testament in the Light of Historical Research*. 4th ed. Nashville: Broadman, 1934.

Rommen, Edward. *Come and See: An Eastern Orthodox Perspective on Contextualization*. Pasadena: William Carey Library, 2013.

Ruas, Terry, et al. "Multi-Sense Embeddings Through a Word Sense Disambiguation Process." *Expert Systems with Applications* 136 (2019) 288–303. https://doi.org/10.1016/j.eswa.2019.06.026.

Runge, Steven E. *Discourse Grammar of the Greek New Testament: A Practical Introduction for Teaching and Exegesis*. Peabody, MA: Hendrickson, 2015.

Sanneh, Lamin. *Translating the Message: The Missionary Impact on Culture*. Maryknoll, NY: Orbis, 2009.

Schleiermacher, Friedrich. *Lectures on Philosophical Ethics*. Edited by Robert B. Louden, translated by Louise Adey Huish. Cambridge Texts in the History of Philosophy. Cambridge: Cambridge University Press, 2002.

Scivetti, Wesley, et al. "Assessing Language Comprehension in Large Language Models Using Construction Grammar." arXiv: 2501.04661 [cs.CL], January 2025. https://doi.org/10.48550/arXiv.2501.04661.

Sellars, Wilfrid. "Counterfactuals, Dispositions, and Causal Modalities." In *Concepts, Theories, and the Mind-Body Problem*, edited by Herbert Feigl et al., 225–308. Minnesota Studies in the Philosophy of Science 2. Minneapolis: University of Minnesota Press, 1958.

Shanahan, Murray, and Beth Singler. "Existential Conversations with Large Language Models: Content, Community, and Culture." arXiv: 2411.13223 [cs.CY], November 2024. https://doi.org/10.48550/arXiv.2411.13223.

Shazeer, Noam. "GLU Variants Improve Transformer." arXiv: 2002.05202 [cs.LG], February 2020. https://doi.org/10.48550/arXiv.2002.05202.

Soskice, Janet Martin. *Metaphor and Religious Language*. Oxford: Oxford University Press, 1985.

Sun, Qi, et al. "Transformer-Squared: Self-Adaptive LLMs." arXiv: 2501.06252 [cs.LG], January 2025. https://doi.org/10.48550/arXiv.2501.06252.

Sun, Yuxi, et al. "ClarityEthic: Explainable Moral Judgment Utilizing Contrastive Ethical Insights from Large Language Models." arXiv: 2412.12848 [cs.CY], December 2024. Withdrawn by the authors April 2025. https://doi.org/10.48550/arXiv.2412.12848.

Thiselton, Anthony C. *The Two Horizons: New Testament Hermeneutics and Philosophical Description with Special Reference to Heidegger, Bultmann, Gadamer, and Wittgenstein*. Grand Rapids: Eerdmans, 1980.

Tillich, Paul. *The Protestant Era*. Chicago: University of Chicago Press, 1948.

Torrance, Alan. *Persons in Communion: Trinitarian Description and Human Participation*. London: Continuum, 1996.
Turkle, Sherry. *Alone Together: Why We Expect More from Technology and Less from Each Other*. 3rd ed. New York: Basic, 2017.
Vanhoozer, Kevin J. *Faith Speaking Understanding: Performing the Drama of Doctrine*. Louisville: Westminster John Knox, 2014.
———. *Is There a Meaning in This Text? The Bible, the Reader, and the Morality of Literary Knowledge*. Grand Rapids: Zondervan, 2009.
Vaswani, Ashish, et al. "Attention Is All You Need." arXiv: 1706.03762 [cs.CL], June 2017. Last revised August 2023. https://doi.org/10.48550/arXiv.1706.03762.
Via, Dan Otto. "The Parable of the Unjust Judge: A Metaphor of the Unrealized Self." In *Semiology and the Parables: An Exploration of the Possibilities Offered by Structuralism for Exegesis*, edited by Daniel Patte, 1–32. Pittsburgh Theological Monograph Series 9. Pittsburgh: Pickwick, 1976.
Wang, Chenglong, et al. "Hybrid Alignment Training for Large Language Models." arXiv: 2406.15178 [cs.CL], June 2024. https://doi.org/10.48550/arXiv.2406.15178.
Wang, Jiaan, et al. "DRT: Deep Reasoning Translation via Long Chain-of-Thought." arXiv: 2412.17498 [cs.CL], December 2024. Last revised February 2025. https://doi.org/10.48550/arXiv.2412.17498.
Warner, Benjamin, et al. "Smarter, Better, Faster, Longer: A Modern Bidirectional Encoder for Fast, Memory Efficient, and Long Context Finetuning and Inference." arXiv: 2412.13663 [cs.CL], December 2024. https://doi.org/10.48550/arXiv.2412.13663.
Wilson, Robert A., and Frank C. Keil. *The MIT Encyclopedia of the Cognitive Sciences*. Cambridge: MIT Press, 1999.
Wimsatt, W. K., and M. C. Beardsley. "The Intentional Fallacy." *Sewanee Review* 54 (1946) 468–88.
Wittgenstein, Ludwig. *Philosophical Investigations*. Translated by P. M. S. Hacker and Joachim Schulte. Chichester, UK: Wiley & Sons, 2009.
———. *Tractatus Logico-Philosophicus*. Edited by Luciano Bazzocchi, Pears-McGuinness translation. Centenary ed. Anthem Studies in Wittgenstein. London: Anthem, 2021.
———. *Zettel*. Edited by G. E. M. Anscombe and G. H. von Wright, translated by G. E. M. Anscombe. Berkeley: University of California Press, 1967.
Yarnold, Edward. *Cyril of Jerusalem*. Early Church Fathers. New York: Routledge, 2000.
Yeago, David S. "The New Testament and the Nicene Dogma: A Contribution to the Recovery of Theological Exegesis." *Pro Ecclesia* 3 (1994) 152–64.
Yuan, Jiaqing, et al. "Right vs. Right: Can LLMs Make Tough Choices?" arXiv: 2412.19926 [cs.CL], December 2024. https://doi.org/10.48550/arXiv.2412.19926.
Zeng, Hongchuan, et al. "Converging to a Lingua Franca: Evolution of Linguistic Regions and Semantics Alignment in Multilingual Large Language Models." arXiv: 2410.11718 [cs.CL], October 2024. Last revised February 2025. https://doi.org/10.48550/arXiv.2410.11718.
Zheng, Tianshi, et al. "LogiDynamics: Unraveling the Dynamics of Logical Inference in Large Language Model Reasoning." arXiv: 2502.11176 [cs.CL], February 2025. Last revised April 2025. https://doi.org/10.48550/arXiv.2502.11176.
Zimmermann, Jens. *Recovering Theological Hermeneutics: An Incarnational-Trinitarian Theory of Interpretation*. Eugene, OR: Wipf & Stock, 2012.

SUBJECT INDEX

AI systems, 5, 11–15, 21–44
aktionsart, 51, 63, 172, 190
allegory, 77, 81, 95, 185
analogy, 88–91, 110, 113–14, 125
anaphora, 74
appropriation, 169, 178–79, 190–92
attention, 27–29, 35–38, 47, 52, 59, 67–68, 78, 87, 90–91, 101, 118, 122, 125, 129
attention matrix, 24–25, 78, 122, 145
authenticate, 3–4, 126, 155, 161, 176, 184, 190–92
authorial intention, 3–4, 63–65, 94–95, 189–90, 192, 197, 205–6
authority, 112–14, 119–22, 128–32, 142–43, 152, 156, 177–80

charity principle, 40, 99, 108, 126, 140, 159, 201
coherence, 27, 33, 55, 59, 66, 89, 100–102, 109, 119, 126, 153, 171, 202
consistency, 135, 153, 188, 202–3
continuation, 32, 59, 77, 89, 111, 114, 176
correspondence, 72, 74–77, 85, 136, 143, 147, 202

determinacy, 46–48, 115, 170, 173, 196
determinate, 8, 40, 79, 170, 189, 199
discourse meaning, 52, 101
distributional semantics, 86–87, 121, 193
divine prerogative, 105, 106–10

epistemic systems, 139
external considerations, 169

Generative Pre-trained Transformer (or GPT), 37–38

icons, 112–13
illocutionary, 64, 67–68, 72–73, 96, 103–5, 110, 141, 147, 170–71, 195, 203
implicature, 119, 176–77
intention, 3–4, 8, 43, 47, 54–55, 60, 61–68, 78–80, 100, 110, 119–21, 126, 128, 141, 147, 154, 177, 189–90, 196–98, 203, 205–6
intrinsic genre, 65, 78–80, 169–70, 174, 199

justification, 56, 90, 103, 135, 143, 156, 161–69, 177, 204

literal, 76, 85–88, 95, 110, 177, 203

meaning, 8–10, 30–36, 47–48, 51–55, 57, 60, 64, 66–68, 73, 83–87, 93, 99, 102, 106, 109, 116, 134, 141, 146–47, 154, 156, 162–63, 165–67, 170, 173, 176, 185–86, 189–90, 192, 196, 199, 203–6
metaphor, 32, 85–88, 92, 125, 152–54, 192
normative, 34, 42, 65, 74, 76–77, 90, 111, 114, 119–24, 134, 137–38, 149, 153–54, 164, 175, 201, 203

obligation, 81, 94, 103 126, 138, 141, 162, 198

perlocutionary, 64, 103, 116, 131, 160, 203
plausibility structure, 113, 158
presence, 7, 17, 66, 110, 112–14, 124, 155–60
private, 62–63, 79, 102–6, 114, 117, 120–21, 145–48, 163, 200–201
public, 62–63, 79, 102–6, 114, 117, 120–21, 134, 141, 145–48, 150–55, 163, 196, 200–201

radical-translation, 9, 58, 98, 126
realism, 56, 75, 84, 91, 146–48
reference, 27, 51, 57–58, 75, 77, 84, 85, 88, 92, 94, 114–15, 122, 137, 147–48, 158–60, 179

responsibility, 76, 97, 129, 170, 176, 188, 197, 198, 205
rule-theory, 123, 136–38, 176

semantic distance, 34, 86, 88, 145, 167
semantic projections, 109
semantic space, 31–32, 52, 60, 87, 90, 109, 118, 129, 138, 141
shared presupposition pool, 52–53, 60
skepticism, 40, 54, 99, 145–51, 200, 207

taken true, 11, 103, 149, 158, 177, 192, 196
tradition, 7, 17–18, 108

utterance, 11–13, 30, 46–70, 84, 91, 96–97, 100, 102, 131–32, 137, 148, 153, 165, 167, 169

AUTHOR INDEX

Alston, William, 85–86, 110, 124
Augustine, 84, 107, 132
Austin, J. L., 65, 156

Barth, Karl, 74–75, 90, 115–16, 142
Brandom, Robert, 43, 128–29
Brunner, Emil, 66, 92, 111, 145, 157
Bultmann, Rudolf, 83, 108, 194, 200

Campbell, Constantine, 51, 57, 172
Cotterell, Peter, 37, 45–57, 92, 101, 201

Davidson, Donald, 32, 40, 50, 53–56, 87, 98–99, 139, 163, 165, 167, 174
Dik, Simon, 35, 101, 162
Dummett, Michael, 64–65, 84, 146, 165

Eagleton, Terry, 48

Fish, Stanley, 58, 204
Frei, Hans, 91–95, 103–4, 123, 126, 138
Fuchs, Ernst, 81, 131, 160

Gadamer, Hans-Georg, 63–64, 77, 106, 147, 154, 158–59, 161, 170, 175

Hauerwas, Stanley, 191, 197, 204
Hays, Richard, 9, 80–82, 86, 105, 152–54, 175, 195

Hector, Kevin, 10, 29, 32, 72, 74–77, 90–94, 102, 111, 115, 119–25, 136, 166, 176, 202
Hirsch, E. D., 9, 46, 50–55, 63, 65, 77–80, 102, 148, 169.170–71, 174

Knapp, Steven, 59–60, 65–66

MacCulloch, Diarmaid, 76
Marshall, Bruce, 9, 84, 105, 119, 122–23, 130, 136, 138–40, 149, 159, 162–67, 170, 171–73, 175, 178–79, 195, 200, 202–3

Pannenberg, Wolfhart, 37, 66, 92, 146
Plantinga, Alvin, 9, 39, 99, 126, 152, 160, 195

Quine, W. V., 39, 53, 58, 99

Ricoeur, Paul, 47, 62, 70, 94–95
Robertson, A. T, 85
Rommen, Edward, 112–14, 158, 195
Runge, Steven, 27, 155, 162, 172

Sanneh, Lamin, 82, 108–9, 124
Schleiermacher, Friedrich, 37, 62, 74–75, 139, 146, 159, 161, 164
Soskice, Janet, 75–76, 85–86, 92

Thiselton, Anthony, 46–47, 64, 74, 81, 86, 96, 117, 131, 143, 168, 194
Tillich, Paul, 185
Torrance, Alan, 89

Vanhoozer, Kevin, 9, 15–16, 46–47, 54–55, 57, 63, 102, 140–42, 155–56, 173–75, 197–98, 204

Wittgenstein, Ludwig, 45, 47, 64, 74, 79, 102, 116, 124, 179, 201–2

Yeago, David, 89